SEX, CRIME AND LITERATURE IN VICTORIAN ENGLAND

The Victorians worried about many things, prominent among their worries being the 'condition' of England and the 'question' of its women. *Sex, Crime and Literature in Victorian England* revisits these particular anxieties, concentrating more closely upon four 'crimes' which generated especial concern amongst contemporaries: adultery, bigamy, infanticide and prostitution. Each engaged questions of sexuality and its regulation, legal, moral and cultural, for which reason each attracted the considerable interest not just of lawyers and parliamentarians, but also novelists and poets and, perhaps most importantly, those who, in ever-larger numbers, liked to pass their leisure hours reading about sex and crime. Alongside statutes such as the 1857 Matrimonial Causes Act and the 1864 Contagious Diseases Act, *Sex, Crime and Literature in Victorian England* contemplates those texts which shaped Victorian attitudes towards England's 'condition' and the 'question' of its women – the novels of Dickens, Thackeray and Eliot, the works of sensationalists such as Ellen Wood and Mary Braddon, and the poetry of Gabriel and Christina Rossetti. *Sex, Crime and Literature in Victorian England* is a richly contextual commentary on a critical period in the evolution of modern legal and cultural attitudes to the relation of crime, sexuality and the family.

Sex, Crime and Literature in Victorian England

Ian Ward

·HART·
PUBLISHING
OXFORD AND PORTLAND, OREGON
2015

Published in the United Kingdom by Hart Publishing Ltd
16C Worcester Place, Oxford, OX1 2JW
Telephone: +44 (0)1865 517530
Fax: +44 (0)1865 510710
E-mail: mail@hartpub.co.uk
Website: http://www.hartpub.co.uk

Published in North America (US and Canada) by
Hart Publishing
c/o International Specialized Book Services
920 NE 58th Avenue, Suite 300
Portland, OR 97213-3786
USA
Tel: +1 503 287 3093 or toll-free: (1) 800 944 6190
Fax: +1 503 280 8832
E-mail: orders@isbs.com
Website: http://www.isbs.com

Hart Publishing is an imprint of Bloomsbury Publishing plc.

British Library Cataloguing in Publication Data
Data Available

ISBN: 978-1-50990-498-3

Typeset by Hope Services, Abingdon
Printed and bound in Great Britain by
TJ International Ltd, Padstow, Cornwall

CONTENTS

Introduction

Dark Shapes

In June 1858, Charles Dickens published a series of notices in the press confirming, in the vaguest possible way, that he had separated from his wife, but denying rumours that the reason lay in his relationship with any 'persons close to my heart'.[1] His long-time friend and later biographer, John Forster, desperately tried to dissuade him, reasoning that the notice would only serve to titillate public prurience. He was, of course, right. The timing was oddly, and rather discomfortingly, resonant, as the doors of the new Divorce Court had only just opened for business; something which had made the subject of adultery and dysfunctional families of particular contemporary interest.[2] If the Dickens family was indeed breaking up, and if the reason lay in an extra-marital indiscretion, it was becoming rather too obvious that there was in this nothing particularly unusual. Moreover, only a decade previously Dickens had confirmed his reputation as a 'serious' novelist, and chronicler of the 'condition of England', by depicting precisely such a familial fragmentation in *Dombey and Son*.[3] We shall return to *Dombey and Son* shortly. At the same time as he was publishing his notice, Dickens was giving some of his first public readings, of which one of the most popular, the death of 'little Paul', was taken from *Dombey and Son*. The ironies abounded, along with the hypocrisies.[4]

Dickens was right to be concerned, even if the manner of his response proved to be entirely misconceived. The rumours, as to both the state of his marriage and his infatuation with a young actress, were well-founded. The 45-year-old Dickens

---

[1] C Tomalin, *Charles Dickens* (Viking, 2011) 298. Notices were published in *The Times*, *The New York Tribune* and *Household Words*. *Punch* declined to publish, something which ensured Dickens's life-long enmity.

[2] Indeed, Charles's brother Fred was one of the first to sue for divorce before the new court, in December 1858, citing the alleged adultery of his wife. Dickens, of course, had no grounds with which he could seek a divorce even if he had wanted to do so. Catherine was not at fault. He was.

[3] See S Marcus, *Dickens from Pickwick to Dombey* (Norton, 1985) 347–48, suggesting that whilst Dickens's marriage was still relatively strong at the time he was composing *Dombey and Son*, warning signs were present; an early infatuation with Christiana Weller, the fiancée of his friend TJ Thompson, and then more suggestively, his bizarre behaviour towards Mrs de la Rue whilst in Genoa. Mrs de la Rue suffered from hallucinations, which Dickens thought he could cure by hypnosis. Catherine protested that Dickens was paying too much attention to the supposed invalid; an accusation that Dickens hotly denied. He refused to stop paying his visits to Mrs de la Rue either during the day, or more troublingly, at night.

[4] On the obvious hypocrisy of Dickens writing about the sanctity of the family, see Marcus, *Dickens*, ibid, 356 and more recently, K Hager, *Dickens and the Rise of Divorce* (Ashgate, 2010) 92.

had fallen in love with the 19-year-old Ellen Ternan.[5] The rumours were not to be easily assuaged. In conversation at the Garrick, a club they shared, Thackeray rather witlessly confirmed that his friend Dickens was indeed conducting an affair with an actress; an error for which he was never forgiven. Elizabeth Barrett Browning expressed herself appalled when she came across one of the notices which appeared to hold Catherine Dickens in large part responsible for the separation. It was, she bluntly said, a 'crime' and a 'dreadful' one.[6] When Angela Burdett Coutts, who was bankrolling the home for fallen women which she and Dickens had set up, heard the rumours she pretty much cut him off.[7] The even greater risk for Dickens, of course, was that his readers might do the same.

As his notices only barely concealed, Dickens had become bored of his wife of 20 years, confiding in increasingly pained, and self-justificatory, correspondence with Forster that they were never really 'made for each other'; a view which he pressed more strongly the older and less pretty Catherine became. She was, Dickens conceded, 'amiable and complying', in this sense the ideal 'angel in the house' so frequently celebrated in contemporary literature, but she was no longer very exciting, in or out of bed.[8] Using a metaphor with a very particular contemporary resonance, Dickens confided that what was 'befalling' him had been 'steadily coming'. Of course, the real fall, prospectively at least, would have been Ellen's. It might be noted that when it came to developing infatuations with younger unmarried women, Dickens already had form; as did a conspicuous number of his fellow male writers, including both Ruskin and Thackeray.[9] As later biographers have lined up to confirm, Dickens anyway struggled to relate in a mature way to most women.[10] He treated Catherine abominably, pointedly telling friends when her sister Mary died that he would have preferred it to have been his wife. Mary was another of those young women for whom Dickens had developed one of his discomforting infatuations. Ellen was not the first, and was probably not the last.

On the matter of his reputation, however, Dickens was right. There was much to be lost if his readers decided that he was indeed responsible for the 'fall' of an

---

[5] He was 'keeping' both her and her sisters in a large house in Ampthill Square in London. Biographers and critics have long tried to comprehend the nature of their relationship, the precise details of which remain maddeningly elusive, particularly for the years 1862–65, during which time, according to Dickens's daughter Kate, Ellen gave birth to an illegitimate child. Confirmed critical sightings of Nelly are intermittent during these years, though she does famously resurface as a travelling companion in a railway crash at Staplehurst in June 1865, from which Dickens had her quickly and discreetly whisked away. See most recently, Tomalin, *Charles Dickens* (above n 1) 326–35, commenting that a 'great many questions hang on the air, unanswered and mostly unanswerable'.

[6] Ibid, 300.

[7] Dickens desperately tried to make his case, suggesting in correspondence that Catherine caused him 'unspeakable agony of mind'. Coutts, who prided herself on her personal propriety, was not persuaded and their relationship never recovered.

[8] See Tomalin, *Charles Dickens* (above n 1) 252, 285.

[9] Ruskin's marriage disintegrated even more spectacularly than Dickens's, his impotence being cited in his wife's divorce proceedings as grounds for voidity. A little later, he became infatuated with the 11-year-old Rose La Touche, something which he was, for understandable reasons, equally as keen to keep from his public. We will encounter Thackeray's infatuations in the chapter one.

[10] His daughter put it bluntly: 'my father did not understand women' quoted in N Auerbach, 'Dickens and Dombey: A Daughter After All' (1976) 5 *Dickens Studies Annual* 95.

innocent young woman, as well as the resultant disintegration of his own family for, as Fitzjames Stephen put it, the family had become the 'supreme object of idolatry' in mid-Victorian England, especially amongst the kind of people for whom Dickens wrote.[11] It was an inherently paradoxical idol, as Edmund Burke had noted in his manual for whimsical conservatives, *Reflections on the Revolution in France*. The English political 'mind' was founded on a shared adoration for an iconography that celebrated the common worship of 'our state, our hearths, our sepulchres, our altars'.[12] The Burkean commonwealth cherished each and every English home as an irreducibly public space even whilst it remained, at least in the cultural imagination, privately inviolable. The house of Paul Dombey, as we shall see, was just such a home; 'in private' and 'in public' (554)[13] so, it had become painfully apparent, was the home of Charles Dickens. As the mainly female readership of the *Home Circle* magazine was reminded, the woman who tends to the hearth exercises a vicarious power 'over the will of the nation'.[14] By now, however, neither the rhetoric nor the iconography was quite so convincing. Few mid-Victorians were more whimsical or more conservative than Walter Bagehot, or more sceptical. Few were more sensitive to the fact that theirs was an 'age of confusion and tumult', not least because ordinary Englishmen and women were no longer so confident in the inviolability of the English 'household'.[15]

For this very reason, mid-Victorian England was also a place of anxiety and of uncertainty. The anxiety bred the questioning. England worried about its 'condition', for which reason it also worried, at length, about the state of its families and more particularly, the 'question' of its women, what they should be doing, what they might be thinking, and what they seemed to be reading.[16] This latter affinity was immediate. The Burkean family presumed a particular 'sphere' within which women lived their married lives.[17] At a remove, it also presumed a particular place within which the sexuality of these women might be regulated, and this place was the institution of marriage. This book is about sex and marriage, and the consequences, legal and otherwise, of transgressing the Burkean norm. It is about families like the Dickenses, about men like Charles Dickens and women like Ellen Ternan.

---

[11] See K Chase and M Levenson, *The Spectacle of Intimacy: A Public Life for the Victorian Family* (Princeton University Press, 2000) 215–16. See also J Tosh, *A Man's Place: Masculinity and the Middle-Class Home in Victorian England* (Yale University Press, 1999) 4–6, exploring the middle-class 'cult of domesticity', and T Hoppen, *The Mid-Victorian Generation 1846–1886* (Oxford University Press, 1998) 316 stating, as baldly as Stephen, that the 'family dominated Victorian life'.

[12] E Burke, *Reflections on the Revolution in France* (Penguin, 1986) 120.

[13] All internal citations are taken from C Dickens, *Dombey and Son* (Penguin, 2002).

[14] H Fraser et al (ed), *Gender and the Victorian Periodical* (Cambridge University Press, 2003) 108.

[15] W Bagehot, 'The First Edinburgh Reviewers' in N St John Stevas (ed), *The Collected Works of Walter Bagehot* vol 1 (The Economist, 1965–86) 261.

[16] See C Hersh, *Subversive Heroines: Feminist Resolutions of Social Crisis in the Condition of England Novel* (Michigan University Press, 1994) 1–16.

[17] See I Hayward, *The Revolution of Popular Literature: Print, Politics and the People 1790–1860* (Cambridge University Press, 2004) 199, noting the lingering influence of the 'neo-Burkean creed' of liberal conservatism in the early and middle parts of the nineteenth century.

It is also about the families that Dickens created for his thousands of devoted readers, about their conformities and nonconformities, indeed about families such as the Dombeys. It is not only about families created by Dickens of course, for it is also about other fictional families we will come across, such as the Newcomes, the Carlyles and the Mellishs, each of which was beset with marital dysfunction. It is also about the fate of those women such as Ellen, who found themselves 'fallen' outside marriage, about women such as Hetty Sorrel, Jessie Phillips and Ruth Hilton, as well as Dickens's own Nancy Sikes. Dickens knew that his age was an interrogatory one, a serious one and an anxious one. He also knew that if he read his audience right, this same anxiety would make his fortune, for the Victorian age, the 'age of so many things', as Margaret Oliphant rather wearily observed, was also a peculiarly literate one; the great 'age of the triumph of fiction', as Edmund Gosse later affirmed in rather more celebratory tones.[18] If there was one thing a Victorian gentleman liked more than worrying, it was reading about worrying things.[19] The same, it was commonly felt, was true of his wife; indeed, of all the worrying things, few were more worrying than the thought that women were reading too much. Indeed, it was commonly supposed that women like Ellen Ternan fell because they read novels written by men such as Charles Dickens.

Angels in the House

Of course, as we have already intimated, the shame that Dickens was so keen to evade was nothing in comparison with that which would have attached to Ellen. The mid-Victorian was obsessed with 'fallen' women, which is precisely why they loved to read about them in the novels that Dickens, and so many of his contemporaries, wrote.[20] There were two distinct species of 'fallen' women: those who fell whilst married, and those who, like Ellen Ternan, fell outside of marriage. The necessary fact of sexual transgression, even its mere insinuation, made both equally thrilling subjects for leisured contemplation; as did the further insinuation, commonly made in the literature of the 'fallen' women, that transgressive sexuality nurtured criminality. Whilst the 'fallen' married woman could easily find herself slipping into a kind of criminality, it was usually of the less violent kind: a 'criminal conversation' perhaps, a spot of bigamy. But for the 'fallen' unmarried woman, the crimes prescribed tended to be rather more dramatic, certainly more violent. A life

---

[18] E Gosse, 'The Tyranny of the Novel' (1982) 19 *National Review* 164. For Oliphant's observation, see 'Modern Novelists Great and Small' (1855) 77 *Blackwoods* 555. In his 'Introduction' to the first Penguin edition of *Dombey and Son* in 1970, at 11, Raymond Williams suggested that 'There has been no higher point in the whole history of English fiction'.

[19] On the Victorian age as one of 'apprehension', see M Wolff, 'Victorian Study: An Interdisciplinary Essay' (1964) 8 *Victorian Studies* 1964.

[20] See N Auerbach, 'The Rise of the Fallen Woman' (1980) 35 *Nineteenth-Century Fiction* 30–34 and 37–52; G Watt, *The Fallen Woman in the Nineteenth-Century English Novel* (Croom Helm, 1984) 1–9; and T Winnifrith, *Fallen Women in the Nineteenth Century Novel* (St Martin's Press, 1994) 1–11.

of prostitution leading as often as not to violent death was commonly prescribed, as was the arrival of an unwanted child and the temptation to commit that most 'unnatural' of crimes, child-murder. Ellen appears to have been luckier than most. She did not fall quite so far, or at least so it seems. We shall, however, encounter some of the less fortunate in due course, as we will the associated literature on female sexuality with which so many Victorian gentlemen, for reasons of science or more commonly simple prurience, were evidently so fascinated.[21]

The alternative to the 'fallen' woman was the 'womanly' woman.[22] Single women could be 'womanly' but they were generally viewed as being odd if they did not sooner or later get married.[23] The cultural presumption was that women should marry. There were exceptional voices, most famously perhaps that of John Stuart Mill, who argued that a wife was in reality the 'bond-servant of her husband: no less so, as far as legal obligation goes, than slaves commonly so-called'. There were, he concluded, alluding to recent emancipation statutes, 'no legal slaves' in England 'except the mistress of every house'.[24] Early feminist contemporaries such as Mona Caird were quick to cite Mill's authority and deploy his metaphor. As late as 1888, Caird likened the marriage market to the 'Mongolian market-place', with 'its iron cage, wherein women are held in bondage, suffering moral starvation, while the thoughtless gather round to taunt and to insult their lingering misery'.[25] But again, the complaint was as much against the practice of marriage as the idea and few in mid-Victorian England even shared this measure of doubt.[26] They may have read innumerable novels which insinuated that there was something awry with marital practice but they were hard pressed to find any that suggested a credible, still less desirable, alternative. Thackeray's Ethel Newcome may articulate some of the most caustic condemnations of marital practice found in the Victorian novel, as we shall see in chapter one, but there is nothing Ethel craves more than marriage to the man of her dreams. The same is every bit as true of her fictive sisters, from bigamous adulteresses to traduced maidens. Each wants, above anything, to be married. Florence Dombey may have watched the brutal disintegration of her father's marriage, but she too is desperate to marry her beloved Walter; and quite rightly, as Mr Sownds the church beadle confirms with a Burkean flourish, 'We must marry 'em . . . and keep the country going' (868).

Once married, the Victorian woman was expected to assume a particular role, and it was adherence to this role that distinguished the 'womanly' wife from the 'fallen' one. The dominant doctrine here was that of 'separate spheres'. In her essay

[21] For an overview, see K Harvey, 'Sexuality and the body' in H Barker and E Chalus (eds), *Women's History: Britain 1700–1850* (Routledge, 2005) 78–99.
[22] See P Ingham, *The Language of Gender and Class: Transformations in the Victorian Novel* (Routledge, 1996) 20–22.
[23] A presumption that Cobbe sought to satirise in her essay 'What shall we do with our old maids?' to which the answer was educate them and put them to useful employment. S Hamilton (ed), *Criminals, Idiots, Women, and Minors: Victorian Writing by Women on Women* (Broadview, 1995) 85–107.
[24] J Mill, *The Subjection of Women* (Hackett, 1988) 32, 86.
[25] M Caird, 'Marriage' in Hamilton, *Criminals, Idiots, Women, and Minors* (above n 23) 279.
[26] See Hager, *Dickens and the Rise of Divorce* (above n 4) 2–5, concluding that 'it sometimes seems as if marriage is everywhere written against, even as it is everywhere desired or assumed'.

Laws Concerning Women, Elizabeth Lynn Linton confirmed that the assumption of 'separate' spheres was 'the very first principle of domestic existence'.[27] Such essays, and such comments, were legion. So too were domestic manuals; inordinately popular and invariably keen to reaffirm the 'natural' distinction between the alternative realms of spousal authority. In her 1838 manual *Women of England*, Sarah Stickney Ellis confirmed that 'there is an appropriate sphere for women to move in, from which those of the middle class of England seldom deviate'. This 'sphere', she continued, 'has duties and occupations of its own, from which no woman can shrink without culpability and disgrace'.[28] It was not simply a matter of maintaining domestic harmony. As Mr Sownds appreciated, the 'nation's moral worth' depended on women 'keeping' these responsibilities; an invocation which necessarily aligned the emergent 'question' of women with larger questions about England's 'condition', of the kind famously asked by Thomas Carlyle and Henry Newman.

As we have already noted, religious and scriptural metaphors commonly reinforced the more prosaic presumptions of domestic utility. Thus Ellis adopted a distinctly Burkean tone in confirming that the 'household hearth', the maintenance of which was at the very top of the good wife's responsibilities, possessed an 'inviolable sanctity'.[29] In *The Woman's Mission*, Sarah Lewis made the theological affinity more patent still:

> Let men enjoy in peace and triumph the intellectual kingdom which is theirs, and which, doubtless, was intended for them; let us participate in its privileges without desiring to share its domination. The moral worlds is ours ours by position; ours by qualification, ours by the very indication of God.[30]

Alongside the domestic manual was the domestic journal, saying pretty much the same. *The Ladies Treasury* assured its readers that between its pages would be found nothing to 'enervate or bewilder the pure female mind'. Rather it was intended to 'illustrate and uphold each dear, domestic virtue, child of home'.[31] The home was sacrosanct indeed. Dickens's *Household Words* was not a woman's journal as such; but he chose the title for a reason. There will be occasions in the chapters which follow when we encounter writers who appear to be rather more sceptical, articulating the kind of doubts as to the veracity of the separation doctrine insinuated in the essays of Mill and nascent feminists such as Barbara Leigh Smith Bodichon and Frances Power Cobbe; voices which sought to raise a distinct 'question' of women, in effect a question of their place in mid-Victorian England. But such voices were few; even amongst those who are so often credited with nurturing the evolution of modern feminist consciousness. 'There is no question' George Eliot observed, 'on which I am more inclined to hold my peace and learn,

---

[27] E Linton, 'Laws Concerning Women' *Blackwood's Magazine*, April 1856, 381.
[28] See P Ingham, *The Brontes* (Oxford University Press, 2006) 128.
[29] S Ellis, *Women of England*, (Fisher and Son, 1839) 1
[30] S Lewis, *The Woman's Mission* (John Parker, 1840) 129.
[31] See N Thompson, *Reviewing Sex: Gender and the Reception of Victorian Novels* (Macmillan, 1996) 123.

than on the Woman Question'.[32] Even Frances Power Cobbe was later moved to
remark, along similar lines, that 'of all theories concerning women, none is more
curious than the theory that it is needful to make a theory about them'.[33] Even as
they wrote novels which appeared to push at the boundaries which sought to con-
fine the mid-Victorian woman, writers such as Eliot, Elizabeth Gaskell and Ellen
Wood did so cautiously.[34] Having articulated her distrust of the 'Woman Question',
Eliot gestured to the reason why. 'It seems to me', she opined, 'to overhang abysses,
of which even prostitution is not the worst'.[35] At the sharp end of the 'Woman
Question' there lay real darkness and real suffering, and real sex too.

The mid-Victorian aesthetic was written accordingly in deference to the broader
presumptions of the separation thesis, affirming the more prosaic declarations
articulated in the myriad domestic manuals published by the likes of Ellis and
Lewis. Coventry Patmore's poem *The Angel in the House* assumed a particular
iconic status. A closer reading revealed that the 'angel' in Patmore's house was
love. But in the minds of his contemporaries, male and female alike, it became a
cultural shorthand for the ideal 'womanly' wife; for if the wife failed to play her
role as prescribed, then the 'house' would be governed not by love but by suspicion, dislike and very probably violence.[36] In his review of Elizabeth Gaskell's *Ruth*,
a novel we shall revisit in chapter three, JM Ludlow confirmed that 'if man is the
head of humanity, woman is its heart'.[37] A generation earlier, Thomas Gisborne's
popular *Enquiry into the Duties of the Female Sex*, confirmed that it was for men to
plumb the 'inexhaustible depths of philosophy', just as they write the 'science of
legislation, of jurisprudence'. Their wives, in return, exercise a 'sympathising
sensibility'.[38]

This prescriptive, and necessarily pejorative, poetic found famous expression in
John Ruskin's 1865 lecture, 'Of Queen's Gardens'. The demarcation of male and
female spheres was not, Ruskin averred, a matter of power or subjugation, but of
nature and harmony. A 'true wife', he urged, was not a 'slave' but rather a 'help-
mate'. Thus:

[32] Ibid, 12.
[33] Adding 'we are driven to conclude' that whilst men grow like trees, 'women run in moulds, like
candles, and we can make them long-threes or short-sixes, whatever we please'. See Newton, *Women*
(above n 29) 2.
[34] For a commentary on this caution, see N Thompson, 'Responding to the woman questions:
rereading non-canonical Victorian women novelists' in N Thompson (ed), *Victorian Women Writers
and the Woman Question* (Cambridge University Press, 1999) 2–4, 6.
[35] See Thompson, *Reviewing Sex* (above n 31) 12.
[36] Virginia Woolf famously denounced the image as one of the most pernicious in English literature.
For commentaries, see S Gilbert and S Gubar, *The Madwoman in the Attic: The Woman Writer and the
Nineteenth-Century Literary Imagination* (Yale University Press, 2000) 20–23; E Showalter, *A Literature
of Their Own: British Women Novelists from Bronte to Lessing* (Princeton University Press, 1977) 14–16,
emphasising the extent to which the lives of mid-Victorian women were defined by an elaborate scheme
of associated icons and rituals of domestic conformity; and J Tosh, *A Man's Place: Masculinity and the
Middle-Class Home in Victorian England* (Yale University Press, 1999) 54–59, 68.
[37] J Ludow, 'Ruth' (1853) 19 *North British Review* 90.
[38] Gisborne's *Enquiry* was first published in 1797, but retained its popularity during much of the
nineteenth century. See J Guy and I Small, *The Routledge Concise History of Nineteenth-Century
Literature* (Routledge, 2011) 173.

The man's power is active, progressive, defensive. He is eminently the doer, the creator, the discoverer, the defender. His intellect is for speculation and invention; his energy for adventure, for war, and for conquest, wherever war is just, wherever conquest is necessary. But the woman's power is for rule, not for battle and the intellect is not for invention or creation, but for sweet ordering, arrangement, and decision. She sees the qualities of things, their claims, and their places. Her great function is Praise; she enters into no contest, but infallibly adjudges the crown of contest. By her office, and place, she is protected from all danger and temptation.[39]

Or at least, this is what an 'incorruptibly good' wife would be.[40] There were, of course, other women, as Ruskin inferred, those who had not been properly 'trained in habits of accurate thought', who thought to 'understand' too much, who read the wrong books, 'frivolous' books, books that engaged notions of 'folly' and 'wit' and romance, for even the 'best romance becomes dangerous if, by its excitement, it renders the ordinary course of life uninteresting, and increases the morbid thirst for useless acquaintance with scenes we shall never be called upon to act'; or so he hoped.[41] We will consider contemporary attitudes to women's reading shortly. It was, as we shall see, a subject which aroused considerable anxieties. Ruskin was certainly anxious, seizing upon Thackeray as just the kind of author who, if not read carefully, might despoil an impressionable female mind; an observation the acuity of which we will again contemplate in chapter one.[42] It was not, as WR Greg confirmed, merely a matter of the 'good' wife not reading such novels; she should also not able to comprehend them:

> Many of the saddest and deepest truths in the strange science of sexual affection are to her mysteriously and mercifully veiled and can only be purchased at such a fearful cost that we cannot but wish it otherwise.[43]

As the century progressed, anxious men of letters could look for some reassurance to men of science, at least on the subject of sexuality. Thus the eminent psychologist, Henry Maudsley, could be found agreeing that the biology of female reproduction confirmed that 'the male organisation is one, and the female organisation is another'.[44] The equally eminent William Acton agreed, straying further into the realm of female sexuality to confirm in his *Functions and Disorders of the Reproductive Organs*, published in 1857, that a 'modest' woman was 'seldom' in need of sexual 'gratification' for its own sake; a supposition which clearly implied that there was something unnatural in women engaging sexual activity for any purpose other than furnishing her husband with progeny.[45] Acton's treatise comprised endless case studies in which the happiness of women, and the harmony of

[39] J Ruskin, *Selected Writings* (Oxford University Press, 2004) 158.
[40] Ibid, 159.
[41] Ibid, 161–64.
[42] Ibid, 164.
[43] WR Greg, 'The False Morality of Lady Novelists' (1859) 7 *National Review* 149.
[44] See L Pykett, *The Improper Feminine: The Women's Sensation Novel and the New Woman Writing* (Routledge, 1992) 14.
[45] Ibid, 15. See also R Clark, 'Riddling the Family Firm: The Sexual Economy in *Dombey and Son*' (1984) 51 *ELH* 70, commenting on the strength of this belief in mid-Victorian culture.

their homes, directly correlated with the extent to which they were over- or under-sexualised; insofar as Acton was prepared, barely, to countenance the idea that any woman might be somehow under-sexualised. Thus in the case of a barrister who was afflicted with impotence, Acton was able to offer the reassurance that no matter how frustrated he might be, his wife, being 'kind, considerate, self-sacrificing, and sensible' and above all 'so pure-hearted as to be utterly ignorant and averse to any sexual indulgence', would be fine.[46]

We will revisit Acton and Maudsley and the discourse of sexuality which they strove so hard to prescribe in chapter four, when we take a closer look at prostitution and obscenity. As we shall see, the discourse of science was just one of many discourses which sought to somehow regulate sexual activity and its depiction. None were particularly successful, for the simple reason articulated by Florence Nightingale; there is nothing more futile than the attempt to regulate the expression of 'passion'.[47] For obvious reasons, the discourse of sexuality was inexorably bound up in the larger 'question' of women; even if it remained, very often, in the darker recesses of the debate. The attempt to regulate one presumed the concomitant necessity of confining the other, both within the walls of the Englishman's home and within the pages of his novels.

At Home with the Dombeys

It is a critical commonplace of Dickensian scholarship to suggest that *Dombey and Son* was Charles Dickens's first serious novel, by which is meant the first novel in which he engaged with larger questions of England and its 'condition'.[48] This was certainly the impression of contemporary admirers such as Thackeray and Forster.[49] The critical inference is that earlier novels such as *Pickwick Papers* and *Oliver Twist* were written, at least in part, in lighter shades. The inference is, of course, questionable. At the same time, it can certainly be agreed that there is precious little that is light about *Dombey and Son*. It is a novel, as the narrator affirms, about 'dark shapes'. The house of Paul Dombey, which assumes such symbolic

[46] E Ermarth, *The English Novel in History 1840–1895* (Routledge, 1997) 186.

[47] F Nightingale, *Cassandra, and Other Selections from Suggestions for Thought* (Pickering and Chatto, 1991) 200.

[48] It was also the first from which he made serious money which is somewhat ironic given that the overarching theme of *Dombey and Son* is the devastating consequences that can follow from the single-minded pursuit of wealth. He earned £3,800 from serialisation in 1847 and 'from this date', as Forster confirmed, 'all embarrassments connected with money were brought to a close'. Tomalin, *Charles Dickens* (above n 1) 200. For influential early comments on the pivotal place of *Dombey and Son* in the evolution of Dickens's canon, see F Leavis and Q Leavis, *Dickens the Novelist* (Penguin, 1994) 22, basing his assessment on the unity of plot, K Tillotson; 'Dombey and Son', in A Dyson (ed), *Dickens: Modern Judgements* (Macmillan, 1968) 158–61, 179; and H Stone, 'Dickens and Leitmotif: Music-Staircase Imagery in *Dombey and Son*' (1963) 25 *College English* 217.

[49] Tomalin, *Charles Dickens* (above n 1) 193.

import, is a 'dark' place, every bit as bleak as the infamous Bleak House.[50] At its best, it can be said to have a 'dreary magnificence' (351). At its worst, it is a 'dismal' house, 'as blank a house inside as outside' (34). Shrouded in seemingly perpetual darkness, Dombey's mansion is a monument to vaunting pride and selfishness, and a fragile one too. The fragility becomes shockingly apparent in chapter forty-seven, the moment when Dickens gets very serious indeed.[51]

At this moment, rebuked by a wife who refuses to do anything 'that you ask', possessed of an impotent fury, Paul Dombey lashes out and assaults his daughter Florence (712, 718). The fragile pretences of domestic harmony are shattered. Sarah Ellis had solemnly warned that: 'There are private histories belonging to every family, which, though they operate powerfully upon individual happiness, ought never to be named beyond the home-circle.'[52] However, the dysfunction of the Dombey family is not something that can be kept under one roof, metaphorically or literally. Florence flees, the 'darkening mark of an angry hand' livid upon her breast, a semiotic that will recur throughout the pages that follow (736). The 'dark shadows' are uncovered, as the narrator famously declaims moments before Dombey loses control:

> Oh for a good spirit who would take the house-tops off, with a more potent and benig-nant hand than the lame demon in the tale, and show a Christian people what dark shapes issue from amidst their homes, to swell the retinue of the Destroying Angel as he moves forth among them! (702)

More than anything else Dombey fears public humiliation, the 'opinion of the world' (774, 776). But his shame cannot be allowed to remain in the shadows.[53] Thirty thousand Englishmen and women would follow the disintegration of Paul Dombey's family month by month for the best part of two years.

The first 46 chapters had charted the gradual disintegration of Paul Dombey, emotionally bereft widower and 'Colossus of commerce' (398). The 'fall' of the house of Dombey is triggered by the early death of Dombey's son Paul, the intended heir to the family business, an event which plunges his father into a deep depression from which he is seemingly unable to recover.[54] The death of little Paul attracted considerable critical applause. Thereafter the novel tends to mark time until Dombey makes the fateful mistake of deciding to remarry, or rather the fate-ful mistake of choosing Edith Granger to be his second wife. Edith proves to be a reluctant bride, or at least a deeply cynical and unsympathetic one. The marriage

---

[50] On the symbolism of Dombey's house, and its conspicuous darkness, see A Jackson, 'Reward, Punishment and the Conclusion of *Dombey and Son*', (1978) 7 *Dickens Studies Annual* 107–11; J Gold, *Charles Dickens: Radical Moralist* (Minnesota University Press, 1972) 157; and H Stone, 'The Novel as Fairy Tale: Dickens' *Dombey and Son*' (1966) 47 *English Studies* 16–17, likening Dombey's mansion to a bewitched and decaying fairy-tale mansion.

[51] On chapter 47 as the pivot of the novel, see C Colligan, 'Raising the House Tops: Sexual Surveillance in Charles Dickens's *Dombey and Son*' (2000) 29 *Dickens Studies Annual* 100–102.

[52] See Chase and Levenson, *The Spectacle of Intimacy* (above n 11) 12.

[53] It is reported that 'The Papers' are 'eager for news' of Dombey's separation and its causes (801).

[54] Critics have long supposed that little Paul is a precursor to David Copperfield, whose conception followed quickly on his heels. See Tomalin, *Charles Dickens* (above n 1) 185.

is a failure from the start, the mutual loathing of both parties quickly intensifying. Sensing a chance to humiliate his hated employer, Dombey's business manager Carker tries to seduce Edith. Edith agrees to elope to France, but has no intention of committing adultery. The rejected Carker falls under a train, terrified that he is being followed by a vengeful Dombey. In fact, Dombey has descended into catatonic depression, broken only by moments of occasional violence, such as that in chapter forty-seven, after which Florence flees the family home, the business collapses, and the bailiffs move in. Dombey is 'fallen' and his house disintegrates, literally and metaphorically, at least until Florence returns to fashion her father's tortuous redemption; a process which consumes the final 15 chapters (904).[55]

There are, of course, myriad interpretations of *Dombey and Son*. A number of critics have, for obvious reasons, read the novel as an assault on the violence of commerce, the belief that 'money' as Dombey tells his little son 'can do anything', seeing in the disintegration of the Dombey family a representation of the disintegration of England's 'condition', and more particularly the condition of its middle-classes (111).[56] Such a reading confirms the opinion of those who see *Dombey and Son* as being Dickens's first 'serious' novel. Of obvious importance for us are those readings which focus on gender issues in *Dombey and Son* including those which align the disintegration of Paul Dombey with a suggested crisis of masculinity in Victorian England, as well as those which read the novel as a reflection on the continuing credibility of the doctrine of separate spheres, and those which address the failure of Dombey's second marriage and its consequences.[57] In comparison with some of Dickens's other novels it might be thought that one of the themes that is rather less prominent in *Dombey and Son* is legal reform. There are occasional references to legal instruments, most obviously the marriage settlement

---

[55] The nature of Dombey's not entirely convincing process of redemption has long troubled critics, not least because Dickens was keen to impress in the Preface to the second edition that his protagonist 'undergoes no violent internal change, either in this book, or in life. A sense of injustice is with him all along' (949). For a commentary, see I Milner, 'The Dickens Drama: Mr Dombey' (1970) 24 *Nineteenth-Century Fiction* 477–48, and L Yelin, 'Strategies for Survival: Florence and Edith in *Dombey and Son*' (1979) 23 *Victorian Studies* 298–300.

[56] In reply to his father's rather pompous advice, young Paul asks why if it can 'do anything', money could not save his mother. Amongst the many interpretations of *Dombey* as a 'parable of mercantile capitalism', are those of J Tambling, *Dickens, Violence and the Modern State* (Macmillan, 1995) 48–70; A Elfenbein, 'Managing the House in *Dombey and Son*: Dickens and the Use of Analogy' (1995) 92 *Studies in Philology* 361–82; J Loesberg, 'Deconstruction, Historicism, and Overdetermination: Dislocations of Marriage Plots in *Robert Elsmere* and *Dombey and Son*' (1990) 33 *Victorian Studies* 456–60; and S Perera, 'Wholesale, Retail and for Exportation: Empire and the Family Business in *Dombey and Son*' in M Hollington (ed), *Charles Dickens: Critical Assessments* (Croom Helm, 1995) 41–58, also noting immediate thematic parallels with Thackeray's *The Newcomes*, a novel that we shall encounter in chapter one.

[57] A number of these also work with the commercial theme, most immediately in terms of the economics of the marriage market. See, for example, Clark, 'Riddling the Family Firm' (above n 45) 69–84; Auerbach, 'Dickens and Dombey' (above n 10) 95–114; and Yelin, 'Strategies for Survival' (above n 55) 297–319, suggesting that *Dombey and Son* can be read as a full-frontal critique of the doctrine of 'separate spheres'; H Moglen, 'Theorizing Fiction/Fictionalizing Theory: The Case of *Dombey and Son*' (1922) 35 *Victorian Studies* 159–84; and J Marsh, 'Good Mrs Brown's Connections: Sexuality and Story-Telling in *Dealings with the Firm of Dombey and Son*' (1991) 58 *ELH* 405–26, arguing that *Dombey* is the first novel in which Dickens ventures into the subject of female sexuality.

between Dombey and his second wife, and her subsequent request for a formal 'separation' agreement (713). Yet, in comparison with the two novels that were to follow, *David Copperfield* and *Bleak House*, both of which place the law more obviously on the surface of the text, this absence might seem to be remarkable in itself. There is no equivalent case law to *Jarndyce v Jarndyce*, and there are no lawyers or legal clerks of the discomforting presence of Tulkinghorn or Uriah Heep. The law, however, is not so much absent as lurking; it is one of the many dark shadows which shroud the house of Paul Dombey. As the novel unfolds, the reader is assaulted with a series of crimes which are written to confirm the dire consequences that follow the disintegration of a dysfunctional family.

There is perhaps most obviously Dombey's assault; a violence which, in her 'shadowy dread' Florence had long feared (712, 718). Florence's is an 'outcast from a living parent's love', her very existence hitherto barely registering with her father; for 'girls' can have 'nothing to do with Dombey and Son' (153, 381).[58] Mrs Tox famously articulates the incongruity: 'Dear me, dear me! To think . . . that Dombey and Son should be Daughter after all' (253).[59] But this is precisely what Paul Dombey cannot think. It is into this emotional void that Edith steps, recognising in Florence a 'good angel' (705).[60] Dombey only begins to take cognisance of Florence as his marriage to Edith collapses, seeing in his daughter an accomplice to his misfortune. When he hits Florence, Dombey imagines himself striking his recalcitrant wife. By this time Edith had already flown, terrified, 'shuddering' (718). Florence will quickly follow. Meeting her father staring at the 'deed of settlement' drawn up on the occasion of his marriage to Edith, Florence moves to console him:

> But in his frenzy, he lifted up his cruel arm and struck her, crosswise, with that heaviness, that she tottered on the marble floor, and as he dealt the blow, he told her what Edith was, and bade her follow her, since they had always been in league. (721)

The reader is left to imagine how Dombey describes his second wife: adulteress, whore? Both are possible, each gesturing towards a further crime with which Dickens challenges his readers.

The insinuation of adultery alludes to the second of these crimes. It is allusive because, although she appears to elope, Edith has no intention of having an affair with the odious Carker.[61] As she subsequently impresses upon Florence, she may be 'guilty of much', but not of adultery (936–37). Even so, the very fact of her eloping creates an impression of 'criminality', as her horrified cousin Feenix concedes, gesturing to a popular prejudice which found sustenance in the arcane jurispru-

---

[58] In another famous passage, Dombey instructs the statuary as to the appropriate inscription for his son's headstone to read 'beloved and only child' (268). He has to be reminded that he has another, Florence.

[59] An observation pointedly reiterated at the close of the novel, following Florence's reconciliation with her father (912).

[60] She is not alone. The same metaphor is repeatedly invoked by Florence's admirers, most readily Walter and Mr Toots (759, 764).

[61] Though it seems that Dickens had originally intended that she should. See Stone, 'The Novel as Fairy Tale' (above n 50) 9, and more recently Hager, *Dickens and the Rise of Divorce* (above n 4) 96.

dence of 'criminal conversation' which we will encounter in chapter one, and with which, as we shall see, Dickens was very familiar (776, 937). Paul Dombey, needless to say, has a very particular view of marriage as a 'social contract', a bargain much like any other bargain (13). As the narrator observes in the very first chapter, 'Dombey and Son had often dealt in hides, but never in hearts' (12). Dombey purchases his wives, exchanging access to his wealth and reputation in return for dutiful governance of his 'house' and sex on demand (13). There is nothing unusual in this. It is a view shared by countless fictive husbands of the period, as we shall see in the following chapters, and nearly as many fictive wives, including, it seems, Dombey's first wife.

Edith, his second wife, is first seen 'carrying her gossamer parasol with a proud and weary air'. She is 'very handsome, very haughty, very wilful' (316). She is also a widow. But more importantly, at least for Dombey and his irksome companion Major Bagstock, Edith is reported to be of good 'blood' (321). Negotiations are conducted between the Major and Edith's mother, the gruesome Mrs Skewton. It is clear to both that there might be issues of compatibility, but as the Major ruminates:

> None of that, Sir. It won't do here. But as to there being something of a division between 'em or a gulf as the mother calls it damme, Sir, that seems true enough. And it's odd enough! Well Sir! ... Edith Granger and Dombey are well matched; let 'em fight it out! Bagstock backs the winner! (410)

Incompatible or not, it is clear that there is a bargain to be had. Edith has 'beauty, blood, and talent' and Dombey has a 'fortune', and 'what more could any couple have?' (411) It is a 'bargain' that Edith appreciates, even if it is one into which she enters reluctantly. She has, as she informs her mother, been 'bought'; as indeed she was in her first marriage (431).[62] For:

> There is no slave in a market: there is no horse in a fair: so shown and offered and examined and paraded, Mother, as I have been, for ten shameful years . . . Is it not so? Have I been made the bye-word of all kinds of men? Have fools, have profligates, have boys, have dotards, dangled after me, and one by one rejected me, and fallen off, because you were too plain with all your cunning: yes, and too true, with all those false pretences: until we have almost come to be notorious? . . . Have I been hawked and vended here and there, until the last grain of self-respect is dead within me, and I loathe myself? (432)

There is certainly something melodramatic about 'angelic' Edith, as the Major deploying a metaphor of pointed inappropriateness, observes.[63] There is also much that is cold. Both qualities are evident in her chilling rejection of Carker,

[62] The bargain on this latter occasion was frustrated by the fact that Edith's first husband died before 'his inheritance descended on him' leaving her effectively penniless (432).

[63] On the melodramatic Edith, see Tillotson, 'Dombey and Son' (above n 48) 170–71; Jackson, 'Reward' (above n 50) 122–24; and more recently, Tomalin, *Charles Dickens* (above n 1) 194. The melodrama enhances the sense that in a number of the Edith 'scenes' Dickens is anticipating the coming vogue for the 'sensational'. The melodrama does not preclude Dickens writing some depth into Edith. Indeed, according to Louise Yelin, Edith is Dickens's 'first attempt to create a complex woman character'. See Yelin, 'Strategies for Survival' (above n 55) 310, and 315.

grasping a knife and threatening to 'murder' him if lays a hand on her (820). But there is also much that is calculated to insinuate the respect, if not the sympathy, of Dickens's readers. On the night before her wedding, Edith is described as wrestling 'with her unquiet spirit, tearless, friendless, silent, proud and uncomplaining' (475) after which she bursts into tears. It is a familiar misery, or at least it would have been to many of Dickens's female readers. At first, she plays the part of Mrs Dombey, 'beautiful and proud', but also 'disdainful and defiant' (555). It is the disdain, the 'intense, unutterable, withering scorn' that ultimately destroys her husband, and their marriage despite her mother's desperate reminders that Dombey has secured her 'settlement' and thus completed his part of the bargain (566). Matters reach their peak when Edith flatly observes 'I will do nothing that you ask'; a declaration which imports an inference of sexual resistance (712).[64] Ultimately, as all communication breaks down, Dombey deputes Carker to spy on his wife and try to persuade her that his 'will is law' (645) but the cause is already lost. All Dombey can do is 'watch', at first in person and then vicariously, and hate (566, 644).[65] In the end, Edith runs off to France, Carker following eagerly in her path.

The third crime written into *Dombey and Son* is that of prostitution. It takes place both within and without the house of Paul Dombey. In the former instance it is again allusive. As we have just noted, Edith Dombey repeatedly likens the operation of the marriage-market to that of a market for concubines or slaves:

> I have been offered and rejected, put up and appraised, until my very soul has sickened. I have not had an accomplishment or grace that might have been a resource to me, but it has been paraded and vended to enhance my value, as if the common crier had called it through the streets . . . I suffered myself to be sold, as infamously as any woman with a halter round her neck is sold in any market-place. (823)

The affinity is sharply drawn in the scene where the notionally 'fallen' Edith comes across the very fallen Alice Marwood. Unlike Edith, Alice had long ago allowed herself to be seduced by Carker, and so now is left with no means of survival other than prostitution. Each, Edith concludes, has 'sold' themselves (624). But only in a sense, for Alice is a real prostitute; something she is determined to impress as she relates the particular legal consequences of her fall:

> There was a criminal called Alice Marwood a girl still, but deserted and outcast. And she was tried, and she was sentenced. And lord, how the gentlemen in the court talked about it! And how grave the judge was, on her duty, and on her having perverted the gifts of nature as if he didn't know better than anybody there, that they had been made curses to her! and how he preached about the strong arm of the Law so very strong to save her, when she was an innocent and helpless little wretch! (531)

---

[64] See Milner, 'The Dickens Drama' (above n 55) 484–85; Jackson, 'Reward', 110; Colligan, 'Sexual Surveillance' (above n 51) 115–18; and Moglen, 'Theorizing Fiction' (above n 57) 164–68, surmising that Dombey may be particularly enraged by the imputation that he is anyway impotent.

[65] On the idea of the 'gaze' in *Dombey and Son*, particularly over the sexualized bodies of Edith and Florence, see Colligan, 'Sexual Surveillance' ibid, 99–123.

To the reader of *Dombey and Son*, Alice would have seemed both more and less familiar. Dickens wrote in the main for the middle classes, for men like Paul Dombey and for women like Edith and Florence, for which reason the crimes inflicted upon each would have had a certain familiarity, particularly following the establishment of the Divorce Court in 1857. Alice, however, falls outside the home of Paul Dombey, for which reason she might also be said to fall outside the experience of Dickens's readers, or at least his female readers. She did not, of course, fall outside Dickens's experience. As he wrote *Dombey and Son* in 1848, he was also busy setting up a home for 'fallen' women at Urania Cottage.[66] To the vast majority of Dickens's readers, however, the fall of Alice Marwood was very much the kind of thing that happened to other people. It was, of course, no less salutary for this, just as the parallel which Dickens creates between the respective fates of Alice and Edith is no less significant. In presenting Alice Marwood to his readers, Dickens brought the working-class 'fallen angel', if not into the house of Paul Dombey, then into the reading-rooms of tens of thousands of middle-class Victorians.[67]

And it was not, of course, just Alice. 'What came to that girl', Alice says of herself, 'comes to thousands every year. It was only ruin, and she was born to it' (531). There would be plenty of Alices in Dickens's novels, as there were in his life, just as there would be plenty more Ediths. Indeed, in the perception of many, far too many Alice Marwoods and Edith Dombeys could be found in the pages of the Victorian novel. For a significant few, however, the depiction of women like Alice and Edith served a vital purpose in writing a rather different female aesthetic. In her 1868 essay 'Criminals, Idiots, Women, and Minors', Frances Power Cobbe took satirical aim at the poetics of the 'angel in the house':

> But where women are concerned, English law ceases to be a dry system, regardful only of abstract justice and policy. Themis, when she presides at the domestic hearth, doffs her wig, and allows herself to be swayed by poetical, not to say romantic, considerations. We are rarely allowed in debating it to examine accurately the theory of conjugal justice.[68]

The marriage of Paul and Edith Dombey may have been fictional, but there was nothing poetic, still less romantic, about it. They were an:

> Ill-assorted couple, unhappy in themselves and in each other, bound together by no tie but the manacle that joined their fettered hands, and straining that so harshly, in their shrinking asunder, that it wore and chafed to the bone. (699)

The house of Paul Dombey, like that of Ebenezer Scrooge, was visited by a spirit for a reason; to present a parallel of the deepest discomfort, between the 'moral pestilence' which everyone knew existed on the streets of London, and the

---

[66] An institution we will revisit in chapter four. See J Hartley, *Charles Dickens and the House of Fallen Women* (Methuen, 2009) 10–11, 43.

[67] The sales figures for the serialised version of *Dombey* hovered pretty consistently around the 30,000 mark. See Tomalin, *Charles Dickens* (above n 1) 191.

[68] See Hamilton, *Criminals, Idiots, Women, and Minors* (above n 23) 112.

'nameless sins' which existed inside the houses of men such as Paul Dombey (701).
By the time *Dombey and Son* hit the presses, it had become increasingly obvious
that too many families were as dysfunctional and violent as the Dombeys, just as
it was becoming equally apparent that far too many women who lived on the
streets outside suffered in the same way as Alice Marwood. Modern critics have
noted the very evident parallels between Edith Dombey and the notorious Caroline
Norton whose husband embarked on an ill-fated 'criminal conversation' suit
against the incumbent Prime Minister, Lord Melbourne, in 1836; an action we will
revisit in chapter one.[69] Dickens was fascinated by Norton, just as he was by the
various 'fallen' women who came through the doors of Urania Cottage. Victorian
gentlemen, and their wives, worried a lot about women such as Edith and Alice;
but they did not just worry. They also tried to work out what to do to make their
lives better; or at least some of them did. Despite the similar uncertainties which
afflicted his private life, or perhaps indeed because of them, Charles Dickens was
precisely such a Victorian.

The Disease of Reading

The fall of the 'house' of Dombey mattered because so many people read about it,
and did so at a time when debates about the 'condition' of England and its women
were becoming increasingly urgent. As literary historians have noted, the mid-
nineteenth century saw an explosion in reading, impelled by rising literacy rates
and technological advances in printing and publishing.[70] More and more people
were reading more and more, and in the main they were reading novels and newspapers. Even those who made their fortunes from this explosion could be found
expressing certain misgivings. Wilkie Collins mused uneasily on the 'unknown
public' which could be 'counted by millions; the mysterious, the unfathomable,
the universal public of the penny-novel-Journals'.[71] Here, Collins was speaking to
a particular affinity which caused much contemporary anxiety, between the novelist and the newspaper editor. As the century progressed the power of the novel, like
that of the press, became ever more crisply apparent, and ever more obviously a
matter of concern.

---

[69] See Hager, *Dickens and the Rise of Divorce* (above n 4) 91, 122–26.

[70] See Thompson, *Reviewing Sex* (above n 31) at 3, noting that by the late 1840s, the 'novel was
universally acknowledged to be the representative artistic form of the period', for which reason the
literary review became the critical 'mediator' between literature and reading public. In her *The English
Novel in History 1840–1895* (Routledge, 1997) Elizabeth Deeds Ermarth refers, at 38, to the mid-century
as 'momentous' in regard to the shaping of the modern English novel. Nicholas Daly refers to a 'dizzying
ascent' of the novel in the mid-century. See N Daly, *Sensation and Modernity in the 1860s* (Cambridge
University Press, 2009) 13–14, noting also that 1859 saw the publication of the first academic study of
the novel, Masson's *British Novelists and Their Styles: Being a Critical Sketch of the History of British Prose
Fiction*, (Macmillan, 1859)

[71] Quoted in Daly, *Sensation and Modernity* (above n 70) 3.

As we have already noted, the fact that *Dombey and Son* was written by Charles Dickens imports a particular authorial context. We shall revisit Dickens on a number of occasions in subsequent chapters, as we will other male novelists and indeed poets. We will also encounter, for the first time perhaps in English literary history, a significant number of female ones, for this was, in the words of the revered contemporary critic ES Dallas, the 'age of the lady novelists'.[72] It was also the age of the lady reader, as a reviewer in the *Church of England Quarterly Review* warned as early as 1842:

> The great bulk of novel readers are females; and to them such impressions (as are conveyed through fiction) are peculiarly mischievous: for, first, they are naturally more sensitive, more impressable, than the other sex; and secondly, their engagements are of a less engrossing character, they have more time as well as more inclination to indulge in reveries of fiction.[73]

Robert Buchanan took a more positive view, confirming that the 'birth of the novel has given speech to many ladies who must otherwise have been silent'.[74] So, rather later, did Josephine Butler, who attested to the importance of the novel in forcing 'us to create a literature of our own' which thus liberated women from a 'conspiracy of silence'; a supposition which has, for understandable reasons, generated especial interest amongst modern feminist literary critics.[75] But few others were quite so welcoming. As late as 1880, Davenport Adams expressed himself no

---

[72] Review of *Lady Audley's Secret* in *The Times* (18 November 1862) 4. WR Greg took the same view, observing in 1859 that 'the number ... of young-lady novelists, extant at this moment, passes calculation, and was unparalleled at any former epoch' before concluding that 'the supply of the fiction market has fallen mainly into their hands'. See his 'False Morality of Lady Novelists' (1859) 8 *National Review* at 148. For commentaries on the particular significance of emergent women writers at this time, see Gilbert and Gubar, *The Madwoman in the Attic* (above n 36) xi–ii, xxxii; C Kaplan, *Victoriana: Histories, Fictions, Criticism*, (Edinburgh University Press, 2007), 39–40, Showalter, *A Literature of Their Own* (above n 36) 3–4; and most recently, Thompson, 'Responding to the woman questions' above n 34 at 1, arguing that 'Women writers dominated the vast novel market in Victorian England'.

[73] 'Moral and Political Tendency of the Modern Novels' (1842) 11 *Church of England Quarterly Review* 287–88.

[74] R Buchanan, 'Society's Looking-Glass', (1862) 6 *Temple Bar* 135. We shall encounter Buchanan again in chapter four, in the immediate context of his notorious critique of Dante Gabriel Rossetti and the 'fleshly school' of poets.

[75] See Hamilton, *Criminals, Idiots, Women, and Minors* (above n 23) 9. According to Gail Cunningham, 'the emancipation of women and the emancipation of the English novel advanced together'. See G Cunningham, *The New Woman and the Victorian Novel* (Macmillan, 1978) at 3. The literature here is, of course, vast. Amongst the most influential commentaries on the impact of the novel on an emergent Victorian female consciousness, can be counted Gilbert and Gubar's *The Madwoman in the Attic* (above n 36); Elaine Showalter's, *A Literature of Their Own* (above n 36); Nancy Armstrong's *Desire and Domestic Fiction: A Political History of the Novel* (Oxford University Press, 1987); Constance Hersh's *Subversive Heroines* (above n 16) and Mary Poovey's *Uneven Developments: the Ideological Work of Gender in Mid-Victorian England* (Virago, 1989). Gilbert and Gubar have famously likened the written word to a 'weapon in a kind of metaphorical warfare'. See Gilbert and Gubar, *The Madwoman in the Attic* (above n 36) at 52. According to Poovey, it was the novel which, more than anything, transformed the female communicant 'from silent sufferer of private wrongs into an articulate spokesperson in the public sphere'. See Poovey, *Uneven Developments*, at 64–65. For a recent comment on the implications of this particular affinity between the novel and the female consciousness, and its more immediate implications in regard to an awareness of legal issues at the time, see K Kalsem, *In Contempt: Nineteenth Century Women, Law and Literature* (Ohio State University Press, 2012) 18–19.

less concerned in regard to the 'fictitious sentiment' that the woman reader 'nourishes by novel-reading, idleness and indulgence in day-dreaming'.[76] Whilst she
likewise acknowledged the role that novels such as Charlotte Bronte's *Jane Eyre*
had played in nurturing the female 'mind', Margaret Oliphant declared that the
emergence of the woman's novel was shaming, to both writer and reader, the only
solution for which was the most careful regulation of its reception.[77] In his influential 1859 essay the 'False Morality of Lady Novelists', WR Greg iterated the same
anxiety and the same prospective solution:

> Novels constitute a principal part of the reading of women, who are always impression-
> able, in whom at all times the emotional element is more awake and more powerful than
> the critical, whose feelings are more easily aroused and whose estimates are more easily
> influenced than ours, while at the same time the correctness of their feelings and the
> justice of their elements are matters of the most special and preeminent concern.[78]

Ruskin agreed. There was nothing wrong with women reading and there was nothing wrong with women being allowed into libraries but it was important that it was
the right books they read and the right libraries they browsed; by which he meant
'old' libraries divested of 'modern' books.[79] Accordingly, much of the debate
moved around which books were right and which were wrong. Ever sensitive to
the moment, and the perceived needs of her readers, Sarah Stickney Ellis duly
produced a dedicated handbook on the subject entitled *The Young Ladies Reader*
in which she urged the particular responsibility of mothers to oversee what their
daughters were reading, alongside the shrewd advice that they would anyway be
better directed towards domestic manuals, such as hers.[80] It was, inevitably perhaps, yet another best-seller.

A few years later in his *Autobiography* Anthony Trollope mused on the state of
the mid-Victorian novel: what had changed and what had stayed the same. What
had stayed the same was a preoccupation with stories about 'love'.[81] What had
changed was the way these stories were being written. Here Trollope famously
identified two dominant genres, both of which at first glance appeared to be new:
the 'sensational' and the 'anti-sensational'. Of course, as Trollope went on to urge,
the distinction was as much one of convenience, for a 'good novel should be both
and both in the highest degree'.[82] It is certainly true that the line between the 'sen-

---

[76] Davenport Adams, *Woman's Work and Worth* (J Hogg, 1880) 97.

[77] See M Allott, *The Brontes: The Critical Heritage* (Routledge, 1974) 390.

[78] Greg, 'False Morality' (above n 43) 144.

[79] Ruskin, *Selected Writings* (above n 39) 164–65. For a broad commentary on strategies of
'paternalistic surveillance' engaged in regulating what young women read, see Flint, *The Woman Reader
1837–1914* (Oxford University Press, 1993) 4.

[80] S Ellis, *The Young Ladies Reader* (Grant and Griffith, 1845) 1, 289–90. There was nothing wrong
with reading, Ellis reassured her readers. Done properly, it could promote the communion of 'mutual
minds', between mothers and daughters as well as wives and husbands. But it had to be done properly.
She was particularly troubled by the thought that daughters might come across Shakespeare
unaccompanied, even more that they might somehow alight upon something French.

[81] A Trollope, *An Autobiography* (Penguin, 1996) 144–45, confirming that 'love' was, with only the
rarest of exceptions, 'necessary to all novelists'.

[82] Ibid, 146.

sational' and the supposedly 'anti-sensational' can at times seem rather blurred. Trollope seized on *Jane Eyre* as instructive.[83] In chapter one, we will in like terms contemplate Ellen Wood's *East Lynne* as a piece of 'domestic sensationalism'.[84] We will also, in due course, encounter various other literary genres which do not seem to fit comfortably into the simpler dichotomy: the late Gothic, the satirical and the pre-Raphaelite. But what these genres and sub-genres all shared in common was an ability to cultivate admiring audiences and anxious reviewers.

The greatest anxiety moved around the 'sensational' novel, examples of which will recur in each of the chapters that follow. Oliphant was peculiarly exercised by the sensational, by novels about sex and crime, most commonly adultery, bigamy and murder. Critics tended to identify in the sensation novel the epitome of all that was wrong with the literature of the time. And here again they were not alone. Medical journals railed against the addictive nature of reading, confirming any number of specific female 'maladies' that the craving for literature nurtured, including neurosis, hysteria, and irregular menstrual cycles; afflictions which, as EJ Tilt warned, were peculiarly prevalent 'among the higher class'.[85] A reviewer in the *Medical Critic and Psychological Journal* in 1863 confirmed that the 'morbid craving for excitement', so alarmingly evident amongst young women, was indeed a pathology; one that demanded instant attention.[86] But all was not lost. Young women, as Acton advised, might be inoculated from the worst symptoms of the 'disease of reading' provided their reading habits were carefully regulated,[87] and provided they did not read alone, Robert Carter added, in his 1853 treatise *On the Pathology and Treatment of Hysteria.*[88]

Pathological metaphors were eagerly adopted by suitably awed literary critics.[89] Alfred Ainger suggested that a 'craving for books' was indeed a 'morbid phenomenon'.[90] The sensation novel, it was opined, worked by 'drugging thought and reason, and stimulating the attention through the lower and more animal

[83] Ibid, 146–47.

[84] Daly discusses the relation of the sensational and the domestic in his *Sensation* (above n 70) suggesting at 27–28, that the former might be read as an 'aberrant strain' of the latter in which the 'darker aspects of courtship and family life seduction, adultery, bigamy, and even murder were foregrounded'.

[85] E Tilt, *On the Preservation of Health of Women at the Critical Periods of Life* (John Churchill, 1851) 31. There was a particular danger, it was generally agreed, in teenage girls reading romance novels and pregnant women too. For a commentary, see C Golden, *Images of the Woman Reader in Victorian British and American Fiction* (University Press of Florida, 2003), 31–38, 96–97.

[86] 'Sensation Novels' (1863) 3 *Medical Critic and Psychological Journal* 513.

[87] See J Phegley, 'Henceforward I Refuse to Bow the Knee to Their Narrow Rule: Mary Elizabeth Braddon's *Belgravia Magazine*, Women Readers, and Literary Valuation' (2004) 26 *Nineteenth Century Contexts* 151, 153.

[88] R Carter, *On the Pathology and Treatment of Hysteria* (John Churchill, 1853) 135–36.

[89] For a commentary, see Flint, *Woman Reader* (above n 79) 53–70.

[90] See A Ainger, 'Books and Their Uses' (1859) 1 *Macmillan's Magazine* 110. The metaphor of morbidity, which appears to have been first coined by Mansel, in H Mansel, 'Sensation Novels' (1863) 113 *Quarterly Review* at 482–83, became pervasive. It was, for this reason, similarly supposed that sensation novels appealed more to the working classes; a supposition that only served to enhance contemporary anxiety. The fact that it quickly became apparent that the most readily addicted were actually middle-class women, did nothing to ameliorate these concerns. See Daly, *Sensation and Modernity* (above n 70) 6–7.

instincts'.[91] Women, needless to say, were thought to be peculiarly susceptible to such an 'appeal to the nerves' precisely because their intellects were more fragile.[92] Indeed, too much reading of the wrong books could render a woman insensible and her home dissolute, as one contributor to the *Christian's Penny Magazine* advised:

> A whole family, brought to destitution, has lately had all its misfortunes clearly traced by the authorities to an ungovernable passion for novel-reading entertained by the wife and member. The husband was sober and industrious, but his wife was indolent, and addicted to reading everything procurable in the shape of a romance.

One child had 'fled' into prostitution; another was shackled to prevent her doing the same. The house was filthy, and when the authorities discovered 'the cause of it sat reading the latest "sensation work" of the season', she simply 'refused to allow herself to be disturbed in her entertainment'.[93] The idea that addictive reading would lead to an inexorable sexual 'ruin' became a recurrent theme in such evangelical and conservative journals.[94]

Revealing a common appreciation of both literary and medical discourse, if not such a resilient remembrance of the correct terminology, Jane Welsh Carlyle observed:

> The appetite for magazine *Tales* and three-volume novels is getting to be a positive lupus? Something! I forget the full medical name of that disease which makes the victim gobble up, with unslaked voracity, pounds on pounds of raw beef and tallow candles! Or anything else that comes readiest.[95]

Against the forces of the market, however, the sober warnings of critics, scientists and Jane Welsh Carlyle were futile. As we shall see, sensation novels took the English literary scene by storm during the 1860s, so much so that their influence reached right into the heart of the canon, eventually leading astray the likes of Trollope and Dickens, Eliot, even Oliphant; each of whom, with varying degrees of apparent distaste succumbed to writing novels which clearly owed much to the sensational.[96]

Whilst Trollope preferred to align himself with the 'anti-sensational', there is perhaps less surprise in his turning to the sensational in his late contribution *The Eustace Diamonds*.[97] There is equally little surprise in finding sensational elements

[91] Unsigned, 'Female Sensation Novelists' *Christian Remembrancer* January 1868, 210.

[92] The ease with which readers might become so addicted is evidenced in Braddon's own wry amusement on receiving correspondence sent by readers who had clearly lost the ability to distinguish properly between real people and those she had invented for her novels. See R Wolff, *Sensational Victorian: The Life and Fiction of Mary Elizabeth Braddon* (Garland, 1979) 164–65.

[93] 'Novel Reading: A Letter to a Young Lady' (1859) 14 *Christian's Penny Magazine and Friend of the People* 155.

[94] See Golden, *Images* (above n 85) 96–97, citing a similar case study published in the 1855 *Wesleyan-Methodist Magazine*.

[95] See Flint, *Woman Reader* (above n 79) 51.

[96] See Daly, *Sensation and Modernity* (above n 70) 35–39. Oliphant's contribution was *Salem Chapel*. It was not a commercial or critical success.

[97] Trollope preferred to seem himself as a 'realist'. See Trollope, *Autobiography* (above n 81) 146.

in a number of Dickens's works of the period such as *Bleak House* and *Great Expectations*, and indeed *Dombey and Son*.[98] The conversion of George Eliot, most apparent in later novels such as *Daniel Deronda* might, however, seem to be more remarkable. In the eyes of many critics, both contemporary and modern, the very idea of the Victorian 'realist' novel is indelibly associated with Eliot.[99] Certainly, Eliot's acute sense of authorial responsibility militated away from the fanciful, from what she famously termed 'silly' novels, those 'mind and millinery' novels which were distinguished 'by the particular quality of silliness that predominates them, the frothy, the prosy, the pious, or the pendantic'.[100] Novels should be serious not silly, as fellow critic Dinah Mulock Craik confirmed, for which reason the putative female writer should 'examine herself' most rigorously before putting pen to paper.[101] It was not enough to write simply to entertain. Novels should be written with a 'purpose', dedicated to depicting that 'rare, precious quality of truthfulness' and, it might be surmised, creating it too.[102] It was this commitment which, as we shall see in chapter three, defined the 'realist' novel, and limited it.

In his 1865 essay entitled *Novels with Purpose*, the Irish historian Justin M'Carthy proclaimed:

> The novelist is now our most influential writer. If he be a man of genius his power over the community he addresses is far beyond that of any other author. Macaulay's influence over the average English mind was narrow compared with that of Dickens; even Carlyle's was not on the whole so great as that of Thackeray. The readers of the *Idylls of the King* were but a limited number when compared with the readers of *Jane Eyre*; nor could Mr Browning's finest poem pretend to attract as many admirers, even among people of taste and education, as were suddenly won by *Adam Bede*.[103]

Aside from the passing irony that the author of *Adam Bede* might be considered a 'man of genius', there is much here of significance. The novel mattered in mid-nineteenth-century England, more than ever before and perhaps more than it ever would again. The men, and the women, who wrote novels exercised, accordingly, an authority and influence that was unparalleled.

Writing a little later in 1895, JC Tarver concluded that, 'the novel from being the resource of idle moments, the dissipation of indolent minds, a thing to be

---

[98] The suggestion that parts, at least, of *Dombey and Son*, most obviously those which import a greater sexuality, including the kidnapping of young Florence by Mrs Brown and Edith's rejection of Carker, might be read as prospectively sensational, is made by Marsh in 'Sexuality and Story-Telling' (above n 57) at 419. Leavis famously dismissed the 'childish' sensational plot as an unwelcome distraction. See Leavis and Leavis *Dickens the Novelist* (above n 48) 22. As we shall see in chapter four, it is often argued that the sensation genre grew out of the 1830s Newgate crime novels, in which case *Oliver Twist* might also be said to be genetically coded.

[99] The triumph of the realists was famously proclaimed by FR Leavis in *The Great Tradition* (Chatto and Windus, 1948).

[100] Eliot identified herself with Gaskell, as well as Martineau and Charlotte Bronte, as women writers of 'patient diligence', as opposed to the too many who wrote simply out of 'vanity'. See G Eliot, 'Silly Novels by Lady Novelists' in *Selected Essays, Poems and Other Writings* (Penguin, 1990) 140, 161.

[101] D Craik, *A Woman's Thoughts About Women* (Hurst and Blackett, 1858) at 53.

[102] Eliot, *Selected Essays* (above n 100) 177.

[103] Quoted in L Rodensky, *The Crime in Mind: Criminal Responsibility and the Victorian Novel*, (Oxford University Press, 2003) 4.

preached against, and put away on Sundays, has become the chosen instrument of the greatest thinkers of our age, of our most earnest preachers', before concluding that 'those who object to the works of George Eliot because they are so disagreeable, to *Madame Bovary* because it is so cruel, and declare that such things ought not be written, are simply stoning the prophets in order to be rid of them in their home-truths'.[104] The two citations are instructive. The allusion to Eliot imports a particular resonance; for few were more attuned to the power as well as the 'purpose' of the novel, later observing that she would 'carry to my grave the mental diseases with which' certain novels 'have contaminated me'.[105] Vernon Lee confirmed the same sense of literary insinuation, albeit in less pejorative tones, suggesting that 'a good third of what we take to be instinctive knowledge, or knowledge vaguely acquired from personal experience, is really obtained from the novels which we or our friends have read'.[106]

Someone who was certainly 'contaminated' by reading the wrong kind of novel was Isabel Gilbert. Isabel was the frustrated adulteress who took centre stage in Mary Elizabeth Braddon's 1864 novel *The Doctor's Wife*, a barely disguised re-writing of Flaubert's *Madame Bovary*; the second of Tarver's citations and one of those novels which appalled critics most commonly identified as carrying some kind of malignant literary virus. In a rather neat piece of literary conceit, however, Braddon has Isabel identify herself, not with Emma Bovary, but with Edith Dombey.[107] As she contemplates her future as Mrs Gilbert, Isabel prays that she might live a life of 'luxury and elegance, not to say Edith Dombeyism' (105). Neither she nor Edith was destined to enjoy that; as Edith at least grimly appreciated. Braddon, one of the most popular and successful of the sensation novelists, varied certain aspects of her version of *Madame Bovary*, most obviously its setting, as well as the more significant fact that Isabel remains a frustrated adulteress, unable to consummate her wicked fantasies. However, she also kept many aspects the same as *Madame Bovary*, including an addiction to reading novels which is shared by both Emma and Isabel. In a passage which echoes that recorded in the *Christian's Penny Magazine*, Isabel is described as being so 'breathlessly' addicted to her novel that she cannot, quite literally, put it down; so that, when first introduced to her later husband, she 'kept her thumb between the pages' until he was gone, the sooner the better (23–24, 27). Even Sigismund Smith, the aspiring sensa-

---

[104] J Tarver, *Gustave Flaubert as Seen in his Works and Correspondence* (Constable, 1895) quoted in A Rouxeville, 'Victorian Attitudes to Flaubert: An Investigation' (1987) 16 *Nineteenth-Century French Studies* at 139.

[105] See T Sparks, 'Fiction Becomes Her: Representations of Female Character in Mary Braddon's *The Doctor's Wife*' in M Tromp (ed), *Beyond Sensation: Mary Elizabeth Braddon in Context* (State of University New York Press, 2000) 206–207.

[106] V Lee 'A Dialogue in Novels' (1885) 48 *Contemporary Review* 390. Vernon Lee was the pseudonym of Violet Paget.

[107] Though not only Edith. Edith is a periodic 'favourite' (184). Being a rather confused reader, Isabel also dreams of being Florence Dombey, wanting 'to look like Florence Dombey on her wedding-day', and innumerable other familiar, and not so familiar, literary heroines (105). All internal citations are from *The Doctor's Wife* (Oxford University Press, 1998).

tion novelist who serves as Braddon's necessarily ironic narrator, concludes that Isabel 'reads too many novels' (30).

So enraptured is Isabel that she barely distinguishes fact from fiction; for which reason she is unable to register the 'dark shapes' that more sensitive readers are supposed to discern in the house of Paul Dombey. Unable to comprehend life 'out of a three volume romance' Isabel 'believed in a phantasmal universe, created out of the pages of poets and romancers' (253). To Isabel, the life of Edith Dombey is one of romance and 'luxury' and above all of excitement, no less so because the romance flirts with the tragic. Thus, as she prepares herself for an assignation with her rather dithery lover Roland, Isabel imagines herself as 'like Edith Dombey in the grand Carker scene'; preferring to ignore the consequences of Edith's crushing rejection of her prospective lover (155).[108] Ironies abound, of course; not the least of which is the fact that Braddon, like Sigismund, wrote precisely for women like Isabel. Furthermore, whilst the likes of Ruskin might have nodded sagely at the consequences of Isabel's craving, it can also be argued that it was in the reading of novels such as *Dombey and Son* that women like Isabel Gilbert were first able to imagine a nascent female consciousness.[109] Moreover, where Flaubert's Emma falls all the way, Isabel does not. Fearful that it might 'tarnish her love', Isabel recoils from the idea of actually eloping, and once both lover and dreary husband have conveniently died, Braddon is able to leave her reader with image of a widow who, because she has started reading more substantial books, histories and biographies in particular, is also a wiser one (274).[110]

Isabel Gilbert came to realise that the 'purpose' of reading is not just to entertain; it is also to learn; a conclusion she would have found endorsed if she had, in her more mature reading, come across Trollope's *Autobiography*. Common to all the various genres and sub-genres of the time, Trollope advised, was a shared aspiration to 'please' and to 'teach'.[111] Critics, both contemporary and modern, have long attested to the didacticism which was written into the novels of 'realists' such as Eliot and Gaskell, but recognition that sensation novelists such as Braddon and Wood shared the same aspiration is perceptive, not least because they, to an even greater degree perhaps, wrote for a peculiarly female audience. As Trollope again correctly observed, the mark of the successful author was an appreciation of what their readers craved, and an ability to satiate that craving. Women readers, as Braddon and Wood surmised, and Eliot and Gaskell, wanted to read about other

---

[108] Her imagination rapidly wanders to alternative tragic heroines, alighting first on Juliet and then on Desdemona: 'Yes, she would do for Desdemona.' (155)

[109] See C Harsh, *Subversive Heroines: Feminist Resolutions of Social Crisis in the Condition of England Novel*, (Michigan University Press, 1994), 15–16, and Flint, *Woman Reader*, 288–91, suggesting that it was in the 'practice of reading' novels such as *The Doctor's Wife* or *Dombey and Son* that Victorian women first began to imagine a 'sense of selfhood'.

[110] Her conversion to history is apparently triggered by Roland giving her a copy of Carlyle's *French Revolution*, at which point she suddenly decides that 'she didn't want to be Edith Dombey any longer' (185, 187–88). The conversion will, however, be a little more protracted. A few days later, on hearing that Roland has left for London, Isabel has changed her mind and begins to think of herself as Edith again (227).

[111] Trollope, *Autobiography* (above n 81) 143.

women who, even if they did not live similar lives, felt similar feelings. They may not be as beautiful as Aurora Floyd, Isabel Carlyle or Edith Dombey, but they could empathise with their frustrations and disappointments, and they could sympathise, just a little perhaps, with the mistakes they made and their consequences.[112] Of course, sympathy was a potentially dangerous emotion. It was all very well, as Arthur Helps observed, deploying a fiction that 'creates and nourishes sympathy'.[113] But it must be the right kind of sympathy, and the problem, once again, lay in the suspicion that, in too many cases, this was no longer the case.

Pleasing and Teaching

The idea that literature might both 'please' and 'teach' has, for us, a final resonance; as indeed does the supposition that it might refine our sympathetic sensibilities. The inter-disciplinary study of law, literature and history is commonly defended on the same terms. If it does nothing more, the introduction of the literary text can leaven the study of law; it can 'please'.[114] As to what it teaches, first it emphasises a shared textual generic. A novel such as *Dombey and Son* is obviously literary, but so too is John Austin's near-contemporary *Province of Jurisprudence Determined*, as was each and every judgment handed down from the Victorian bench. As texts, each is subject to the same disciplinary and critical exercises of reading and interpretation. All law, as Kieran Dolin has recently affirmed, 'is invariably a matter of language'.[115] It is also a matter of context, as Robert Cover rightly argued as long ago as 1983: 'No set of legal institutions or prescriptions exists apart from the narratives that locate it and give it meaning.'[116]

It is also a matter of history, for every text is written at a particular 'moment' and then read in a different one.[117] Our moment is the mid-nineteenth century, for our immediate purposes inaugurated by the publication of Dickens's *Oliver Twist* in 1838 and closed with the controversy generated by the publication of Dante Gabriel Rossetti's *Jenny* in 1870. It is also a 'moment', or as contemporaries understood it an 'age', of legal reform.[118] This is true of many periods but the determination to rationalise and reform, driven by two generations of utilitarian agitation,

---

[112] On the deployment of empathy in the Victorian woman's novel, see J Radway, *Reading the Romance: Women, Patriarchy and Popular Literature* (University of North Carolina Press, 1984) 97.

[113] A Helps, *Friends in Council: A Series of Readings and Discourse Thereon* (Pickering, 1847) 90. Helps was Clerk to the Privy Council and a close friend of Dickens.

[114] See I Ward, 'The Educative Ambition of Law and Literature' (1993) 13 *Legal Studies* 323–31.

[115] K Dolin, *A Critical Introduction to Law and Literature* (Cambridge University Press, 2007) 2.

[116] R Cover, 'Nomos and Narrative' (1983) 97 *Harvard Law Review* 4.

[117] For a persuasive example of applying such a historicist methodology to the literary text, see James Chandler's extended study of Shelley's sonnet 'England in 1819' in J Chandler, *England in 1819: The Politics of Literary Culture and the Case of Romantic Historicism* (Chicago University Press, 1998) xv, 4–6. For a recent comment on the importance of the 'law and literature' scholar appreciating the historicity of particular texts, see Kalsem, *In Contempt* (above n 75) 6–7.

[118] G Himmelfarb, *The Spirit of the Age: Victorian Essays* (Yale University Press, 2007), 4–5.

and the scale and the prospective reach of legislative enactment, makes this a peculiarly significant one in English legal history; and a novel such as *Oliver Twist* or *Dombey and Son*, or indeed *The Doctor's Wife*, is part of the fabric of this historical 'moment', in just the same way as is Austin's *Province of Jurisprudence*. Each chronicles the history, and each comprises it. Indeed, it might be argued that the influence of the literary text on debates regarding legal and political reform was greater in Victorian England than it ever had been or would ever be again, which makes it perhaps all the more odd that the Victorian period has until recently remained a relatively fallow field of law and literature scholarship.[119] Dickens has, for obvious reasons perhaps, always proved to be an exception. So too, at the end of the era, has Hardy. Otherwise, there remains some consonance in Margot Finn's observation that in the nineteenth century context the disciplines of law and literature have tended to pass one another like 'ships in the night'.[120]

In the chapters which follow we will encounter a number of debates regarding the putative reform of English law in the mid-nineteenth century, most particularly the reform of matrimonial and criminal law, those areas of jurisprudence which were respectively intended to regulate sex within marriage and sex without marriage. The idea of justice might have occasionally risen, but as we shall see time and again, the impetus for reform was far more commonly derived from concerns as to efficacy.[121] The jurisprudential mentality was set, in large part, by Benthamites such as Austin and Sidgwick, for whom questions of what law is and what law ought to be were quite separate. It was not just jurists scribbling away in their studies, but also critics and journalists of like persuasion, either Benthamite or just plain conservative such as Elizabeth Lynn Linton who, in decidedly Austinian tones, confirmed that the role of the law was not to somehow regulate 'love', but to maintain the 'peace of families', and above all to keep them together. The law, she firmly concluded, should never be invited 'into the heart of the house', but rather 'must be dragged across the threshold' like an 'evil spirit'.[122] There is nothing benign about this spirit.

The following two chapters will focus on matrimonial law and its particular failings; a morass, as we shall see, of often conflicted canon and common law doctrine, amended by the occasional, and often just as conflictive, statutory enactment.[123] As Cobbe observed 'it is not thanks to the Common Law, but in spite

---

[119] In recent years, the number of law and literature scholars engaging nineteenth-century texts has steadily increased. For a very recent contribution, discussing a specific law and literature course on the Victorian novel, see L Rodensky, 'Making Crime Pay in the Victorian Novel Survey Course' in A Sarat, C Frank and M Anderson (eds) *Teaching Law and Literature*, (Modern Language Association, 2011), 126–35.

[120] See M Finn, 'Victorian Law, Literature and History: Three Ships Passing in the Night' (2002) 7 *Journal of Victorian Culture* 134–46. For a similar observation, see S Petch, 'Law, Literature and Victorian Studies' (2007) 35 *Victorian Literature and Culture* 361–84.

[121] See A Norrie, *Crime, Reason and History: A Critical Introduction to Criminal Law* (Butterworths, 1993) 17–33.

[122] Lynn Linton, 'Laws Concerning Women' (above n 27) 382, 386.

[123] A 'mess' as Lawrence Stone bluntly concludes. See L Stone, *Road to Divorce: England 1530–1987* (Oxford University Press, 1990) 135.

thereof, that there are so many united and happy homes in England'.[124] The extent of its dysfunction was particularly apparent when it came to working out what to do with adulterous and bigamous wives. Adulterous and bigamous husbands, as we shall see, although hardly applauded, generated rather less concern. Demand that the law relating to divorce and separation should be reformed, gained pace during the 1840s and 1850s, leading ultimately to the passage of the 1857 Matrimonial Causes Act and the establishment of a dedicated Divorce Court; at which point, as we have already noted, it became all too obvious that England was full of families like the Dombeys. And as we shall also see, whilst the debate was conducted with some intensity in Parliament, it was just as significantly debated outside Parliament, by precisely the kind of people who read the novels of Charles Dickens and Thackeray, and Braddon and Wood, and so many others.

The final two chapters will turn to sex outside marriage, and the extent of its possible regulation. The jurisprudential focus will accordingly move from matrimonial law to criminal law. It will also move from the 'crimes' of the middle class to those of the working class, for which reason the mood will change, becoming in a tangible sense more sympathetic, if also more patronising. The law, however, though undoubtedly patronising, was nothing like so sympathetic to those who were perceived to have transgressed the narrow boundaries of acceptable sexuality. It was particularly unsympathetic to those who were generally perceived as being the most culpable, women. In chapter three we will consider illegitimacy and infanticide, both of which 'crimes' were the subject of a jurisprudence every bit as confused and incoherent as that which attached to the adulterous wife. The subject of chapter four is prostitution. Here, the problem was generally perceived to be less one of incoherence, and more one of neglect. The law did not need to be rationalised; it needed to be written. The result was the Contagious Diseases Act; perhaps the most iniquitous of all the variously iniquitous and ineffective statutory reforms we will encounter. Here again in the cases of illegitimacy and infanticide and prostitution, we will discover that the debate regarding the reform of their legal regulation was conducted with just as great an interest outside Parliament as it was within. If the mid-Victorian picked up the latest Dickens or Eliot or Gaskell, as often as not they would come across an illegitimate child, a straitened mother, or an angel who had fallen on times so hard that there was nothing she could do but walk the streets. These characters were not, as Trollope noted, there simply to entertain. They were there to 'teach'; again not just about what the law was or was not doing, but also what the law could do and what it could not.

It is here, at the margins of the 'could' and the 'should' that a third 'strategy' of law and literature, the 'poethical', is often situated; the supposition that literature has a peculiar capacity to humanise the practice of law.[125] Here we come closer still to Trollope's inference, for when he suggested that literature should 'teach', the

---

[124] Cobbe, 'Criminals, Idiots, Women, and Minors' in Hamilton, *Criminals, Idiots, Women, and Minors* (above n 23) 123.

[125] R Weisberg, *Poethics and Other Strategies of Law and Literature* (Columbia University Press, 1992).

kind of education he had in mind was moral and didactic. In this he was certainly not alone. As we shall see, it is an aspiration common to pretty much all the literary texts that we will encounter in the chapters to come, from Ellen Wood's *East Lynne* to Mary Braddon's *Aurora Floyd* and George Eliot's *Adam Bede*. There is nothing new in the idea that literature humanises readers, whether they be mid-Victorian gentlemen and their wives or twenty-first-century law students and their tutors. It was, after all, a defining precept of Enlightenment, its veracity attested by the likes of Samuel Johnson, David Hume, in whose opinion men were best governed through their sympathetic 'imagination' and, of course, Edmund Burke, whose *Reflections* remains one of the most brilliant examples of empathetic narrative history.[126] It was also attested by Adam Smith, in whose *Theory of Moral Sentiments* could be found the assertion that the faculty of 'pity of compassion' was most effectively stimulated in the 'spectator' when he or she was made to 'conceive it in a lively manner', by seeing it performed or by reading it in novels.[127]

It is a perception which Martha Nussbaum has placed at the heart of her idea of 'poetic justice', an idea of justice which is designed to better nurture within the lawyer an enlarged 'imagination' and thus an enhanced 'sympathy', whilst also raising the 'voices' of those otherwise silenced before the law; a thought which will assume an especial resonance in the cases of many of the women we will encounter in the chapters which follow, such as Hetty Sorrel and Marian Erle and, most starkly of all perhaps, Dante Gabriel Rossetti's Jenny.[128] It is the creator of Marian Erle who, as we shall see, elsewhere raises the spectre of 'Women sobbing out of sight/Because men made the laws'.[129] Both these aspirations, to enhance sympathy and to raise voices, have a particular pertinence in the context of testamentary literature; yet another literary genre which took off during the middle decades of the nineteenth century, and which is commonly associated with the woman's novel of the period. The common denominator here again is the originality of writing from female experience.

Whilst there is indeed much that is shared by a novel such as *Dombey and Son* and a treatise such as Austin's *Province*, in terms of their common texuality and their complementary ability to chronicle contemporary attitudes to law and legal reform, there is here something different. In *Dombey and Son*, Dickens demands that his readers exercise both faculties, of sense and sensibility. Here, once again, he was not alone. Indeed, it is commonly argued that the nineteenth-century woman's novel was defined by precisely this aspiration. This is something else

---

[126] See M Drakopoulou, 'Feminism and the Siren Call of Law' (2007) 18 *Law and Critique* 336–42; and Kaplan, *Victoriana* (above n 72) 46, discussing Johnson's appreciation of literature, particularly testimonial literature, as a means of engaging reader empathy; and I Ward, 'The Perversions of History: Constitutionalism and Revolution in Burke's *Reflections*' (2010) 31 *Liverpool Law Review* 207–32, discussing Burke's use of literary strategies in order to generate sympathetic and empathetic responses in readers of his *Reflections*.
[127] A Smith, *A Theory of Moral Sentiments* (Oxford University Press, 1976) 6.
[128] M Nussbaum, *Poetic Justice* (Beacon Press, 1995) 118–19.
[129] That creator being Elizabeth Barrett Browning. The quote is from *Casa Guidi Windows* in H Scudder (ed), *The Complete Poetical Works of Elizabeth Barrett Browning* (Bucaneer, 1993) lines 637–39, at 251.

which we will bear in mind in the chapters that follow, for whilst the mid-century reader was supposed to look askance at the activities of Hetty, Marian and Jenny, and so many of their similarly fallen fictive counterparts, this was not intended to preclude empathy; quite the contrary indeed.[130] The same, however, cannot be said of Austin's *Province*. Few texts in modern jurisprudence are more 'positive' in their determination to detach the study of law from the romance of sensibility. However, as even Linton was forced to concede, somewhere between the 'authoritative hardness of legal phraseology' and 'the sweet jargon of nonsense', a space had to be found by those who wanted to improve the lot of Victorian women.[131] The problem was where that space would be found.

The distinction between Dickens and Austin matters for another reason too, that of audience. Austin wrote, in the main, for a cadre of fellow jurists and political scientists, for which reason his readership was necessarily circumscribed. Dickens, conversely, wrote for a public that was numbered in its hundreds of thousands. Today, he is read in the millions. It may seem crude, but numbers matter.[132] We need to read his novels, as we do those of Thackeray, Eliot and Gaskell, and Wood and Braddon and so on, because thousands and thousands of Victorians did.[133] As Henry James affirmed, whilst in 'every novel the work is divided between the writer and the reader', ultimately it is writer who 'makes the reader very much as he makes his characters'.[134] *Dombey and Son*, *The Newcomes*, *East Lynne*, *Adam Bede*, *Jessie Philips*, *Oliver Twist*, *Jenny*; these, and many more that we will now encounter, are the texts which shaped the Victorian mind, what it thought about women and their sexuality, about marriage, and about the law which was somehow supposed to regulate it.

---

[130] See S Mitchell, 'Sentiment and Suffering: Women's Recreational Reading in the 1860s' (1977/78) 21 *Victorian Studies* 35, 45.

[131] Linton, 'Laws Concerning Women' (above n 27) 380.

[132] A point made by Kate Flint, in *Woman Reader* (above n 79) at 34.

[133] According to Geoffrey Best, if the modern historian wants to know what the mid-Victorian thought, he or she can do no better than read the novels they read. See G Best, *Mid-Victorian Britain 1851–75* (Fontana, 1979), 14.

[134] See Fraser, *Gender and the Victorian Periodical* (above n 14) 57–58.

1

Criminal Conversations

On 22nd June 1836 Charles Dickens sat down comfortably in the reporter's pew at the Court of Common Pleas. The room was packed. The case, *Norton v Lord Melbourne*, had been eagerly awaited for weeks. The suit alleged that the incumbent Prime Minister had committed adultery with the noted society hostess Caroline Sheridan Norton, the wife of the Honourable George Norton, Tory MP and minor party functionary and, as it turned out, serial wife-beater.[1] The claim was for damages, and was grounded in the ancient common law action of criminal conversation. A criminal conversation, or 'crim-con' action was in fact founded in tort, and was based on the fiction that a male co-respondent had, in committing adultery, trespassed on the goods of the husband.[2] A few years before, Mr Justice Kelyng had felt emboldened to observe that adultery was indeed the 'highest invasion of property'.[3]

Criminal conversations were fun at least for those who were not too closely involved. And there were plenty of laughs to be had in June 1836, not least when various servants trooped into the witness box to be questioned by prosecuting counsel as to the timing and duration of Lord Melbourne's visits to the Nortons' house. There was tittering when prosecuting counsel tried to ascertain how much thigh Caroline had exposed during one of Melbourne's visits. There was an altogether more raucous reaction when it was suggested, by one servant, that his Lordship 'invariably went in' by the 'passage behind'. Supposed love letters were read out, most of which confirmed little more than a mutual liking for piebald ponies and beechwood nuts. Defence counsel fared little better, eliciting from one servant confirmation that there was nothing special about Melbourne's visits, as Mrs Norton had 'a great many gentlemen' to call.[4] As he sat watching the proceedings gradually

---

[1] Caroline was the granddaughter of Richard Brynsley Sheridan. The enterprising manager of the Haymarket honoured the occasion of the trial by reviving Sheridan's *The Rivals*. Caroline repeatedly alluded to her husband's violence in her writings, most notably in her account of *Norton v Lord Melbourne* in her 'English Laws' in J Huddlestone (ed), *Caroline Norton's Defense* (Academy Chicago, 1982) at 31.

[2] The action reached its height in the late eighteenth century when, according to Lawrence Stone, there was an 'explosion' of crim-con litigation. By the mid nineteenth century, conversely, crim-con litigation was notably rarer. For modern commentaries, see W Cornish et al., *The Oxford History of the Laws of England*, vol 13 (Oxford University Press, 2010) 733–74, and more extensively, L Stone, *Road to Divorce: England 1530–1987* (Oxford University Press, 1990) chapter 9.

[3] Stone, *Road to Divorce* (above n 2) 242.

[4] For an account of the proceedings, see A Chedzoy, *A Scandalous Woman: the Story of Caroline Norton* (Alison & Busby, 1992) 9–22, and R Craig, *The Narratives of Caroline Norton* (Palgrave, 2009) 79–85.

descend into farce, Dickens conceived in his notebook the 'Memorable Trial of Bardell against Pickwick'.[5]

A crim-con suit was not, however, merely entertaining. It was also deadly serious, importing a shame that could blight the lives of all concerned. A gentleman, it was commonly felt, would be better advised to resolve the matter at dawn with a pistol.[6] A cuckolded husband who went to court was opened up to ridicule; his wife, as a distraught Caroline noted in private correspondence, was made to 'appear a painted prostitute in a Public Court'.[7] Equally, there were good reasons for launching such an action. Simply getting rid of an unwanted spouse was one, and it had become ever-more evident that a number of crim-con suits were 'collusive', with all three parties agreeing to go through the motions of the action as a prerequisite for a more final separation or divorce.[8] Conversely, cuckolded husbands might be tempted to endure the momentary humiliation of admitting their shame in order to see their wife's lover incarcerated in debtors' gaol from which, as often as not, they were unlikely ever to emerge.[9] If a 'man cannot pay with his purse', Lord Kenyon declaimed in *Walford v Cooke* in 1789, 'he must pay with his person'.[10]

Norton's claim was for £10,000, which would certainly have come in useful. But he also had a rather different reason for initiating his suit, aside from the fact that he loathed his wife and she loathed him. Keen to invigorate his rather lacklustre political career, George decided that he might use his wife's alleged indiscretions to bring down Melbourne and his administration.[11] He miscalculated badly. First, Melbourne rather relished his depiction in court as an ageing roué, one that was capable of seducing the beautiful young wives of political opponents.[12] Secondly, it quickly became apparent that the evidence, whilst thrillingly suggestive, was wholly circumstantial. The fact that the prime witness for the prosecution con-

---

[5] See Chedzoy, *Woman* (above n 4) 13, and Craig, *Narratives* (ibid) 93–94.

[6] See Cornish, *History* (above n 2) at 734, referring to the 'prim distaste' which many felt for actions brought into court rather than settled outside.

[7] K Chase and M Levenson, *The Spectacle of Intimacy: A Public Life for the Victorian Family* (Princeton University Press, 2000) 38.

[8] On collusive actions, see Stone, *Road to Divorce*, (above n 2) 19–20, 282–93, and L Stone, *Broken Lives: Separation and Divorce in England 1660–1857* (Oxford University Press, 1993) 24. Courts, unsurprisingly, took a dim view of such actions, as they did an alternative species of collusion which saw a husband and wife lure a third party into having an affair as a pretext for claiming substantial damages, an activity which was perceived as resembling a kind of prostitution. Fielding used precisely this plot in his 1751 novel *Amelia*. A successful crim-con suit had been a pre-requisite for a parliamentary divorce since 1798.

[9] Juries were commonly encouraged to make large awards in proven instances of crim-con as a deterrent against prospective adulterers. See A Manchester, *A Modern Legal History of England and Wales* (Butterworths, 1980) 374–75; Stone, *Broken Lives* (above n 8) 22–23; and Stone, *Road to Divorce* (above n 2) 234–35.

[10] Quoted in Stone, *Road to Divorce* ibid, 274.

[11] Norton had been elected MP for Guildford in 1826, but had failed to make much progress in terms of political preferment. The idea that he precipitated legal action in order to promote his political career was insinuated by Caroline in her 'English Laws' (above n 1).

[12] Melbourne was not new to the experience of being accused of adultery, having been cited in the similarly notorious *Brandon* case. Whether he and Caroline actually committed adultery remains uncertain.

fessed that he had been offered £500 to give evidence against Mrs Norton hardly supported his case. Thirdly, he lost; the jury not even bothering to retire before it gave its verdict in Melbourne's favour. Norton looked a fool; so it might be surmised, did the law. As a foreign visitor remarked, clearly alluding to the *Norton* case:

> I have heard of £10000 sterling awarded in some cases, which is certainly rather dear for a conversation! . . . The publicity which such prosecutions necessarily occasion, and all the details and proofs of intrigue, are highly indelicate and scandalous.[13]

However, the biggest loser was Caroline. At least a husband had a decision to make. A wife enjoyed no such luxury; she was quite powerless if her husband decided to furnish eager journal editors with salacious details of her alleged affairs. Moreover, she was equally powerless when it came to court proceedings. George might have his day in court; so too Melbourne. But Caroline did not, instead she was 'condemned', as she put it, 'to remain perfectly neuter; perfectly helpless; excluded, by the principles of our jurisprudence, from all possibility of defence'.[14] It was to become a familiar experience over the following decades, as the Nortons repeatedly found themselves in various courtrooms and chambers squabbling over the terms of separation deeds, debts and settlements, and the custody of their children. The trials of Caroline Norton would be many, and would keep the British public entertained intermittently for 30 years. Denied her voice in court, Caroline would later revisit the events of June 1836 in successive essays written in the 1850s in support of matrimonial law reform. By then, as one reviewer observed, in the broader public perception the cause of matrimonial law reform had become essentially indistinct from the seemingly endless saga of 'Mrs Norton's case'.[15]

It was not just in the perception of the essay-reading public. Fictive Caroline Nortons could be found all over the Victorian canon of fallen middle-class women, from Meredith's eponymous Diana Warwick in his hugely popular, if now largely forgotten, *Diana of the Crossways*, to Trollope's Laura Kennedy in *Phineas Finn*, Disraeli's Berengaria Montfort in *Endymion*, and Elizabeth Lynn Linton's Charlotte Desborough.[16] Dickens repeatedly found himself inspired by a woman he famously appraised as a 'sight for the Gods'. A decade after the more jocose account of *Bardell v Pickwick*, Dickensian Carolines reappeared in rather more sombre from, first as Edith Dombey and then as Lady Dedlock. When a novelist came to write about adultery the image of Caroline Norton loomed large, not just as an inspiration, but as a reader referent. Accordingly, as we shall shortly see, when William

---

[13] L Simon, *A Journal of a Tour and Residence in Great Britain during the Years 1810 and 1811 by a French Traveller*, quoted in Stone, *Road to Divorce* (above n 2) 231–32.

[14] C Norton, *Plain Letter to the Lord Chancellor on the Infant Custody Bill* (J Ridgway, 1839) 9–10.

[15] Unsigned, 'The Non-Existence of Women: Letter to the Queen on Lord Chancellor Cranworth's Marriage and Divorce Bill' 23 *North British Review* May/August 1855, at 560, in Craig, *Narratives* (above n 4) at 175.

[16] The 'true story' of Charlotte Desborough was told in Linton's essay 'One of Our Legal Fictions' published in *Household Words* April 1854, at 259. It closed with the depressing observation that the 'marriage idyll' for most young girls ended up resembling a 'dirge for ruined hopes and wasted youth'. For a comment, see Craig, *Narratives* (above n 4) 196.

Makepeace Thackeray and Ellen Wood decided to write about the legal consequences of adultery in the cases of *Newcome v Lord Highgate* and *Carlyle v Carlyle*
they raised a familiar spectre.

One Person in Law

As we have already noted, the institution of marriage lay at the very heart of
Victorian society, bringing together religious, social and cultural expectations.
Men and women were supposed to marry, which is why, as Lord Brougham noted,
the appropriateness of its legal regulation was so important:

> There is no one branch of law more important, in any point of view, to the great interests
> of society, and to the personal comforts of its members, than that which regulates the
> formation and the dissolution of the nuptial contract. No institution indeed more
> nearly concerns the very foundations of society, or more distinctly marks by its existence
> the transition from a rude to a civilized state, than that of marriage.[17]

Few Victorian writers, no matter how critical of marital practice, disagreed with
the idea of marriage or the need for its proper regulation. It was, as even Frances
Power Cobbe conceded, 'manifestly the Creator's plan for humanity'.[18] But the
practice of marriage, as Dickens had noted in *Dombey and Son*, was very different.
Too many marriages were abusive, too many dysfunctional. And the law of marriage was, in substantial part, to blame.

Marriages in nineteenth-century England failed for different reasons. Boredom
was common, particularly in marriages of so-called 'convenience'. At an extreme,
this boredom could migrate from indifference to dislike and, rather too
commonly, to violence. Many such journeys were taken in the pages of the mid-
Victorian novel. Edith Dombey took it, as did Anne Bronte's Millicent Hattersley
in *The Tenant of Wildfell Hall*, and George Eliot's Janet Dempster in the third of
the *Scenes from Clerical Life*. The abuse suffered by Caroline Norton's Eleanor
Raymond, in her now largely-forgotten 1851 novel *Stuart of Dunleath*, imported a
particular poignancy. For such women, as we shall see, solutions were limited. The
law preferred wives, and indeed husbands, to put up with their mutual dislike and
not to make too much of a fuss. Desertion happened rarely, particularly, given the
financial constraints, for women. Bigamy was more common, and far more titillating. As we shall see in chapter two, for a brief moment in the early 1860s, fuelled
by the revelations of the newly-established Divorce Court, middle England was
possessed of a 'bigamy scare': the delicious possibility that its collective drawing
rooms were teeming with bigamous spouses.

---

[17] Quoted in Stone, *Road to Divorce* (above n 2) 1.
[18] FP Cobbe, 'Celibacy v Marriage' in S Hamilton (ed), *Criminals, Idiots, Women, and Minors:
Victorian Writing by Women on Women* (Broadview, 1995) 83.

Equally satisfying, because it imported a similar sexual inference, was adultery. No-one condoned adultery. But everyone liked to read about it. Adultery was, of course, a sin against God, proscribed in the Mosaic commandments. It was also widely presumed to be an offence against social propriety, for which the punishment could be severe and unremitting, as Caroline Norton found to her cost. A woman suspected of having committed adultery could expect to be shunned by polite society, and, as Norton put it, to 'be slandered, tormented, insulted'.[19] Her humiliation was considerable. Ideally, so too should have been her sense of regret, and her urge to repent. As we shall see, Ellen Wood inflicted an agonizing repentance on her 'fallen' protagonist in *East Lynne*. Thackeray, typically, did not. Needless to say, if there was one thing which troubled a mid-Victorian critic more than a fallen woman, it was fallen woman who declined to repent. We shall encounter a few more of these women in the following chapters.

The legal consequences of adultery were various. To the regret of many, it was no longer a crime; a fact which continued to exercise members of both Houses when discussing proposed divorce law reform during the 1850s.[20] It remained, however, a jurisprudential sin, most immediately against the sanctity of property. Whilst the common law seemed uninterested in adultery, it was very concerned about property. Prior to the enactment of the 1857 Matrimonial Causes Act, the legal options open to unhappily married couples were limited. A divorce *a vinculo* was a possibility, albeit for mostly a remote one. Such a divorce, which could only be petitioned by a husband, was secured by parliamentary statute and could be granted on grounds of adultery, mental incompetence, sexual impotence or fraud. If granted, both parties were free to marry again. The process was, however, prohibitively expensive, primarily because the proceedings were so convoluted.[21] Before seeking parliamentary approval, a husband would need to have secured an ecclesiastical separation *a mensa et thoro*, as well as a successful crim-con suit. Only rarely did the number of parliamentary divorces exceed two or three a year.

Decrees *a mensa et thoro*, literally 'from bed and board', were granted at the discretion of an ecclesiastical court, and could be granted on grounds of adultery, sodomy or cruelty, but did not facilitate re-marriage. Critically, matters of property also remained beyond ecclesiastical jurisdiction. A third alternative was a purely private settlement which was, unsurprisingly, similarly devoid of legal force. The Nortons separated on these terms, leaving Caroline to spend 30 years squabbling for intermittent maintenance payments.[22] As the century progressed, campaigners for marriage law reform focussed their attention ever more acutely

---

[19] Stone, *Road to Divorce* (above n 2) 169.

[20] This made England almost unique in Europe at the time. See Stone, *Road to Divorce* ibid, 233.

[21] A petitioner might expect to pay upwards of £800 in legal costs. In today's money this would be in excess of £70,000.

[22] See Cornish, *History* (above n 2) 769–74, and Stone, *Road to Divorce* (above n 2) 154–58, noting that common law courts were stolidly disinclined to intervene in order to enforce any aspect of a private settlement, including even the proprietary. At the centre of a private settlement would commonly be found an agreement whereby a wife would agree to take responsibility for her own debts in return for the granting of annuity, usually from within her own marriage portion. The Norton settlement, which George intermittently recognised, was written along these lines.

on the issue of matrimonial property in separation cases.[23] According to the prominent reform campaigner Lord Brougham, the 'absolute' financial authority of the husband, and the inevitable 'pecuniary dependence' of his wife, was one of the 'manifold evils occasioned by the present law'.[24] Once married, as another reformer wrote in 1855, a woman was 'despoiled' of her 'money, goods and chattels' and 'condemned to prison for life'.[25] A year later, Lord Lyndhurst referred to the 'state of outlawry' which a separated wife might find herself in, 'homeless, helpless, hopeless'.[26] Perhaps the most famous deployment of jurisprudential allusion was found in Frances Power Cobbe's alignment of 'Criminals, Idiots, Women and Minors' in her essay of that name, published a little later in 1868.[27]

The reason for this precarious financial dependence lay in the continuing authority in English matrimonial law of the ancient common law doctrine of coverture. Blackstone's *Commentaries* defined coverture thus:

> In marriage the husband and wife are one person in law: that is, the very being or legal existence of the woman is suspended during the marriage, or at least is incorporated and consolidated into that of the husband: under whose wing, protection and cover, she performs everything ... For this reason, a man cannot grant any thing to his wife, or enter in to covenant with her: for the grant would be to suppose her separate existence; and to covenant with her, would be only to covenant with himself.[28]

Harriet Taylor Mill identified the root of marital 'slavery' as being in the fiction of coverture.[29] It was coverture which, in denying the separate legal personality of a wife, also limited the prosecution of crim-con suits to husbands.[30]

---

[23] The 'first condition of free marriage', as Mona Caird was still to argue at the end of the century. See Hamilton, *Criminals* (above n 18) 283.

[24] Chedzoy, *Norton* (above n 4) 248.

[25] *Remarks on the Law of Marriage and Divorce; suggested by the Honourable Mrs Norton's Letter to the Queen* (James Ridgway, 1855) 4, quoted in M Shanley, *Feminism, Marriage and the Law: Victorian England 1850–1895*, (Princeton University Press, 1989) 9.

[26] Manchester, *Legal History* (above n 9) at 386. It was not just real estate that a separated wife might lose. She could also lose her children. It was this latter realisation that inspired Norton's first forays into political journalism: 'The Separation of Mother and Child by the Custody of Infants Considered' (Roake and Varty, 1837) and 'A Plain Letter to the Lord Chancellor on the Infant Custody Bill' (James Ridgway, 1838), a year later. The bill to which Norton referred became the Infant Custody Act in 1839, which for the first time granted very limited rights to separated mothers: to petition Chancery for custody of children up to the age of seven, and for access up to the age of 16. In private correspondence Caroline railed against the 'cruel tyranny' that George exercised in refusing to allow her to see her own children. He did so in an effort to wring a more favourable financial settlement out of Caroline as part of ongoing negotiations regarding the terms of their separation. A Acland, *Caroline Norton* (Constable, 1948) 107–109.

[27] Hamilton, *Criminals* (above n 18) 108–31.

[28] W Blackstone, *Commentaries on the Laws of England* (William Walker, 1828) 1.130.

[29] See Shanley, *Feminism, Marriage and the Law* (above n 25) 160; J Hammerton, *Cruelty and Companionship: Conflict in Nineteenth Century Married Life* (Routledge, 1992) 57–58; and K Kalsem, *In Contempt: Nineteenth-Century Women, Law and Literature* (Ohio State University Press, 2012) 22–23.

[30] Caroline Norton compared the legal 'fiction' of the separated husband and wife as one person to 'those ingenious twisted groups of animal death we sometimes see in sculpture; one creature wild to resist, and another fierce to destroy'. See C Norton, *A Letter to the Queen on Lord Chancellor Cranworth's Marriage and Divorce Bill* (Longman, 1855) 28.

The consequences of this allied fiction, of coverture and criminal conversation, were shaming, and not just to the parties involved, as Mr Justice Maule famously made clear in the 1845 bigamy case of *R v Hall*:

> Prisoner at the bar, you have been convicted before me of what the law regards as a very grave and serious offence: that of going through the marriage ceremony a second time while your wife was still alive. You plead in mitigation of your conduct that she was given to dissipation and drunkenness, that she proved herself a curse to your household while she remained mistress of it, and that she had latterly deserted you; but I am not permitted to recognise any such plea ... Another of your irrational excuses is that your wife had committed adultery, and so you thought you were relieved from treating her with any further consideration but you were mistaken. The law in its wisdom points out a means by which you might rid yourself from further association with a woman who had dishonoured you; but you did not think it proper to adopt it. I will tell you what that process is. You ought first to have brought an action against your wife's seducer, if you could have discovered him; that might have cost you money, and you say you are a poor working man, but that is not the fault of the law. You would then be obliged to prove by evidence your wife's criminality in a Court of Justice, and thus obtain a verdict with damages against the defendant, who was not unlikely to turn out a pauper. But so jealous is the law (which you ought to be aware is the perfection of reason) of the sanctity of the marriage tie, that in accomplishing all this you would only have fulfilled the lighter portion of your duty. You must then have gone, with your verdict in your hand, and petitioned the House of Lords for a divorce. It would cost you perhaps five or six thousand pounds, and you do not seem to be worth as many pence. But it is the boast of the law that it is impartial, and makes no difference between the rich and the poor. The wealthiest man in the kingdom would have had to pay no less than that sum for the same luxury; so that you would have no reason to complain. You would, of course, have to prove your case over again, and at the end of a year, or possibly two, you might obtain a divorce which would enable you legally to do what you have thought proper to do without it. You have thus wilfully rejected the boon the legislature offered you, and it is my duty to pass upon you such a sentence as I think your offence deserves, and that sentence is, that you be imprisoned for one day, and in as much as the present assizes are three days old, the result is that you will be immediately discharged.[31]

There was nothing particularly unusual about novelists ridiculing the law, as we shall see in Thackeray's account of *Newcome v Lord Highgate*. Less common were instances of real judges adopting a tone of equivalent irony. In fact, crim-con suits had become increasingly rare by the 1840s to the dismay of newspaper editors. The sober-minded Victorian preferred to think of them as a symptom of Regency excess, and they would be abrogated in the 1857 Matrimonial Causes Act, although a facility for claiming damages against a wife's lover was preserved.[32] They were not, as we shall see, so quickly abrogated from the literary imagination.

[31] *R v Hall* (1845) reported in *The Times* 3 April 1845, and quoted in Stone, *Road to Divorce* (above n 2) 369.

[32] See Stone, *Road to Divorce* ibid, 290–95, and Cornish, *History* (above n 2) 785, suggesting that the power remained as 'a deterrent of a kind against the biblical sin'. Any such damages remained at the discretion of the jury, and were after 1857 subject to the discretionary disbursement of the presiding judge who would take into account such matters as maintenance and provision for children, and legal costs incurred, as well as compensation for the former husband.

The sense that English matrimonial law was in urgent need of reform had gained pace by the middle of the century; and one of its most enthusiastic advocates was Caroline Norton, who published two essays on the subject, both of which drew on her personal experience of injustice and misfortune; 'English Laws for Women in the Nineteenth Century' and 'A Letter to the Queen on Lord Chancellor Cranworth's Marriage and Divorce Bill', published in 1854 and 1855 respectively.[33] Avowed admirers ranged from nascent feminists, such as Barbara Leigh Smith Bodichon, to prominent Whig reformers such as Lord Brougham and Lord Chancellor Cranworth, who introduced successive Matrimonial Causes bills in 1854 and 1856. For Brougham and Cranworth, however, the cause of reform rested less on principle than on practice, and its prospects relied on appealing to vested interests. The common lawyers were lured by the possibility of riches that might follow the sequestration of matrimonial affairs from the 'cosy, dozy, old-fashioned, time-forgotten, sleepy-headed' courts of canon law.[34] To allay tender consciences, Cranworth confirmed that whilst divorces might henceforth be easier for husbands, they would be rather more difficult for wives; an argument he justified in simple terms, for whilst a husband might be a 'little profligate' from time to time, a straying wife was a whore.[35] Not everyone was persuaded of course. Lord Redesdale warned of moral 'pollution', whilst the opposition of Lords Spiritual was unremitting.[36] Gladstone thundered for hours on the impending doom. But a third Matrimonial Causes bill was passed, just, in 1857.[37]

The consequences of the 1857 Act were variously institutional, jurisdictional and substantive. The institutional is perhaps the most famous: the establishment of a dedicated Divorce Court. The jurisdictional reform necessarily complemented the institutional, confirming the transfer of authority to approve divorce and separation decrees from ecclesiastical to civil courts. More controversial were the substantive reforms, especially the double-standard written into provisions relating to grounds for divorce. Whilst husbands would only need to evidence the adultery of a wife, a wife would need to evidence not just adultery, but also bigamy, rape, sodomy or bestiality, or cruelty or desertion. Lord Lyndhurst had argued against Cranworth that 'in principle there ought to be no distinction made between the adultery of the husband and that of the wife', but their Lordships were more troubled by the thought that scheming wives might find it all too easy to bribe maids into entrapping their husbands.[38] If a wife could only evidence adultery, she was left with the option of seeking a judicial separation.[39]

[33] As Caroline Norton admitted at the outset of her 'English Laws', which was printed for private circulation in 1854, (above n 1) 2 'Arguing my case from my own example'. See C Norton, *A Letter to the Queen on Lord Chancellor Cranworth's Marriage and Divorce Bill* (Longman, 1855).

[34] As Dickens famously lampooned them in *David Copperfield*.

[35] See M Poovey, *Uneven Developments: The Ideology of Gender in Mid-Victorian England* (Virago, 1989) 51; Shanley, *Feminism, Marriage and the Law* (above n 25) 39–40, 43; and Stone, *Road to Divorce* (above n 2), 24–27, 371, 380.

[36] Stone, *Road to Divorce* ibid, 371.

[37] The bill passed a final reading in the Lords by just two votes.

[38] See Shanley, *Feminism, Marriage and the Law* (above n 25) 39–40, 43, and Stone, *Road to Divorce* (above n 2) 380.

[39] A remedy which replaced separations *a mensa et thoro*.

The extent to which the 1857 Act represented some kind of victory for women remains a matter of debate. Later historians have tended to support Lawrence Stone's conclusion that the Act was an expression of 'defensive conservatism'.[40] Contemporary opinion was mixed. Whilst common lawyers welcomed the jurisdictional reform, others remained agitated by the double-standard in regard to grounds for divorce, together with the unresolved issue of matrimonial property. In cases of both divorce and judicial separation, the problem of adequate financial settlement remained. Whilst a newly-divorced woman regained her status as a feme sole, and so could retain future earnings, the settlement of matrimonial property remained a matter of judicial discretion as regards both alimony in the Divorce Court and settled estates in Chancery courts.[41] A woman suspected of adultery could expect little judicial sympathy in either court, before or after 1857. A Married Women's Property bill had been presented to Parliament a year before the enactment of the 1857 Act. It failed, Lord Campbell warning his fellow peers that the idea that the law might intervene to reward straying wives would be 'shocking to all the habits of the people of the country'.[42]

The Act was, however, unambiguously embraced by newspaper proprietors and their readers. Members of both Houses had been repeatedly advised of the 'terrible evils which will flow' from the establishment of the Divorce Court and more particularly the reporting of its proceedings.[43] They were right to be concerned, for the Court quickly assumed the role of a legal 'confessional', where day by day fractious spouses could be found rolling up to tell their various tales of sexual transgression and domestic dysfunction; a place of 'hideous revelations' as Frances Power Cobbe confirmed, with a sense of grim satisfaction.[44] Just two years after the Act came into force Queen Victoria protested to her Lord Chancellor that editors should be dissuaded from publishing accounts 'of so scandalous a character that it makes it almost impossible for a paper to be trusted in the hands of a young lady or boy'. 'None of the worst French novels', she added, could 'be as bad' or more 'pernicious to the public morals of the country'.[45] The appeal fell on deaf ears. The husbands of Middle England were left to shake their heads in dismay as they trundled

[40] Stone, *Road to Divorce* (above n 2) 383, adding at 389 that the Act was ultimately a 'botched and bungled job, cobbled together over months of wrangling by a dwindling band of weary legislators'.
[41] A discretion strongly reaffirmed in *Robertson v R* (1883) 8 PD, 94. As its jurisprudence evolved, it became apparent that the Divorce Court would ordinarily order a deed of settlement for wives who initiated proceedings securing an annual payment or capital sum; though the precise nature of the settlement remained a matter of discretion. The Court remained far less inclined to support respondent wives. For a commentary, see Cornish, *History* (above n 2) 787–88.
[42] Shanley, *Feminism, Marriage and the Law* (above n 25) 46.
[43] Stone, *Road to Divorce* (above n 2) 416.
[44] For Power Cobbe's comment, see Cobbe, 'Celibacy v Marriage' (above n 18) 82; B Leckie, *Culture and Adultery: the Novel, the Newspaper and the Law 1857–1914* (Pennsylvania University Press, 1999) 67; and G Savage, 'Erotic Stories and Public Decency: Newspaper Reporting of Divorce Proceedings in England' (1998) 41 *Historical Journal* 513–14, quoting Lord Chancellor Campbell's misgivings, that 'like Frankenstein, I am afraid of the monster I have called into existence'. See also Stone, *Road to Divorce* (above n 2) 30 and 295, citing Judge Lewis's observation to the 1912 Royal Commission on Divorce: 'I think they are spicy reading: a great many people take up the paper and the first thing they do is turn up and read about the Divorce Court.'
[45] Quoted in Stone, *Road to Divorce* (above n 2) 295.

off to work each morning. Their wives meanwhile retired to the morning room, where their appetite for scandal could be further satiated by similar accounts found in far too many novels of the period, English as well as French.

Newcome v Lord Highgate

Clara Newcome is not, as we shall see, a major figure in Thackeray's *The Newcomes*, published between 1853 and 1855 and generally reckoned to be his last significant novel.[46] Her 'awful falling away' takes place largely off-stage; its consequences are related by various narrators of differing sympathies and reliability (741).[47] But this does not diminish the significance of Clara's fall or the legal consequences which were to follow. Divorces were not as rare in Victorian fiction as they were in Victorian life prior to 1857 but neither were they common. The 'famous suit of *Newcome v Lord Highgate*' is one of the more notorious of the fictive variety, mainly because it lay at the heart of one of the most caustic critiques of marital practice in nineteenth-century English literature (620).[48]

The Newcomes is a vast novel, the baggiest of Henry James's 'loose baggy monsters'.[49] Whilst no less a figure than Thomas Carlyle would recommend it as one of the greatest of contemporary novels, today *The Newcomes* is largely forgotten, particularly in comparison with Thackeray's breakthrough novel, *Vanity Fair*.[50] Where the latter sold over 10,000 copies in its first edition, and a further 20,000 in a second, more competitively-priced print-run, *The Newcomes* only achieved 14,000 sales during Thackeray's lifetime, and was only rarely re-published after his death. The figures imply a reasonably substantial readership, particularly when calibrated in terms of library circulation but they pale in comparison with the kind

---

[46] It was not his final novel. Although increasingly blighted by ill-health, he struggled through two more: *The Virginians* and *Philip*. Neither has earned critical acclaim. Much of his energy in these final years was devoted to editing the *Cornhill*. In this he was a striking success, the magazine achieving sales figures of roughly 80,000 per edition.

[47] All internal citations are from W Thackeray, *The Newcomes* (Dent, 1994).

[48] On the significance of the matrimonial critique in *The Newcomes*, see M Lund, *Reading Thackeray*, (Wayne State University Press, 1988) 108–10, and J McMaster, *Thackeray: the Major Novels* (Manchester University Press, 1971) 133–35.

[49] For James's famous comment on the great Victorian 'baggy monsters', and his particular suggestion that *The Newcomes* was probably the baggiest of all, see H James, *The Art of the Novel* (Scribner, 1934) at 84. In the final chapter of *The Newcomes*, Thackeray apologises for the length of the novel and the fact that it has taken 23 months to complete its serialisation (772–73).

[50] See D Taylor, *Thackeray* (Chatto & Windus, 1999) 275–76, suggesting that *The Newcomes* now lies relatively undisturbed in the 'remainder bin' of Victorian literature, and surmising that in his seeming inability to get the novel finished Thackeray may have suspected his own 'slide into mediocrity'. The same conclusion is reached by Juliet McMaster in 'Theme and Form in *The Newcomes*' (1968) 23 *Nineteenth Century Fiction* 177, and again in J McMaster, *Thackeray: the Major Novels* (Manchester University Press, 1971) 153. Whitwell Elwin adopted the same laudatory tone as Carlyle, suggesting that *The Newcomes* was Thackeray's 'masterpiece' and indeed 'one of the masterpieces of English fiction' (1855) 4 *Quarterly Review* 350. Elwin's review was both the most extensive and the most positive of those published on completion of the serialisation of *The Newcomes*.

of sales achieved by the man with whom Thackeray most commonly liked to compare himself, Charles Dickens, and, as we shall see, they represent only a fraction of the sales figures that would be achieved by Ellen Wood for *East Lynne*.

The first parts of Thackeray's novel appeared in autumn 1853, and began to sketch the story of the newly-moneyed banking Newcomes and their attempts to scale the heights of late Regency and early Victorian English 'society'. Introducing a vast cast of characters, and a complementary mass of plots and sub-plots, *The Newcomes* bears all the hallmarks of Thackeray's trademark satire; some gentle, some less so. Amongst the former is the relationship between Colonel Thomas and his son Clive Newcome. Having spent most of his career with the Indian army, the Colonel returns to England in order to retire and spend more time with his son. His arrival is treated with 'condescension' by his banking half-brothers and their families. This condescension, however, gives way to something more sinister when the Colonel interferes with their matrimonial strategies in order to try to secure Clive's marriage to his half-cousin Ethel (75). At this point, Ethel's brother Barnes sets out to destroy the Colonel who has invested his life savings in an uncertain Indian bank, the liquidity of which is dependent on the continuing support of the Financial House of Hobson Brothers and Newcome. Barnes ensures that this support is withdrawn, and the Colonel is ruined.[51] Readers are expected to despise the mendacious Barnes, 'as loathsome a little villain as crawls the earth' (550).[52] It is Barnes who petitions the court in *Newcome v Lord Highgate*.

The Newcomes have lots of money, but what they want is social standing.[53] The marriage-market provides them with an opportunity to gain social status, and it is for this reason that the Colonel's interference is so unwelcome. 'Those banker fellows', as old Major Pendennis observes, 'are wild after grand marriages' (232). The Newcomes offer two marriageable children, Barnes and Ethel, plus cash. They require titled spouses in return, and there are plenty of takers. Negotiations proceed, bargains are struck, and gambles taken, not least in the prospective happiness of the children. As the ultimately rebellious Ethel declaims: 'There never were, since the world began, people so unblushingly sordid! We own it, and are proud

---

[51] He thereby loses what is rumoured to be around £60,000 of stock (520), a sum which today would be worth in the region of £5 million. Barnes brings down the Bundelcund Bank by refusing to re-secure £30,000 of bills. The narrator's observation is both wry and contemptuous: 'We understand that sort of thing. London bankers have no hearts' (646). Thackeray's stepfather lost much of his fortune in the same way in the 1830s when a series of Indian banks collapsed, most prominently the Cruttenden Bank in 1834. See R McMaster, *Thackeray's Cultural Frame of Reference: Allusion in* The Newcomes (Macmillan, 1991) 116.

[52] As the narrator confirms 'That Mr Barnes Newcome was an individual not universally beloved, is a point of history of which there can be no doubt' (288). Evidence of Barnes's cowardice is repeated, not least when the Colonel challenges him to a duel. Barnes responds by seeking police protection. Evidence of his earlier indiscretions with local working-class girls comes back to haunt Barnes when he aspires to become the MP for Newcome and when his crim-con suit comes to trial (561). Given the centrality of money in *The Newcomes*, and Barnes's position as the effective head of the family bank, Juliet McMaster has suggested that he can be read as the 'focal character' of the whole novel. See McMaster, 'Theme and Form' (above n 50) 182.

[53] The local journal *The Independent* runs a series of satirical commentaries on the 'Screwcomes' and their desperate attempts to buy influence (146–47).

of it! We barter rank against money, and money against rank, day after day' (324–25). A century earlier, Mary Manley had lamented that 'Hymen no longer officiates at their marriages', but rather 'Interest is deputed in his room, he presides at the feast, he joins their hands'.[54] The market may indeed facilitate social mobility, and it is fun to read about, as Thackeray appreciated, but it does not make for secure, still less for happy, marriages. Not all the marriages written about in *The Newcomes* fail but most, to varying degrees, do. As Edward Burne-Jones observed, no comparable novel 'teems' with quite so many 'marriages that should never have been made'.[55] And in the main, respective spouses do what is expected: they put up with each other. In this, however, if in little else, Clara Newcome proves to be an exception.

The marriage market is not, of course, a free market. On the contrary, it is closely regulated, not just by harridans such as the dowager Lady Kew, but by a rigid culture of marital ritual, a subject that lends itself all too easily to Thackeray's satire. Thackeray was not, of course, alone in registering the affinity of the grotesque and the comic in the rituals of middle-class English marriage. His contemporary, John Boyd Kinnear, advised anyone who doubted just how grotesque these rituals might be that they only need to:

> Frequent the fashionable London drive at the fashionable hour, and there he will see the richest and the most shameful woman-market in the world. Men stand by rails, criticising with perfect impartiality and equal freedom while women drive slowly past, some for hire, some for sale in marriage, these last with their careful mothers at their side, to reckon the value of the biddings and prevent lots from going off below the reserved price.[56]

The seemingly endless balls and soirées that comprise so much of *The Newcomes* are given over to the rituals of matrimonial bargaining. And when the 'season' comes to an end, everyone decamps to Baden and Bonn to continue their negotiations around the 'green tables' and the hunting lodges, where fortunes are won and lost, 'virgins' bought and 'sold' (275–76).[57]

One of the most famous scenes in the novel occurs at an exhibition of paintings in London, yet another occasion at which parents can pander their offspring. In conversation with her redoubtable grandmother, Lady Kew, the 'spirited' Ethel suggests a parallel between the exhibiting of art and the exhibiting of daughters

> we young ladies in the world, when we are exhibiting, ought to have little green tickets pinned on our backs, with 'Sold' written on them; it would prevent trouble and any

---

[54] M Manley, *New Atlantis* (J Morphen, 1714–20) 1.2–4, quoted in Stone, *Broken Lives* (above n 8) 28.

[55] Burne-Jones's review was published in the *Oxford and Cambridge Magazine*, January 1856, and quoted in G Tillotson and D Hawes (eds), *Thackeray: The Critical Heritage* (Routledge, 1968) 255.

[56] JB Kinnear, 'The Social Position of Women in the Present Age' in Shanley, *Feminism, Marriage and the Law* (above n 25) 62.

[57] Like many of his contemporaries Thackeray deployed fashionable European resorts in his novels in order to conjure images of particular sexual and moral lassitude; most famously perhaps in *Vanity Fair*.

future haggling you know. Then at the end of the season the owner would come and carry us home. (277)

Later that evening as the Newcomes assembled for dinner, 'Ethel appeared with a bright green ticket pinned to the front of her white muslin frock' (278).[58]

The 'dazzling' Ethel is the Newcome 'trump', and much of the first volume of the novel revolves around Lady Kew's attempt to negotiate a suitable settlement between Ethel and her grandson Lord Kew, a match which would consolidate the two branches of the family, the moneyed and the landed (110, 332). The Colonel's suggestion that Ethel and Clive might marry because they love each other and would be 'happy ever after' is treated with barely concealed incredulity (256–57). As Lady Kew reminds Ethel: 'Had he money, it would be different. You would receive him, and welcome him, and hold out your hands to him; but he is only a poor painter, and we, forsooth, are bankers in the City' (324).[59] And so, after much persuasion, and many balls, Ethel becomes engaged to young Kew. However, troubled by 'the surveillance' which he had begun to exert over her, and by reports of his propensity for impregnating working-class girls, Ethel later breaks the engagement (338). A reluctant Kew is left to wonder 'whether I was right to give up sixty thousand pounds, and the prettiest girl in London', and then to locate a suitable alternative with which to mollify his grandmother (384–85). Ethel, meanwhile, is placed back on the market to be 'bandied about from bidder to bidder' once more; not, as the narrator affirms, a 'very dignified position', especially as the 'season' is nearly ended (386, 457). The situation is rapidly appraised and Ethel, along with large quantities of 'old Kew port', is targeted at the Marquis of Farintosh (457). In time, she will rebel once again. In the still more distant future, her fate will be consigned to Thackeray's famously inconclusive conclusion. She may end her days happily married to Clive. There again she may not.[60]

Clara Pulleyn, like Ethel Newcome, is expected to marry for money, and is placed on the market on these terms. As Lord Kew observes, there is a 'brood' of Pulleyn daughters and their father has 'nothing to give them' (300). There is nothing exceptional here. Isabel Carlyle finds herself in the same predicament in Ellen Wood's *East Lynne*, as we shall shortly see; so does Edith Dombey. Edith rebels, but only after her marriage. Ethel Newcome is more remarkable in that she rebels before, though only just. Clara Pulleyn is not remarkable. She does what virtually every Victorian girl in her situation, as the daughter of an aristocratic but impoverished family, did. Clara Pulleyn gives in and becomes Clara Newcome, wife of

[58] Thackeray very probably borrowed the image from a notorious cartoon which appeared in *Punch's Pocket Book for 1847*. The cartoon, entitled 'The Matrimonial Tatersalls', pictured various unmarried women being auctioned off to the highest bidders, with those already bought having 'Sold' tags pinned to their chests.

[59] Clive Newcome is an aspiring painter, something which, as critics have noted, allows Thackeray to revisit his youthful ambitions to pursue a career as an artist.

[60] The concluding passages of the novel, in which the possibility of Ethel and Clive marrying is hazarded, are famously compromised; Thackeray reminding his audience that they spent 23 months in 'fable-land', and if they hoped for a certain conclusion they had entirely misunderstood the practice of reading his novels.

Barnes. Of course, Barnes has been speculated in the same market. But he is happy
with his lot, consoling himself with the thought that whilst his prospective wife has
a 'history', a 'silly little affair' with a childhood sweetheart, she is also a daughter
of the 'ancient' house of Pulleyn and if the right in-laws die in the right order,
he might even secure himself a place 'in the Peers' (275, 284). In terms of 'rank'
the match is eminently suited, satisfying the complementary yearnings of both
families (305).

In many ways the 'fall' of Clara Newcome is entirely prosaic, and just as familiar.
Barnes is reported to be 'very cruel to her' (480). Intimations of violence recur,
Clara's 'bruised cheek' assuming the same semiotic import as the 'mark' which
appears on Florence Dombey's breast (563).[61] Thackeray indulges a 'long paren-
thesis' on the broader subject of spousal abuse in chapter thirty-six, inviting his
readers to wonder 'how many murderous assaults there are by husband or wife',
metaphorical and literal (360). In the next chapter the splendid 'union' of the two
'noble families', Newcome and Pulleyn, is described in tones of darkest irony
(362–63).[62] For a while Clara tries to put up with it. But in the end it proves too
much, and so she re-kindles a 'little affair' with her former sweetheart, the now
ennobled Lord Highgate, before eloping with him.[63] Contemporaries such as Sir
William Scott and Thomas Erskine appreciated that in many instances a crim-con
suit arrived in court, not because a wife had found a lover, but because a husband
had driven her to despair.[64] Certainly Clara Newcome was driven to despair. But
'patient timid little' Clara was also resilient (323, 331). There is nothing, as the
perceptive if disapproving Laura Pendennis suggests, 'artless' about Clara; quite
the contrary (499). Through everything Clara, who predictably enough likes nothing better than to immerse herself in dangerously suggestive French novels, clings
on to her 'dream' of living happily with the man she loves (578). In a sense it is
Clara's determination to realise this 'dream', despite everything, which makes her
extraordinary. But it is again the ordinariness of Clara which is significant, the
grim familiarity of her miserable marriage. Thackeray's female readers might
have admired Ethel's beauty as well as her spirit. But they probably felt a more
immediate affinity with 'timid little' Clara, and in the end a still greater admiration
for her.

[61] Clive casts the early aspersion, in argument with Barnes, observing 'I thought you only swore at
women' (303). Highgate finally agrees to the elopement as the only practical way to protect Clara from
Barnes. When rumours of violence become public, Barnes is visited by a disapproving Lady Kew who,
needless to say, is more concerned by the publicity than by the violence.
[62] The narrator making the passing observation that the marriage was perhaps just a little 'too soon';
news coming shortly afterwards that the previously impoverished Jack Belsize, her childhood
sweetheart, was now the rather wealthier and altogether more marriageable, Lord Highgate.
[63] The 16-year-old Clara first met Highgate at her elder sister's wedding. Their love is presented as
being genuine, the proof of which lies in the fact that Highgate, newly enriched and ennobled, is still
prepared to risk his reputation in marrying her once her divorce from Barnes is secured. Clara's family
had originally been appalled at the prospect, in large part because the young Jack soon ends up in
Insolvency Court and in due course the Queen's Bench prison, his financial failings 'smartly chronicled
by the indignant moralists of the press' (283).
[64] As Scott opined in Parliament and Erskine in private correspondence. See Stone, *Road to Divorce*
(above n 2) 266.

Humiliated by his wife and her lover, Barnes embarks on a crim-con suit at the Queen's Bench. Lord Highgate offers a more gentlemanly alternative (592). But Barnes, savouring the prospect of £20,000 damages, prefers to go to law. Proceedings are opened by Barnes's barrister, who it is reported 'wept freely during his noble harangue'. He begins by making a stand 'for the rights of British husbands!':

> With what pathos he depicted the conjugal paradise, the innocent children prattling round their happy parents, the serpent, the destroyer, entering into that Belgravian Eden; the wretched and deserted husband alone by his desecrated hearth, and calling for redress on his country! (593)

The reporter for the *Day* was surely persuaded as to the 'monstrosity of the crime' (593). The following day, however, the Newcome cause suffers a setback when it is discovered that the servants have defected, and there are no witnesses available to 'prove' the veracity of this picture of 'connubial happiness'. Whilst he cannot defend his client's 'conduct', Highgate's counsel proceeds to paint a very different picture of life in the Barnes Newcome household, of a man 'whose cruelty and neglect twenty witnesses in court were ready to prove, neglect so outrageous, cruelty so systematic, that he wondered the plaintiff had not been better advised than to bring this trial, with all its degrading particulars, to a public issue' (593). After this, despite the urgent protests of opposing counsel, he acquaints the court with all the gruesome details of Barnes's previous philandering, of his 'castaway children pleading in vain for bread' (593). Various corroborative witnesses duly appear, to be 'mauled and slain' by rival counsel (594). The 'whole country' meanwhile 'looked on' fascinated and horrified though mainly fascinated. As a reviewer in the *Spectator* observed, as Thackeray's novel reached its eventual conclusion:

> Were we not all present at the case of 'Newcome, Bart v Lord Highgate', and did we not clap our inward hands with keen applause as the defendant's counsel painted, as only that distinguished mover of juries can paint, the character and brutal conduct of the injured husband?[65]

The behaviour of Barnes Newcome, it is universally agreed, has been appalling. Nevertheless, and with a suitably grim sense of irony, he wins his case and is awarded 'immense damages' (594). The law had run its course. The suit won, the 'Newcome Divorce Bill' is filed in the House of Lords, much to the delight of newspaper editors and their readers, who are once again invited to contemplate 'the whole story of Barnes Newcome's household' (593).

There is much here that would have been familiar to followers of crim-con cases, particularly those who could recall the proceedings of *Norton v Lord Melbourne*. On a personal level, Thackeray was just as enamoured of Caroline Norton as Dickens; for which reason his novels are similarly populated by a

---

[65] Anonymous reviewer, 'Thackeray's Newcomes' *Spectator*, 18 August 1855, 859–61.

number of fictive Carolines.[66] Indeed, in *The Newcomes*, it can be argued that there are two prospective Carolines: a 'womanly' Caroline in the figure of Ethel and a 'fallen' Caroline in the figure of Clara.[67] The Norton allusion is further strengthened by Thackeray's evident replication of certain aspects of the *Norton* case in *Newcome v Lord Highgate*.[68] There are differences, of course; not least the fact that Clara's adultery is undoubted and Barnes's suit thus successful. But the similarities are still striking: a common preoccupation with putative damages; the role of patently unreliable servants giving evidence of doubtful veracity; the inability of allegedly adulterous wives to do the same; darker allegations of spousal violence; and the unavoidable shame that attaches to respective parties. There is also a hint of collusion. Neither Newcome and Highgate nor Norton and Melbourne, colluded overtly but respective husbands in both cases seemed peculiarly happy to allow their wives to flirt with their alleged paramours.[69]

Ultimately, however, the most marked similarity between the cases of Clara Newcome and Caroline Norton is that of disappointment. Clara's divorce might save her from Barnes's ill-temper and she is more fortunate than the fated Isabel Carlyle who, as we shall see, is quickly abandoned by her lover. Even so, the new Lady Highgate is 'not much happier than the luckless Lady Clara Newcome had been', and certainly not as happy as she had liked to 'dream' (623). There is only so much that the law can do. Clara is given her divorce but she will never recover from marrying Barnes Newcome. She may have arrived from the fabulous

[66] Critics have long surmised the presence of Caroline in the character of Becky Sharp in *Vanity Fair*, just as they have discerned parallels between Melbourne and Becky's elderly admirer Lord Steyne. Other possible sources for Becky are of course numerous, including not least, Thackeray's own wife Isabella, who apparently bore a striking physical resemblance to Becky Sharp. It has also been suggested that another Thackerayan Caroline can be found in the character of Lady Lyndon in *Barry Lyndon*. Of Caroline, Thackeray once remarked rather tawdrily that there were 'very few more beautiful bodkins in the world'. See M Clarke, 'William Thackeray's Fiction and Caroline Norton's Biography: Narrative Matrix of Feminist Legal Reform' 18 (1989) *Dickens Studies Annual* 337–50.

[67] On the presentation of two Carolines in *The Newcomes*, see Clarke, 'Narrative Matrix' ibid, 338. The idea that Thackeray would have chosen to present counter-allusions is characteristic of his liking for literary 'doubleness'. Of all Victorian novelists Thackeray was undoubtedly the most determinedly allusive.

[68] Thackeray reported in correspondence that he had been reading the *Norton* case as part of his research for writing *Newcome v Lord Highgate*. See McMaster, *Frame of Reference* (above n 51) 161. He was also able to draw on his experiences, however disagreeable, of being a frustrated law student. He found the study of law to be boring, and constantly interrupted his studies, as often as not to go on jaunts abroad. Once Thackeray's nascent career was established, writing for various literary journals, perhaps most importantly *Punch*, and then composing his first short stories, he abandoned the law with alacrity. For a commentary on obvious parallels between the *Norton* and *Newcome* cases, see Craig, *Narratives* (above n 4) 103–105.

[69] Various narrators in *The Newcomes* express their surprise at Barnes's apparent willingness to allow his wife to spend so much time with her former lover, though they also note the fact that the newly-enriched Highgate has invested a considerable amount of his fortune with Hobson Brothers and Newcome. In the same conversation in which Pendennis and his wife discuss rumours of Clara's adultery, reference is made to their travelling alone together in cabs; something which might have struck a chord with a later generation of readers who encountered Flaubert's *Madame Bovary*. The resonance which Thackeray's narrator strikes between that 'attitude' taken by Clara and Highgate in public and that painted by Hogarth in his *Marriage à la Mode* would have been more immediate (554).

Chanticlere, the ancient seat of the Pulleyns, but there will be no happy ever after for Lady Clara Highgate, destined to be cut off from her children and 'all the friendship of sisterhood' (594–95). As for Barnes, at first glance he too might be thought to be luckier than some at least when compared to the dodgy financiers who find themselves broken in the novels of Dickens and Trollope. It will take more than a spot of adultery to bring down Hobson Brothers and Newcome.[70] However, he is just as unable to find happiness and significantly unable to find a second wife.[71]

No-one emerges with much credit from *Newcome v Lord Highgate*. Certainly the law does not.[72] However, it remains instructive; not least to Ethel, whose scepticism as regards successive proposed matches to Lords Kew and Farintosh is strengthened by reports of Clara's unhappiness.[73] In his perceptive review of *The Newcomes*, published on the completion of its serialisation in 1855, Whitwell Elwin noted this precise point, concluding that Thackeray's novel would 'open the eyes of many a girl who is dimly conscious of her position, and lead some, perhaps, to avoid the error of Ethel, or, more difficult still, enable them, like her, to retrace their steps'.[74] In the notorious 1794 'crim-con' case *Howard v Bingham*, Thomas Erskine placed the responsibility for the alleged adultery on the parents of the unfortunate wife:

> You must behold her given up to the plaintiff by the infatuation of parents, and stretched upon this bridal bed as upon a rack torn from the arms of a beloved and impassioned youth, himself of noble birth, only to secure the honours of higher title: a legal victim on the altar of Heraldry.[75]

It was the plea that might just as readily have been made by Lord Highgate's counsel. Erskine went on to conclude that the marriage in question represented 'the legal prostitution of parental choice in the teeth of affection' and, so long as the practice continued, courts would be invited to mediate its often unhappy consequences. Thackeray, whom we might reasonably suppose to have been familiar with the case, would have nodded.

---

[70] Thackeray pointedly observes that whilst most gentlemen shun Barnes, his fellow bankers and his creditors, do not (631).

[71] It is reported that Barnes is turned down by one prospective bride 'to his surprise and indignation, for a beggarly clergyman with a small living' (624). The notoriety of the case also operates against Barnes's attempt to secure one of the Newcome seats in subsequent elections.

[72] See A Humphreys, 'Breaking apart: the early Victorian divorce novel' in N Thompson (ed), *Victorian Women Writers and the Woman Question* (Cambridge University Press, 1999) 46.

[73] The disgrace encapsulated in *Newcome v Lord Highgate* persuades Farintosh to request that Ethel release him from their engagement; something which Ethel is only too happy to do.

[74] *Quarterly Review* (above n 50) 373–76.

[75] Erskine was counsel for the defence in the case. See Stone, *Road to Divorce* (above n 2) 264.

Carlyle v Carlyle

A bare four and a half years after the final part of *The Newcomes* was published, the *New Monthly Magazine* began running another, but very different, account of the same rather thrilling transgression, Ellen Wood's *East Lynne*. Much had happened in those four and a half years, not the least of which was the passage of a new Matrimonial Causes Act. Perhaps more significant, however, was the sudden emergence of a new, and wildly popular, genre of literature, the 'sensation' novel. The Act and the genre were intrinsically related; the sudden publicity of familial dysfunction in the newly-established Divorce Court nurturing a complementary appetite for ever-more thrilling stories of sex and crime.[76] The coincidence made Wood's fortune, as it did the fortunes of other prominent sensationalists such as Wilkie Collins and Mary Elizabeth Braddon, whose infamous 'bigamy novels' will be discussed in chapter two. But no-one sold copy quite as effectively as Wood whose *East Lynne* was quite simply the most successful novel published in Victorian Britain, selling out five three-volume editions within the first year of its publication, and a further 31 in the next 20 years.[77] In all, over a million copies had been sold by the end of the century; the kind of sales figures of which authors such as Thackeray, Collins and Braddon could only dream.[78] Sales do not necessarily translate into readers but the figures are suggestive. Many Victorians read about the fall of Wood's notorious adulteress, Isabel Carlyle and not just frustrated middle-class wives. Avowed admirers of Wood's novel also included Harriet Martineau, General Gordon and the future Edward VII.[79]

The plot of *East Lynne* centres around the adultery of Isabel Carlyle. Isabel is the daughter of an impoverished aristocrat Lord Mount Severn. When he dies, she is

[76] See V Sanders, 'Marriage and the antifeminist woman novelist', and A Humphreys, 'Breaking apart', both in Thompson, *Women Writers* (above n 72) at 24 and 42 respectively.
[77] The conjecture that *East Lynne* was commercially the most successful novel of the century was ventured in a survey published 'What do the Masses Read?' (1904) *Economic Review*, April 170. In *The Argosy* in March 1887, Alexander Jupp hazarded a guess that at least half a million copies had by then been sold. According to Winnifred Hughes, *East Lynne* along with Braddon's similarly sensationalist *Lady Audley's Secret* were easily the most successful novels of the century. See W Hughes, *The Maniac in the Cellar: sensation novels of the 1860s* (Princeton University Press, 1980) 112.
[78] In addition to the readers of these copies might be added the thousands, perhaps even millions, who witnessed dramatic reproductions of the novel. In 1909 the *Pictorial Leader* claimed that 'more millions have witnessed *East Lynne* than have seen any other play that was ever written'. *East Lynne* was far and away Wood's most successful novel. But it was not her only novel or her only success. *The Channings*, published in 1862, sold in excess of 300,000 copies, whilst the shorter *Johnny Ludlow* stories would consistently sell between 20,000 and 45,000 copies each. Between 1861 and 1873, Wood published at least one novel each year. For a commentary on the commercial success of *East Lynne*, see J Elliott, 'A Lady to the End: The Case of Isabel Vane' (1976) 29 *Victorian Studies* 330, suggesting that the figure of one million copies by the end of the century was 'probably a conservative one', and E Liggins and A Maunder, 'Ellen Wood, Writer' (2008) 15 *Women's Writing* 150.
[79] For the women of Holloway prison, as was noted by 1911 parliamentary commission on 'Books for Prisoners', *East Lynne* was an 'especial favourite'. See D Birch, 'Fear among the Teacups' *London Reviews of Books*, February 2001, 22, and Liggins and Maunder, 'Wood' (above n 78) 150.

destitute. In such straightened circumstances, she agrees to marry a rather dull provincial lawyer, Archibald Carlyle. Increasingly bored and isolated, she eventually succumbs to the charms of Sir Francis Levison and runs away with him to France in much the same way as the similarly bored and isolated Clara Newcome runs away with Highgate. In doing so, she abandons her young son William. On hearing that Isabel has eloped with Levison, Archibald takes advantage of the provisions of the new Matrimonial Causes Act and secures a divorce. Meanwhile, Isabel is abandoned by Levison following the discovery that she is pregnant, and shortly after is reported to have been killed in a railway accident. Archibald now feels morally entitled to remarry and does so.[80] Although her baby died in the accident, Isabel survived, but is so disfigured that she feels able to return to England unrecognised. This she does and, pining for her first son, takes up employment as governess to the Carlyle family. In this capacity she suffers any number of emotional torments, including the death of the sickly William, before herself finally dying. Her identity is only discovered at the very end of the book. Alongside the main plot, there is a subplot involving the murder of a local farmer, Hallijohn, for which the brother of Archibald's second wife, Barbara, is wrongly blamed. Rather conveniently, it is subsequently discovered, in large part due to Archibald's detective diligence, that the real murderer was Levison, who is duly tried and sentenced to death, later commuted to hard labour.

The plot is, of course, thoroughly preposterous. But as we have already noted, sensation novels which included Wood's despite its more didactic pretensions were supposed to be preposterous. All the ingredients of a popular sensation novel were present: the uncovering of a marriage that was, in some form or other, scandalous; illicit sexuality; at least one thrilling murder; and the insinuation if not the instance of bigamy.[81] Wood, like her fellow sensationalists, was acutely conscious of what her readers wanted to read. Above all they wanted 'distraction' from the 'cares and perfidies of life'.[82] She knew that when they were not reading her novels, they were reading newspaper reports of Divorce Court hearings, along with more notorious accounts of famous bigamy and murder trials. In the England of 1860, it seemed, rakish seducers, murderous lovers and fallen women were everywhere, and if an author wanted to be sure of thrilling her readers, there was no better way of doing so than by depicting a sexually-frustrated wife succumbing to the temptations of violent passion.[83]

---

[80] It is typical that Archibald chooses not to remarry until he hears of Isabel's reported death. In doing so he cites scriptural authority, Luke 16:18: 'Whosoever putteth away his wife, and marrieth another, committeth adultery' (319).

[81] For modern overviews of the sensation genre, see P Brantlinger, 'What is Sensational about the Sensation Novel?' (1982) 37 *Nineteenth Century Fiction* 1–28; A Maunder, 'Mapping the Victorian Sensation Novel: Some Recent and Future Trends' (2005) 6 *Literary Compass* 1–33, and M Knight, 'Figuring out the Fascination: Recent Trends in Criticism on Victorian Sensation and Crime Fiction' (2009) 37 *Victorian Literature and Culture* 323–33.

[82] Wood's comment on 'distraction', made in a letter to Richard Bentley, is cited in Liggins and Maunder, 'Wood' (above n 78) 151.

[83] As Dinah Birch observes what the readers of a Wood novel expected was 'crime, sorrow and death'. See Birch, 'Fear' (above n 79) 23.

The fact that Carlyle is a lawyer by profession is significant. He is an unusual one, at least when compared to those more commonly found in the mid-Victorian novel. He is not one of the 'pettifogging lawyers' (37).[84] Archibald is a model of the aspiring mid-Victorian gentleman, steady, honest, successful.[85] He may have been left money, but Archibald Carlyle has also made money, so much that he can buy the East Lynne estate from the destitute Lord Mount Severn (8–9).[86] He is also a 'good' husband. 'I assure you, justice', he replies when challenged by his second wife's father, 'I keep her in order' (425). And most importantly, perhaps, at least for our purposes and for reasons which will become apparent, he is also perspicacious. Along with the presence of a lawyer as the lead male protagonist, there are various other legal referents in *East Lynne*, from mundane matters of estate management, settlements and entails, to ghoulish accounts of corpses being seized for payment of debt.[87] Further legal resonance can be discerned in the events surrounding the murder sub-plot, including the arraignment and trial of Levison; scenes which attracted the pointed approval of critics.[88] However, by far the most important legal commentary attaches to the consequences of Isabel's adultery. By the end of chapter two Isabel is attracted to the 'unscrupulous' Levison who hap-

---

[84] All internal citations are from E Wood, *East Lynne* (Oxford University Press, 2005).

[85] Wood has her narrator allude to the obvious anxieties that social mobility engaged in Victorian England, noting that 'A man who could purchase East Lynne was worthy of being received as an equal' to any lord of the realm 'though he was but a country lawyer' (65–66).

[86] Archibald has in all a 'large fortune', £20,000 of which he inherited. It is observed that his elder sister, the redoubtable Cornelia received only a 'small portion' (38). In negotiation with Lord Mount Severn Archibald refuses to meet the £70,000 asked for the East Lynne estate, emphasising that 'forced sales' can never be expected to 'fetch their value' (8–9). The final price is not revealed, nor the extent to which the capital might be raised by mortgage. But it is clear that Carlyle can lay his hands on a sum of money far in excess of what he has inherited. It also noticeable, in passing, that East Lynne is not entailed as part of the apparently rather fragmentary Mount Severn settlement. In the immediate context of rapacious creditors swarming across the estate following the death of Lord Mount Severn, even Carlyle admits to being uncertain as to what precisely is and is not included in the 'entail' (97).

[87] It is the recently-deceased Lord Mount Severn whose corpse is seized for debt (88–93). The fact that two men 'each with a remarkably hooked nose' pretending to be undertakers, sneaked into the house to seize the body, adds a discomfortingly anti-Semitic tone to the depiction of events in chapter 10. The Mount Severn family lawyer articulates the same prejudice a few pages later (102). Reference to a similar fate having previously befallen the 'body of a church dignitary' alludes to a relatively recent case of 1841, which saw the seizure of the corpse of the bishop of Worcester for debts amounting to £100,000. It was, for understandable reasons, an event of great popular interest, and jocularity. It was also lawful. Mount Severn's body is only released for burial once his son has paid off the creditors from his own pocket (104).

[88] Not that they provided a particularly reassuring vision of legal process. Aside from the narrator's distaste for the 'primitive' surroundings of the justice's meeting-room, at the time of Levison's arraignment there are clear breaches of hearsay rules, as his lawyer rightly observes, and an awful lot of 'useless questions' (537, 540, 549). The *Saturday Review* commented in glowing terms that 'what is most wonderful is that the legal proceedings taken, when the murder is finally discovered, are all, or almost all right', concluding that 'Mrs Wood has an accuracy and method of legal knowledge about her which would do credit to many famous male novelists'. The review, dated 15 February 1862, is quoted in C Wood, *Memorials of Mrs Henry Wood* (Bentley, 1894) 241. It is possible that the Levison trial and sentencing was intended to resonate with contemporary debate regarding the prospective 1861 Offences Against the Person Act, and the question of appropriate punishment for acts of violence. Levison's initial sentence to be executed is later commuted to hard labour and the prospect, however remote, of parole. The jury recommends leniency because his actions were not 'planned' and had been carried out 'in a moment of wild rage' (573–74, 607).

pily insinuates that Archibald may be conducting an affair with a former paramour, Barbara Hare (219, 270–71).[89] Isabel marries Archibald not because she loves him, but because she has to; the same predicament which drove Clara Pulleyn to marry Barnes Newcome. Her first 'emotion' when Archibald proposes is 'one of entire opposition' (119). But needs must; Isabel has no portion and no settlement.[90] She might already fancy that she is in love with Levison, but she is not in a position to pick and choose.[91] Marriage disappoints, unsurprisingly. Unsuited to domestic governance, her position is usurped by Archibald's sister Cornelia who descends on the house and assumes control, something which leads Isabel's sympathetic maid Joyce to later conclude about the adultery, 'I say she was driven to it. She has not been allowed to indulge a will of her own, poor thing, since she came to East Lynne' (279). Isabel feels increasingly alone; the servants gossip about Archibald and Barbara, and Levison keeps dropping by to flirt (177–78, 197–98, 244).[92] Before long, the crushingly bored Isabel is experiencing the 'symptoms of sinful happiness throbbing in her heart' (212–13, 216, 223). Levison has a reputation, having apparently conducted numerous previous affairs, including one with a local girl, Afy Hallijohn.[93] Afy, however, is lower class which makes her sexual transgressions rather less troubling. Isabel Carlyle is not. The fall and the shame is all the greater. When Joyce suggests that her disappeared mistress might be dead, Carlyle responds that the truth 'is worse than that' (281). The entire family, as his sister Cornelia adds, is 'dishonoured' (282).[94] Isabel's despairing brother spells out the implications: 'You are an earl's daughter! Oh, Isabel! How utterly you have lost yourself!' (308).

Whilst Wood expected her audience to enjoy the vicarious thrill of Isabel's terrible mistake, she also expected them to note the legal consequences. It is here

---

[89] Barbara is stunned when she hears that Archibald has proposed to Isabel. She herself expected a proposal imminently, as did pretty much everyone else in the neighbourhood, not least an astonished Cornelia who, on hearing of her brother's actions, only half-jokingly suggests that he should be placed before a panel of lunacy commissioners (129–30). Barbara remains supremely jealous of Isabel for much of the first and second volumes of the novel, indeed until she eventually realises her ambition and becomes the second Mrs Carlyle (163).

[90] As the new Lord Mount Severn observes, of his father's carelessness and his sister's predicament: 'Wicked improvidence! Shameful profligacy! Callous-hearted man! To live a rogue, and die a beggar, leaving his daughter to the charity of strangers!' (102) Following his death, it quickly becomes apparent that the old Lord had engaged in a series of fraudulent attempts to raise cash which had resulted in massive indebtedness. With the alienable parts of the estate, including East Lynne, already sold off and the rest heavily encumbered, there is little prospect of many of the debts being discharged. Isabel inherits nothing, although she is initially uncertain that she is without a settlement (98–99). The old Lord had been unable to settle any estate on his daughter in part because of his own intemperate marriage, conducted at Gretna Green without the approval of either set of parents, or more importantly, the security of a settlement; all the fault of 'thoughtless, runaway marriages', as he admits to Carlyle (9).

[91] She hopes that she might come to 'love my husband in time' (136).

[92] Isabel has reasonable grounds for her suspicion. Archibald singularly refuses to divulge why he keeps meeting Barbara in secret. The reason is the Hallijohn murder and Barbara's belief in her brother's innocence but Isabel could not know this.

[93] The narrator also dwells on 'that hushed-up business with Mrs Charlton' whilst implying that it is not an isolated rumour (19–20).

[94] Much later, as her brother contemplates marrying again, Cornelia reminds him of the 'slur' that his last marriage left upon the family (373).

that Archibald's perspicuity is significant. Sensation novels were peculiar in eschewing historical distance. *East Lynne* is set in 1860 just two years after the Divorce Court opened its doors for business. Archibald's options are therefore rather more attractive, certainly rather cheaper, than those which had faced Barnes Newcome a few years earlier. Without pausing to contemplate chasing after his wayward wife, still less bothering to confront her lover, Archibald goes to court and petitions for divorce. Within months, Isabel is cut adrift, her ruin complete; for as Levison confirms, if rather heartlessly, no gentleman would dream of marrying a divorced woman, at least not a penniless one (292). Under the 1857 Act Isabel's adultery was alone sufficient grounds for a successful petition. Of course, if Archibald had committed adultery, Isabel would still have had to evidence another of the collateral grounds enumerated in the Act. Following her husband's arrest for murder, Alice Levison consults Archibald as to her chances of securing a divorce. She might have been able to evidence spousal abuse, along with adultery, but only if she could have persuaded a court that it was sufficient to amount to cruelty. In summary, her chances, compromised further by her lack of money, are 'none' and all Archibald can do is offer 'a few kind words of sympathy' (560).[95]

The 1857 Act, as we have noted, abrogated the need for a petitioner to first secure a successful crim-con suit. Even so, in 1860 crim-con suits were still fresh enough in the memory to justify an allusion in *East Lynne*. Wood was not obviously enamoured of Caroline Norton as a furious correspondence between the two in 1871 on the subject of plagiarism confirmed. But as the same correspondence insinuated, when Wood came to contemplate the case of *Carlyle v Carlyle* she evidently had that of *Norton v Lord Melbourne* in mind.[96] Isabel certainly perceived herself as having committed a 'criminal' offence and it is likely that Wood's readers would have shared a similar perception (432). Moreover, the 1857 Act, as also noted, did not preclude the possibility of visiting financial ruin upon seducers. Levison is clearly troubled by the prospect, demanding that he be kept abreast of all developments in the 'suit, *Carlyle v Carlyle*' (285).[97] It has been suggested that after 1857 courts became ever more reluctant to grant substantial damages in divorce cases. But Wood's court was not, preferring perhaps to recall Lord Kenyon's notorious advice to hesitant juries in such cases, that 'exemplary damages' were necessary for the 'protection of the peace of families'.[98] It is reported that Carlyle, with a typical sense of moral integrity, had declined to claim damages,

---

[95] Alice expresses particular disappointment when she hears that her husband's sentence has been commuted to imprisonment, reconciling herself to the fact that she will thus remain 'tied to him' (607).

[96] The exchange conducted in the letters pages of *The Times* in October 1871 attracted George Eliot's attention, and censure. Wood was quick to reject the accusation of plagiarism, which moved around the supposition that she had based much of Isabel Carlyle's case on a short story which Norton had published many years earlier. The fact that Norton was unable to remember the title hardly helped her case. Wood's repost was suitably contemptuous.

[97] It is clear that Levison is broke, hounded by 'obdurate' creditors (251). It is the primary reason why he escapes to France, and then on return to England strives to move around incognito, before seeking election to Parliament in order to secure 'his threatened person' from 'prison' (205–207, 211, 455).

[98] This was articulated in *Walford v Cooke* in 1789, and quoted in Stone, *Road to Divorce* (above n 2) 274.

but that the jury in his case 'feeling for his wrongs, gave unprecedentedly heavy ones' (307). The fact that Carlyle then gives his damages to charity chimes with contemporary expectation. In the run up to the 1857 Act, supporters of reform urged that a true gentleman would anyway disdain damages awarded 'in compensation for their dishonour', and if received immediately donate them for the public good.[99]

Finally, in getting his divorce Carlyle took the further precaution of securing himself against any subsequent accusation of bigamy. As we shall see, by 1860 bigamy had emerged as one of the most 'fashionable' of literary crimes beloved of the sensation novel reader, its proscription in criminal law having been recently reaffirmed in the 1857 Offences Against the Person Act. Aside from the criminal penalties which were chiefly of application to the witting bigamist, Hardwicke's 1753 Marriage Act had confirmed that a bigamous marriage was void in law, regardless of intent.[100] Those who argued the case for the Matrimonial Causes Act a century later advised that statutory reform might better protect gentlemen from the risk of unwitting bigamy in such cases where the report of a first wife's death is later proved to be false. That is precisely what happens in the case of Isabel Carlyle. Of course, they would still need to be as perspicacious as Archibald unlike the variously oblivious husbands we shall encounter in Mary Braddon's 'bigamy novels'. But Archibald is nothing if not cautious. There is here a final variant on the same essential lesson that Wood intended her readers to contemplate. A wandering wife could no longer, after 1857, fall back on the likelihood that her cuckolded husband would still be married to her, and thus obliged, if nothing else, to service her debts. An adulterous wife could be replaced, and with relative ease. Isabel Carlyle was divorced without her knowing, her place taken by a second Mrs Carlyle within a matter of months.

Oh Reader!

Sensation novels such as *East Lynne* were in general savaged by contemporary critics. But, with one or two exceptions, Wood's novel was not. Margaret Oliphant suggested that *East Lynne* was an especially 'dangerous and foolish work'.[101] The *Athenaeum*, however, concluded that *East Lynne* was 'one of the best novels

---

[99] Stone, *Road to Divorce* (above n 2) 291.

[100] The Act was not especially effective. As John Boyd Kinnear observed, despite its 'strictness', the Act provided 'not the least security' in law against the dangers of bigamous marriage, witting or unwitting. J Fahnestock, 'Bigamy: The Rise and Fall of a Convention' (1981) 36 *Nineteenth Century Fiction* 59. In large part due to popular anxieties fanned by novels such as those of Braddon and Wood, a Royal Commission was established in 1865, tasked with investigating the possibility of root and branch reform of civil and criminal provisions relating to bigamy.

[101] See J Phegley, 'Henceforward I Refuse to Bow the Knee to Their Narrow Rule: Mary Elizabeth Braddon's *Belgravia Magazine*, Women Readers, and Literary Valuation' (2004) 26 *Nineteenth Century Contexts* 165.

published for a season'.[102] In his *Memorials*, Wood's son Charles proudly quoted *The Daily News* reviewer who observed that the 'story displays a force of description and a dramatic completeness we have seldom seen surpassed'.[103] A reason for this approval could be discerned in another review eagerly quoted in the *Memorials*. The *Morning Post* paid tribute to *East Lynne*'s 'strong appeal to women by a woman, who would urge upon her fellows the invincible truth that the only ways of wisdom are those of pleasantness, and only her paths are those of peace'. The author had, in writing about adultery, 'selected a difficult subject'. But her moral purpose was clear. Rather than 'merely providing amusement', Wood had composed a story which could only serve to advise young women of the hazards that will inevitably follow 'through the breach of the most sacred law of God'.[104] For a few the didacticism was rather too richly coated in evangelical moralism but only a few, as Charles was eager to affirm.[105] According to the *Conservative*, the author of *East Lynne* had 'served the interests of morality in holding up to society a mirror in which it may see itself exactly reflected', an observation which, on closer inspection, imported a rather more unsettling insinuation.[106]

It has been suggested that the fall of Isabel Carlyle was intended to articulate the fears of a generation of Victorian women who aspired to be 'ladylike', but who also feared the sexual and emotional suffocation that came with the attribution.[107] The temptation to which Isabel succumbed was not, Wood insinuates, peculiar. It was only too easy to empathise with a suddenly impoverished young woman who finds herself obliged to marry a dreary lawyer, not just in order to maintain appearances, but to survive; 'an expensive girl without a shilling' as the ever-blunt Cornelia observes (131).[108] Nevertheless the temptation to stray had to be resisted because it was contrary to the law of God and because it was also contrary to the newly-revised law of man. In a note left behind, the eloping Isabel asks her husband to tell her abandoned children that they had 'outraged and betrayed' their mother 'driving her to the very depth of desperation, ere she quitted them in her despair'

---

[102] Unsigned, 'New Novels' in *Athenaeum*, 12 October 1861, 474. The *Saturday Review* was rather more temperate, agreeing that the novel was one of the best of the season, but concluding that in the longer term it was likely to be thought of as 'unmistakably of the second class'. See the *Saturday Review*, 15 February 1862.

[103] Charles Wood's *Memorials* (Bentley, 1894), remains the only 'modern' biography of his mother. It is unsurprisingly flattering. Lucy Sussex suggests that it takes the form of a 'hagiography' in L Sussex, 'Mrs Henry Wood and her Memorials' (2008) 15 *Women's Writing* 157–59. Amongst various peculiar facts, Charles was keen to impress that his mother's most famous work was so popular that it was translated into Hindustani and Parsee. See also, A Sergeant, *Women Novelists of Queen Victoria's Reign* (Hurst & Blackett, 1897) 178–79.

[104] Wood, *Memorials* (above n 88) 244.

[105] Charlotte Riddell was moved to observe that 'Mrs Wood is simply a brute; she throws in bits of religion to slip her fodder down the public throat' in B Palmer, 'Dangerous and Foolish Work: Evangelicalism and Sensationalism in Ellen Wood's *Argosy* Magazine' (2008) 15 *Women's Writing* 188.

[106] In Wood, *Memorials*, (above n 88) 243–44.

[107] Elliott, 'Lady' (above n 78) 331–33.

[108] Adding with similar brusqueness that the prospective marriage would be between a 'Beauty' and a 'Beast' (135).

(280).[109] This may be true, but it is not an excuse, as Wood's narrator impresses in one of the passages that contemporary critics most admired:

> Oh, reader, believe me! Lady-wife-mother! Should you ever be tempted to abandon your home, so will you awake. Whatever trials may be the lot of your married life, though they may magnify themselves to your crushed spirit as beyond the endurance of woman to bear, *resolve* to bear them; fall down upon your knees and pray to be enabled to bear them: pray for patience; pray for strength to resist the demon that would urge you so to escape; bear unto death, rather than forfeit your fair name and your good conscience; for be assured that the alternative, if you rush on to it, will be far worse than death. (283)

And just in case the reader had waded through all 62 chapters and still missed the point, the novel closes with Archibald reminding his second wife: 'Oh, Barbara, never forget never forget that the only way to ensure peace in the end, is, to strive always to be doing right, unselfishly, under God' (624).

In terms of Wood's canon, the moral didacticism of *East Lynne* was not exceptional. As Dinah Birch has more recently commented, everything that Ellen Wood wrote was 'unremittingly moral in tone'.[110] And this in turn was hardly surprising. Wood lived a life of studious propriety, in sharp contrast to fellow sensationalists such as the bigamous Braddon and Wilkie Collins with his collection of mistresses. The 'Hand of God', Charles was keen to confirm, was always upon his mother and 'she was ever in His keeping'.[111] Wood craved the same respectability as her readers, even as she shared their liking for vicarious literary thrills. Certainly she wanted her readers to deplore the fall of Isabel Carlyle, just as they may have felt inclined to sympathise, if only a little, with her predicament. She clearly wanted them to contemplate rather more closely the implications of the 1857 Divorce Act but she also wanted them to be reassured. Isabel is one of the remorseful adulteresses, and she suffers. On her deathbed, as she pleads for Archibald's forgiveness, she confesses:

> When I think of what you were, and are, and how I requited you, I could sink to the earth with remorse and shame. My own sin I have surely expiated: I cannot expiate the shame I have entailed on you, and upon our children. (615)

Archibald does, of course, 'forgive' Isabel, just as he pointedly refuses to condone her sin (616). Whilst Isabel might be more pitiable than likeable, quite 'one of the silliest young women that ever existed in the realms of fiction', as Adeline Sergeant put it a few years later, Wood clearly intends to tempt her readers.[112] The didactic effect of her novel would be all the greater on those impressionable young women who might have identified their prospects with those of the evidently and similarly

[109] The abandonment of her children would have attracted the unalloyed criticism of Wood's readers. 'A brute animal, deaf and dumb, clings to its offspring', as Afy observes, 'but she abandoned hers' (396).
[110] Birch, 'Fear' (above n 79) 22. In like terms, Hughes notes a rigid 'propriety' that characterises all of Wood's novels. See Hughes, *Maniac* (above n 77) 112.
[111] Wood, *Memorials* (above n 88) 143.
[112] Sergeant, *Women Novelists* (above n 103) 175.

impressionable Isabel Carlyle.[113] Isabel fell in large part because she felt alienated, unable to articulate her fears and suspicions; a position with which many of the readers of *East Lynne*, just as emotionally bereft and sexually frustrated, might readily have sympathised.

Much the same, it might be argued, can be said of Clara Newcome. As we have already noted, Clara is not the leading female character in *The Newcomes*, still less the most attractive or the most articulate. It is Ethel Newcome who so devastatingly denounces the hypocrisies of marriage law and custom. However, as we have also already noted, whilst many of Thackeray's female readers might have liked to imagine themselves as Ethel Newcome, it is more likely that they felt a closer visceral affinity with 'timid' little Clara; as indeed they might with the observations of Thackeray's narrator:

> Oh, me! What a confession it is, in the very outset of life and blushing brightness of youth's morning, to own that the aim with which a young girl sets out, and the object of her existence, is to marry a rich man; that she was endowed with beauty so that she might buy wealth, and title with it . . . By long cramping and careful process, their little natural hearts have been squeezed up, like the feet of their fashionable little sisters in China. (458–59)

The responsibility is broad, but it is also particular:

> How will you have the story? Worthy mammas of families if you do not like to have your daughters told that bad husbands will make bad wives; that marriages begun in indifference make homes unhappy; that men whom girls are brought to swear to love and honour are sometimes false, selfish and cruel; and that women forget the oaths which they have been made to swear if you will not hear this ladies, close the book, and send for some other. Banish the newspaper out of your houses, and shut your eyes to the truth, the awful truth, of life and sin . . . We arrange such matches every day; we sell or buy beauty, or rank, or wealth; we inaugurate the bargain in churches with sacramental services, in which the parties engaged call upon heaven to witness their vows we know them to be lies, and we sell them with God's name . . . is there a bishop on the bench that has not amen'd the humbug in his lawn sleeves and called a blessing over the kneeling pair of perjurers? (560, 584)

Thackeray wrote from conviction. Replying to an American correspondent at precisely the same time as he was struggling his way through *The Newcomes*, he observed of his fellow countrymen and women:

> They never feel love, but directly its born they throttle it and fling it under the sewer as poor girls do with their unlawful children. They make up money marriages and are content. Then the father goes to the House of Commons or the Counting House, the mother to her balls and visits. The children lurk upstairs with their governess, and when

---

[113] For critical confirmation, see A Cvetkovich, *Mixed Feelings: Feminism, Mass Culture and Victorian Sensationalism* (Rutgers University Press, 1992) 98–99, suggesting that phenomenal success of the novel had 'as much to do with its capacity to make its audience cry as it does with its capacity to generate mystery of suspense'.

their turn comes are bought and sold as respectable and heartless as their parents before them.[114]

He also wrote from the heart, necessarily poignant correspondence with his daughters confirming a deep sense of responsibility as both parent and novelist.[115] Reflecting on his previous novel *The History of Henry Esmond*, Thackeray concluded that it was 'a failure besides being immoral', continuing 'we must take pains and write careful books when we have made 10000 for the young ladies'.[116] Aside from the rather optimistic expectation as regards projected sales figures, the observation betrays an acute sense of what the likely audience for *The Newcomes* might be, and the particular responsibilities that would therefore attach to its writing.

It was perhaps this conviction which made Thackeray so uncompromising. GH Lewes famously castigated Thackeray for eschewing overt moral commentary of the kind which saved Ellen Wood from greater critical discomfort.[117] He was not alone.[118] Conversely, others, such as Thomas Hardy writing a little later, recognised in this a virtue.[119] So did Whitwell Elwin, writing in the *Quarterly Review*, who applauded the deployment of 'stern upbraidings' in the place of 'hacknied discourses on vice and virtue'.[120] It certainly earned Thackeray the reputation of being an angry writer. On his death George Gilfillan testified that: 'He was a minor scourge of God, the Attila of fashionable life. He lashed flesh and bone alike to ribbons. His blows were aimed at vital parts, the head and the heart.'[121] Some contemporaries thought they detected a softening in later novels such as *The Newcomes*.[122] In the opinion of a contemporary reviewer in *The Times*, this apparent change of tone was entirely appropriate as England in 1855 was 'more equitable' and had 'wider plans and loftier objects'. The age of the harsher 'satirist' was past.[123] Elwin was again the more perceptive. The older Thackeray, he suggested, was no less angry. But he was more compassionate in regard to those who suffered most, better able to portray the 'sacredness of sorrow' which attaches to them, and better able to cultivate the 'sorrowful emotions' of his readers in their cause.[124] Edward Burne-Jones agreed, suggesting that the distinguishing feature of the

---

[114] See Taylor, *Thackeray* (above n 50) 348–49. The observation was made in a letter to Sally Baxter, a young and as yet unmarried, Bostonian, Thackeray had met during one of his lecture tours in America. He had evidently become rather infatuated with Sally.

[115] Winnifrith suggests that Thackeray's reluctance to write anything too overtly sexual reflected a personal sense of responsibility as a father of daughters who necessarily sought social acceptance. See T Winnifrith, *Fallen Women in the Nineteenth Century Novel* (St Martin's Press, 1994) 71–72.

[116] Quoted in Taylor, *Thackeray* (above n 50) 350.

[117] Ibid, 352.

[118] The reviewer in *The Times* concluded that whilst Thackeray was 'a great humorist', it was to be regretted that he was 'not a great moralist too'. Tillotson and Hawes, *Critical Heritage* (above n 55) 230.

[119] See Taylor, *Thackeray* (above n 50) 443.

[120] *Quarterly Review* (above n 50) 351–53.

[121] See Taylor, *Thackeray* (above n 50) 447–48.

[122] See, for example, Winnifrith, *Fallen Women* (above n 115) 73–74, 86–87, and J Wheatley, *Patterns in Thackeray's Fiction* (MIT Press, 1969) 96, 103.

[123] See Tillotson and Hawes, *Critical Heritage* (above n 55) 229.

[124] *Quarterly Review* (above n 50) 357.

Thackeray who wrote *The Newcomes* was the articulation of the 'widest sympathy unsurpassable'.[125]

East Lynne and *The Newcomes* were both novels about marriage, adultery and dysfunctional families. They were also novels about the law, or more accurately, the legal consequences of adultery and familial dysfunction. They were thus novels written with a 'purpose'. However, that purpose was very different, for where the fall of Isabel Carlyle was intended to reinforce the institution of marriage, the experience of Clara Newcome was designed to precipitate its reform. Written and published in the middle of the 1850s, it is obvious that Thackeray expected his audience to read *The Newcomes* in the context of wider debates not just about matrimonial law reform, but also about alternative ideas of 'companionate' marriage; marriages of 'love' as 'God has designed', in the words of Frances Power Cobbe, as opposed to 'marriages of interest'.[126] It is just as obvious where his authorial sympathies lay. A 'prudent marriage', his narrator confirms, is one sealed by 'warm friendship, and thorough esteem and confidence' (374–75). The idealistic Thackeray is, however, forever challenged by the cynical. Discussing the alternative hypotheses with Clive, the young Lord Kew confirms that 'love' may be 'good for romances, and for Misses to sigh about, but any man who walks through the world with his eyes open, knows how senseless is all this rubbish' (301). It is not simply that Thackeray might have agreed; it is that he sensed that too many of his countrymen probably did. The case of *Newcome v Lord Highgate* was intended to focus attention on the legal consequences which attended a matrimonial culture which was endemically dysfunctional. Thackeray died in 1863. He would have noted the immediate impact of the 1857 Matrimonial Causes Act, and recognised what it had achieved, and what it had not.

In her essay 'The Law Concerning Women', written on the eve of the 1857 Act, and as part of the same debate which *The Newcomes* enjoined, Elizabeth Lynn Linton warned that there was only so much the law could, or indeed should, do. Linton was not sympathetic to the feminist cause, arguing that the fiction of coverture should be judged on grounds of utility rather than principle.[127] Most importantly, she argued against the fallacy that Victorian England might be able to legislate for domestic happiness:

> The law has nothing to do with that union of souls and sympathies of which lovers dream; but it has to do with the common security, the peace of families, the safe foundation of the social world . . . Bad husbands and bad wives will be in the world, we are

[125] E Burne-Jones, 'Essay on the Newcomes' in *Oxford and Cambridge Magazine*, January 1856, 50, and quoted in Tillotson and Hawes, *Critical Heritage* (above n 55) 253.
[126] For Cobbe's observations, see FP Cobbe, 'What shall we do with our old maids?' in Hamilton, *Criminals* (above n 18) 87. See Clarke, 'Narrative Matrix' (above n 66) 347, arguing strongly that *The Newcomes* 'constitutes a commentary' on 'debates then raging in Parliament' on prospective matrimonial law reform, and further arguments at 349. For a commentary on 'companionate' marriages or, as he terms them, marriages of 'affective individualism', see Stone, *Road to Divorce* (above n 2) 60.
[127] See N Thompson, 'Responding to the woman question: rereading non-canonical Victorian women novelists' in Thompson, *Women Writers* (above n 72) 3.

afraid, so long as evil people are in the human race; but the remedies do not lie in the hands of the legislature.[128]

The law might be 'dragged' into the English home. But it 'cannot end' the 'quarrels' of fractious spouses, nor 'defend them from each other'.[129] Here at least there was something upon which Thackeray and Wood might have agreed. Much changed in 1858; and much stayed the same. As late as 1886, Chief Justice Coleridge felt moved to regret that fact that, insofar as English law was concerned, a wife was still 'regarded as some kind of inferior dog or horse'.[130] According to Dinah Birch, the contemporary success of mid-Victorian novels such as *The Newcomes* and *East Lynne* lay in the fact that they articulated the 'deepest fears' of a generation.[131] Both novels assumed a didactic purpose, one that was intrinsically jurisprudential. But neither, in the end, assumed a better future certainly not for women. Indeed, both traded in the converse imputation as, of course, did their near contemporary Mary Elizabeth Braddon, to whose novels we will now turn. Women like Clara Newcome and Isabel Carlyle would continue to fall in the pages of the Victorian novels for decades to come, and few would land happily; middle-class wives such as Laura Kennedy and Gwendolen Grandcourt, and working-class girls such as Lydia Glasher and Tess Durbeyfield. Victorian England would continue to worry about marriage, just as much after 1857 as before: about the fidelity of wives and daughters and the brutality of their husbands, about the integrity of families and their settlements, and about the apparent and continuing inability of the law to make the lives of married women, in particular, very much happier.

---

[128] E Linton, 'The Laws Concerning Women' in *Blackwoods Magazine*, April 1856, 381, 384.

[129] Linton, *Laws* ibid, 386.

[130] See M Wiener, *Men of Blood: Violence, Manliness and Criminal Justice in Victorian England*, (Cambridge University Press, 2004) 161.

[131] Birch, 'Fear' (above n 79) 23.

2

Fashionable Crimes

Gustave Flaubert wrote the following dedication to the first full-length edition of *Madame Bovary*:

> To Marie-Antoine-Jules Senard, Member of the Paris Bar, Ex-President of the National Assembly and Former Minister of the Interior
>
> Dear and Illustrious Friend, allow me to inscribe your name on the first page of this book, which I dedicate to you as having been chiefly responsible for its publication. As a result of the magnificent way in which you conducted my case, my work has conferred upon me, its author, an authority which I had no reason to anticipate. I should like you, therefore, to accept this token of my gratitude. However great it be, it can never adequately repay either your eloquence or your devoted loyalty.[1]

The dedication was dated 12 April 1857.

Just four months earlier, Flaubert had been indicted before the sixth chamber of the *Tribunal Correctional* in Paris for 'offense to public and religious morality and to good morals'. He had in the end been acquitted but with a severe reprimand and his request for costs denied.[2] The case was, for obvious reasons, notorious and, as the dedication implies, did wonders for sales figures.[3] *Madame Bovary* had first appeared in serialised form in the *Revue de Paris*, a journal which had long been the object of government suspicion.[4] The prosecution case invited the court to

---

Some of the material which follows in this chapter was previously published as 'Things little girls have no business to know anything about: the crimes of Aurora Floyd', in (2011) 22.2 *Columbia Journal of Gender and Law* 430–78. My thanks to the editor of the journal for permission to reuse this material.

[1] G Flaubert, *Madame Bovary* (Oxford University Press, 2004) 3.

[2] The Court accepted that *Madame Bovary* did not seek to prescribe immorality, but noted that the book did depict immorality in a coarse way. The judgment observed: 'The work in question merits severe blame, since the mission of literature should be to beautify and enhance the spirit by elevating the intelligence and purifying morals rather than to inspire disgust for vice by offering a portrait of disorder that may exist in society.' Six months later, the poet Charles Baudelaire would be indicted for the same offence. Baudelaire's counsel was, unfortunately, altogether less impressive than Senard. Baudelaire was, accordingly, convicted and the six poems that comprised his *Les Fleurs du Mal* remained censored until 1949. For a recent commentary on the Flaubert trial, and the judgement handed down, see E Langdon, *Dirt for Art's Sake: Books on Trial from Madame Bovary to Lolita* (Cornell University Press, 2007) particularly 22–26, 32–34. For a recent commentary on Baudelaire's trial, see M Hannoosh, 'Reading the Trial of the *Fleurs du Mal*' (2011) 106 *Modern Humanities Research Association* 374–87.

[3] In a private letter to his brother, Flaubert confirmed: 'My *Bovary* continues to be a hit. It has become spicy. Everyone has read it, is reading it, or wants to read it . . . My persecution has won me endless sympathy.' Langdon, *Dirt for Art's Sake* (above n 2) 18.

[4] For this reason the editor of the *Revue*, who was convinced that the prosecution was a pretext for suppressing his journal, was also indicted. See D LaCapra, 'Two Trials' in D Hollier (ed), *A New History*

consider the offence written into certain passages of Flaubert's novel, most immediately those which addressed the 'defilements of marriage' and the 'poetry of
adultery'. *Madame Bovary* was condemned for being 'realist', meaning that it was
'the negation of the beautiful and the good'.[5] Ultimately, however, the prosecution played with anxieties regarding prospective readership. Prosecutor Pinard
asked:

> Who will read the novel of Monsieur Flaubert? Will it be men who busy themselves with
> political or social commentary? No! The light pages of *Madame Bovary* will fall into
> even lighter hands, into the hands of young women, sometimes married women. Well,
> when the imagination has been seduced, when seduction has descended into the heart,
> when the heart has spoken to the senses, do you believe that a very cold reasoning will
> be very strong against this seduction of the senses?[6]

Senard did not dispute the prospective readership, but argued that, on the contrary, *Madame Bovary* was entirely conventional, and if anything would serve as a
moral corrective, dissuading any young woman who read it from making the same
mistakes as Emma Bovary.[7] Ellen Wood's *East Lynne* would be defended in the
pages of various critical reviews on the same terms just three years later. There is
an obvious affinity here between Flaubert's novel and Wood's novel. Critics of the
sensational genre commonly supposed that its poisoned roots lay across the channel. The French 'novel' had become critical shorthand for a genre of literature
which was morally corrupted, 'diseased and indecorous' according to WR Greg,
and which most importantly should not be permitted to fall into the hands of
impressionable young readers, especially female ones.[8] Whilst French novels were
growing in popularity among English middle-class audiences, in fact, the danger
was not that these readers were importing novels from Paris and exercising their
rather shaky appreciation of French syntax, it was that English writers were allowing themselves to be influenced by the novels of Flaubert, Hugo and Balzac,
thereby infecting themselves with a kind of literary virus which they carried into
the hitherto tranquil homes of Middle England.[9]

of French Literature (Harvard University Press, 1989) 727, and C Haynes, 'The Politics of Publishing in
the Second Empire: The Trial of *Madame Bovary* Revisited' (2005) 23 *French Politics, Society and
Culture* 2–4.

[5] LaCapra, 'Two Trials' (above n 4) 730.

[6] Ibid, 728–29.

[7] See Langdon, *Dirt for Art's Sake* (above n 2) 21–22.

[8] For a commentary on the reception of French literature amongst English critics including Greg,
see B Leckie, *Culture and Adultery: The Novel, the Newspaper and the Law 1857–1914* (Pennsylvania
University Press, 1999) 25–26, and K Flint, *The Woman Reader 1837–1914* (Oxford University Press,
1993) 138–40 and 287, referring to the French novel as a 'signifier of immorality'.

[9] The *Saturday Review* denounced *Madame Bovary* as typical French 'garbage' and advised readers
against going to the trouble of ordering a copy from France. The novel was not available in English until
1886, and until that date existed as much by its reputation in Victorian England as by its reading. When
it did appear in English its publication, along with that of other French 'realist' novels including those
of Emile Zola, led to the prosecution of the London publisher Henry Vizetelly, at the behest of the
National Vigilance Association. See A Rouxeville, 'Victorian Attitudes to Flaubert: An Investigation'
(1987) 16 *Nineteenth Century French Studies* 133–34, and N Daly, *Sensation and Modernity in the 1860s*
(Cambridge University Press, 2009) 15.

And so it transpired. Wood's novel was a stunning success, as we have already noted, while the sensation genre which it appeared to herald took the English literary scene by storm during the early years of the 1860s. Critics pointed to a particular and, in the opinion of many, unhappy coincidence, the growing inspiration of French realist novels on English writers and the passage of the 1857 Matrimonial Causes Act. The complementary passage of an Obscene Publications Act in 1857, the purpose of which was never entirely clear, provided little reassurance. The Act was certainly never intended to prevent from English women reading about sexually frustrated French women, nor was it intended to stop them reading about other sexually frustrated English women such as Isabel Carlyle, Edith Dombey or indeed Isabel Gilbert, yet another prospective English adulteress who was, in fact, notorious less for her transgression than for reasons of literary genetics. We have already come across Isabel Gilbert, and more particularly her reading habits. Isabel was the flighty heroine of Mary Elizabeth Braddon's 1864 novel *The Doctor's Wife*, a very obvious, and very lucrative, rewriting of Flaubert's *Madame Bovary*.[10] In one sense Braddon did not feel the need to alter much in her re-write. The scene was shifted from a dreary provincial town in Normandy to a dreary provincial town in the English Midlands but much of the rest of the book remained essentially the same. The doctor was as dull as the town in which he practised medicine, the marriage as love-less, the growing sexual frustration just as destructive in its intensity.[11]

There was, however, one significant exception which distinguished Isabel Gilbert very sharply from both Emma Bovary and indeed, Isabel Carlyle. Isabel Gilbert remained a frustrated adulteress, and thus not only was she less troubled by the deeper emotional and metaphysical anxieties which afflicted Emma Bovary, but she was also saved from the same desperate demise. Isabel Gilbert lived very happily ever after, an unusual fate for the Victorian adulteress, frustrated or otherwise. As we have already noted, one of Isabel's many fictive heroines is Edith Dombey. Insofar as their adultery remains frustrated, they did indeed have something in common. In other ways, there was rather less. Edith does not suffer in quite the same way that Emma Bovary does; neither does her future look quite as rosy as that of Isabel Gilbert. More important, perhaps, is the difference in purpose of their respective creations. It was in writing *Dombey and Son*, as modern critics

---

[10] Braddon openly admitted the influence, confessing herself 'struck' by the 'style' of Flaubert's novel 'in spite of its hideous immorality'. Quoted in N Schroeder and R Schroeder, *From Sensation to Society: Representations of Marriage in the Fiction of Mary Elizabeth Braddon* (Delaware University Press, 2006) 162–63. For an early commentary on the various obvious affinities between the two, see C Heywood, 'Flaubert, Miss Braddon and George Moore' (1960) 12 *Comparative Literature* 151–58.

[11] The object of Isabel's lust is the Byronic Roland Lansdell, who is not only handsome, wealthy and aristocratic but also of poetic inclination, sceptical and atheistic; something which was clearly borrowed from the character of Homais in *Madame Bovary*. It is this scepticism which allows Lansdell to justify his invitation to adultery as a species of 'free' love, in opposition to the 'farce of duty and submission' to 'the laws which other people have made for us'. Lansdell converts to Christianity and repents on his deathbed. His death, which quickly follows that of Isabel's husband, saves Isabel from committing the ultimate sin and her creator from risking still greater critical displeasure. Even so, the reviewer in the *Athenaeum* felt obliged to point out that whilst he may have been unable to seek redress in the new Divorce Court, Isabel's imagined transgressions might themselves have furnished 'no small ground for complaint'. See Schroeder and Schroeder, *From Sensation to Society* (above n 10) 182.

have commonly supposed, that Dickens got serious. The same might be said of Flaubert's *Madame Bovary*; it certainly was by Flaubert's counsel. Braddon's ambition was rather more prosaic. *The Doctor's Wife* was written to entertain and to sell as were, all too obviously, her two previous best-selling 'bigamy novels', *Lady Audley's Secret* and *Aurora Floyd*. We will revisit these two novels, and especially the scandalous 'case' of Aurora Floyd, shortly.

The Sensational Moment

The moment may have comparatively brief, but for a few years during the early 1860s 'sensation' novels such as Braddon's enjoyed an extraordinary popularity.[12] It has been estimated that their ready audience was around five million, predominantly female and middle class.[13] Years later, Braddon would concede that *The Doctor's Wife* was 'not a story which I would care to place in the hands of "the young person"'.[14] But that was many years later. In 1864 she did not hesitate to publish. The first instalments of Braddon's first and most notorious novel, *Lady Audley's Secret* had appeared in late 1861, keeping the nation engrossed in the various crimes of the murderous Lucy Graham for much of the following spring and summer. A three-volume edition followed in October, by which time Braddon had already begun drafting the first instalments of the barely less shocking *Aurora Floyd*. *Aurora Floyd* appeared at the start of 1862 and was even more successful than *Lady Audley's Secret*. Publishers clamoured for *Aurora*. In the end, following its initial serialisation in *Temple Bar*, the Tinsley brothers paid Braddon the vast sum of £1,000 for just two years copyright.[15] Within months she had begun to write *The Doctor's Wife*, which hit the presses in early 1864, to the consternation of appalled critics, harassed librarians, and bemused parents. By now she had secured a readership that would remain 'blindly devoted' for the next 50 years.[16]

The public, Trollope wryly advised, appeared to consume 'sensational' novels 'as men eat a pastry after dinner not without some inward conviction that the taste is vain if not vicious'.[17] Few critics were so sanguine. 'There is', Dean Mansel observed deploying a still less edifying gastronomic metaphor, 'something unspeakably dis-

---

[12] Nicholas Daly notes that while a novel such as Dickens's *Our Mutual Friend* achieved 30,000 sales in its first three days, Reynold's relatively-unknown sensation novel, *The Soldier's Wife*, published in two parts over 1862 and 1863, achieved at least double those sales figures. See Daly, *Sensation and Modernity* (above n 9) 14.

[13] According to Natalie and Ronald Schroeder, 'readers of sensation literature were female, middle-class and legion'. See Schroeder and Schroeder, *From Sensation to Society* (above n 10) 15, and J Loesberg, 'The Ideology of Narrative Form in Sensation Fiction' (1986) 13 *Representations* 115–17.

[14] R Wolff, *Sensational Victorian: The Life and Fiction of Mary Elizabeth Braddon* (Garland, 1979) 204.

[15] Approximately £80,000 in today's money.

[16] In the words of her biographer Robert Wolff, in *Sensational Victorian*, ibid, 407.

[17] A Trollope, *An Autobiography* (Penguin, 1996) 140.

gusting in this ravenous appetite' for sensationalist 'carrion'.[18] Critical anxieties were various. First, there was a concern about decency. Sensation novels, it was observed, appealed to the 'animal part of our human nature'.[19] Unsurprisingly, the depiction of female sexuality and passion attracted especial critical ire.[20] Writing in 1868, the Reverend Paget railed against a generic 'teaching' that was 'so infamous', its principles 'so utterly demoralising', the 'conversations' so 'revolting for their looseness, wickedness, and blasphemy', and the presentation of scenes 'so licentious or so horrible'.[21] A year later, Alfred Austin expressed similar regret in the distasteful species of 'love had we better call it lust?' that seemed to pervade the sensation novel, one 'which begins with seduction and ends in desertion . . . whose agreeable variations are bigamy, adultery, and, in fact, illicit passion of every conceivable sort'.[22] Margaret Oliphant was particularly troubled by the presentation of a 'fleshly and unlovely' sexuality. Heroines of sensation novels 'marry their grooms in fits of sensual passion', lust after 'flesh and muscles, for strong arms that seize her, and warm breath that thrills her through, and a host of other physical attractions that she indicates to the world with charming frankness'. As often as not, rather than tending to their domestic responsibilities, they 'pray their lovers to carry them from husbands and homes they hate'. But the 'peculiarity of it in England', she added, is that 'this intense appreciation of flesh and blood, this eagerness of physical sensation, is represented as the natural sentiment of English girls, and is offered to them not only as a portrait of their own state of mind, but as their amusement and mental food'.[23]

Sensation novels, it was quickly appreciated, were generally written by women and for women.[24] More particularly, they were written for bored women who had the time, and the inclination, to peruse libraries in search of vicarious thrills. The

---

[18] H Mansel, 'Sensation Novels' (1863) 113 *Quarterly Review* 502. Mansel was Dean of St Pauls.

[19] The observation was made in an anonymous article 'Our Female Sensation Novelists' (1863) 46 *Christian Remembrancer* 212. Another of the sensationalists, Charles Reade, was typically brazen, declaring that his readers would be entertained rather than subjected to the 'clap-trap morality' pedalled by so-called 'domestic novels'. See W Hughes, *The Maniac in the Cellar: Sensation Novels of the 1860s* (Princeton University Press, 1980) 41, 58, 68–69, noting Reade's particular dislike of George Eliot as the most prominent domestic novelist. Reade liked to claim that Eliot plagiarised most of her plots from his novels.

[20] See D Liddle, 'Anatomy of a "Nine Days Wonder": Sensation Journalism in the Decade of the Sensation Novel' in A Maunder and G Moore (eds), *Victorian Crime, Madness and Sensation* (Ashgate, 2004) 97.

[21] The comments were written as a serious conclusion to his otherwise satirical pseudo-sensational novel *Lucretia* (Joseph Masters, 1868) 11–12, 301–302.

[22] A Austin, 'The Poetry of the Period: Mr Swinburne' (1860) 26 *Temple Bar* 468.

[23] M Oliphant, 'Novels' (1867) 102 *Blackwoods* 259. The metaphor of reading as eating, and more particularly of voracious reading as species of 'gluttony', was common, perhaps most famously deployed by Ruskin who argued in his 1876 essay 'Fors Clavigera' that 'Gluttonous reading is a worse vice than gluttonous eating'. See Flint, *The Woman Reader* (above n 8) 50–51. For further commentaries, see Hughes, *The Maniac in the Cellar* (above n 19) 30; A Maunder, 'Mapping the Victorian Sensation Novel: Some Recent and Future Trends' (2005) 2 *Literature Compass* VI, 12; and J Phegley, 'Henceforward I Refuse to Bow the Knee to Their Narrow Rule: Mary Elizabeth Braddon's *Belgravia Magazine*, Women Readers, and Literary Valuation' (2004) 26 *Nineteenth-Century Contexts* 165.

[24] See E Showalter, *A Literature of Their Own: British Women Novelists from Bronte to Lessing* (Princeton University Press, 1977) 154–58.

Saturday Review gloomily concluded that 'Mr Mudie's lending library will soon become a sort of Newgate calendar', adding that the contemporary passion for 'crime and crinoline' novels was 'enough to take away the breath of any quiet middle aged gentleman'.[25] Braddon, the acknowledged 'queen' of Mudie's, was in fact rather more concerned about taking away the breath of her female readers. But the point was well made as Braddon readily confessed. 'I have', she once observed, 'learned to look at everything in a mercantile sense, and to write solely for the circulating library reader whose palette requires strong meat, and is not very particular as to the qualities thereof'.[26] On a different occasion she deployed a little irony, observing to her editor, as she despatched another contribution, that the 'amount of crime, treachery, murder, slow poisoning, and general infamy required by the Halfpenny reader is something terrible. I am just going to do a little parricide for this week's supply'.[27] If he is to succeed, Sigismund Smith, the aspiring writer of 'highly-spiced fictions' who serves as a narrator in *The Doctor's Wife*, is fully aware that he must give his readers what they want, 'plot, and plenty of it; surprises, and plenty of 'em; mystery, as thick as a November fog', and above all, lots of 'bodies' (11, 45, 47).[28] Occasionally Braddon expressed a desire to write something 'better', to somehow deflect the 'pelting' of the critics and, to a limited extent, *The Doctor's Wife* evinced this aspiration.[29] However, Braddon remained, above all, sensitive to her audience writing, as Henry James noted, 'at any hazard to make a hit, to catch the public ear'.[30]

In this Fraser Rae attested her success; everyone wanted to read the latest Braddon.

> Others before her have written stories of blood and lust, of atrocious crimes and hard-ened criminals, and these have excited the interest of a very wide circle of readers. But the class that welcomed them was the lowest in the social scale, as well as in mental

[25] Unsigned, 'Homicidal Heroines' 21 *Saturday Review*, 7 April 1866, 403–404. The Newgate novel, along with the later Gothic novel, was commonly seen by contemporary critics as the progenitor of the sensation novel. Mudie's circulating library was probably the most influential of such libraries and the power it exercised in regard to shaping what its subscribers read was considerable. See Flint, *The Woman Reader* (above n 8) 26–27, 144, 171–79.

[26] For which reason, she further confessed that she was 'a patcher up of sham antiquities as compared to a Grecian sculptor, a dauber of pantomime scenes, all Dutch metal, glue, and spangles, as compared with a great painter'. See J Carnell and G Law, 'Our Author: Braddon in the Provincial Weeklies' in M Tromp et al. (eds), *Beyond Sensation: Mary Elizabeth Braddon in Context* (State University of New York Press, 2000) 150, and Wolff, *Sensational Victorian* (above n 14) 155–56, 163. In *The Doctor's Wife*, Braddon's aspiring novelist Sigismund Smith cuts the same Faustian bargain and is similarly reconciled to its consequences.

[27] Hughes, *The Maniac in the Cellar* (above n 19) 9.

[28] All internal citations are to *The Doctor's Wife* (Oxford University Press, 1998). When he is first introduced to the reader, Smith is struggling to work out how best to describe a suicide. When his friend queries whether he needs to bother, Smith returns that any sensation novelist has to be able to present his reader with a convincing suicide. His novel, accordingly 'teems with suicides' (12).

[29] See Wolff, *Sensational Victorian* (above n 14) 154–55, noting Braddon's desire, in particular, to impress her early mentor Bulwer Lytton. Commenting on the publication of her novel *John Marchmont's Legacy*, which began serialisation in 1863, she hoped that he would appreciate the raising of an 'ambition', which was hitherto 'utterly dead', to 'be artistic [and] to please you'.

[30] H James, Review of *Aurora Floyd* for *The Nation* in 1865, and quoted in Wolff, *Sensational Victorian* (above n 14) 152.

capacity. To Miss Braddon belongs the credit of having penned similar stories in easy and correct English, and published them in three volumes in place of issuing them in penny numbers. She may boast, without fear of contradiction, of having temporarily succeeded in making the literature of the Kitchen the favourite reading of the Drawing Room'.[31]

Aristocratic daughters and their scullery maids were brought together in one voracious common readership. Rae was not, however, an admirer. Sensation novels, he observed, were 'one of the abominations of the age'.[32] Mansel invoked a familiar metaphor: 'Action, action, action is the first thing, needful, and the second, and the third.' Both the reader and the author were trapped by the ever more pressing need to satisfy 'the cravings of a diseased appetite'.[33] The *Westminster Review* suggested that there was, quite literally, a 'sensational mania' abroad in the country, 'its virus is spreading in all directions, from the penny journal to the shilling magazine to the thirty shillings volume'.[34] To Mansel it was a matter of authorial irresponsibility, a failure to acknowledge the fact that their novels would play 'no inconsiderable part in moulding the minds and forming the habits and tastes of its generation', particularly its female generation. As we have already noted, the reading matter of women was already a issue of no little concern and, for many critics, of no little regret. It was hardly surprising, therefore, that intimations of young women eagerly devouring tales of sex and violence were viewed with horror.[35]

Deploying a metaphor clearly inspired by newspaper reports of cases heard before the new Divorce Court, a typically concerned reviewer of Braddon's *Aurora Floyd* noted in the *Westminster Review* that sensation novels such as *Aurora Floyd* had put the 'institution of marriage . . . just now upon its trial'.[36] Opponents of the 1857 Act had warned of the potential for harm, and took a grim pleasure in witnessing the realisation of their worst fears. According to Mansel, the newspaper court report was 'to the full-grown sensation novel what the bud is to the flower' and the responsibility of unscrupulous editors was every bit as great as that of unscrupulous novelists; they were confederates in the demeaning search for ever greater profit.[37] But neither party was easily shamed. 'Never mind the books',

[31] F Rae, 'Sensation Novelists: Miss Braddon' (1865) 43 *North British Review* 204.

[32] Ibid, 203.

[33] Mansel, 'Sensation Novels' (above n 18) 482. Similarly, see Hughes, *The Maniac in the Cellar* (above n 19) at 24, quoting GH Lewes's similar observation, 'whether the movement be absurd or not matters little, the essential thing is to keep moving'; and Rae, 'Miss Braddon' (above n 31) at 203, quoting the Archbishop of York's denunciation of 'stories aimed at this effect of exciting in the mind some deep feeling of overwrought interest by means of some terrible passion or crime'.

[34] Unsigned review of Wilkie Collins's *Armadale* in (1866) 86 *Westminster Review* 126.

[35] Mansel, 'Sensation Novels' (above n 18) 482. For commentaries on this concern, see L Hart, 'The Victorian Villainess and the Patriarchal Unconscious' (1994) 40 *Literature and Psychology* 19; L Pykett, *The Improper Feminine: The Women's Sensation Novel and the New Women Writing* (Routledge, 1992) 32–33; and Flint, *The Woman Reader* (above n 8) 15, 50–53.

[36] Schroeder and Schroeder, *From Sensation to Society* (above n 10) 16.

[37] Mansel, 'Sensation Novels' (above n 18) 482–83. Oliphant likewise bemoaned the 'violent stimulant of serial publication'. M Oliphant, 'Sensation Novels' (1862) 91 *Blackwoods* 569. For a comment on the close affinity of sensation novels with popular print, and the impact of a more competitive publishing industry driving down prices, see Maunder, 'Mapping the Victorian Sensation

fellow sensationalist Charles Reade advised a young Braddon, 'read the newspapers'.[38] She did so, observing to one editor as she struggled to hit a deadline, 'I
think I shall once more make my dip into the lucky bag of the Newgate Calendar.'[39]
Braddon, like Reade, readily appreciated the role that papers played in framing the
interests of her readers, and the extent to which the latter were most comfortable
when encountering plots that chimed with contemporary 'mysteries'.[40] Sensation
novels had immediacy. It was not just that writers such as Braddon had 'introduced into fiction those most mysterious of mysteries, the mysteries that are at our
own doors'.[41] As we noted in the case of *East Lynne*, they also eschewed historical
distance. As the *Christian Remembrancer* concluded regretfully, 'however extravagant and unnatural' they might seem, sensation novels were clearly intended to be
read as 'a sign of the times'.[42] Henry James noted precisely the same thing.
Reviewing *Lady Audley's Secret*, he observed that:

> The novelty lay in the heroine being, not a picturesque Italian of the fourteenth century,
> but an English gentlewoman of the current year, familiar with the use of the railway and
> the telegraph. The intense probability of the story is constantly reiterated. Modern
> England the England of today's newspaper crops up at every step.[43]

Any aspiring sensation novelist, Mansel observed with distaste, need 'only keep an
eye on the criminal reports of the daily newspapers' and 'he has the outline of his
story not only ready-made but approved beforehand as the true sensation cast'.[44]

Crime and accounts of crime became mutually sustaining and the same, it
was commonly feared, could be true of sexual transgression. Sex and crime was

Novel' (above n 23) 24–25, and A Cvetkovich, *Mixed Feelings: Feminism, Mass Culture and Victorian
Sensationalism* (Rutgers University Press, 1992) 16–17. See also A Mangham, *Violent Women and
Sensation Fiction: Crime, Medicine and Victorian Popular Culture* (Palgrave, 2007) 5–6; Pykett, *The
Improper Feminine* (above n 35) 30–31; and J Carnell, *The Literary Lives of Mary Elizabeth Braddon: A
study of her life and work*, (Sensation Press, 2000) 142, quoting from Fortescue's article in the (1864)
120 *Edinburgh Review* entitled 'The Queens English' which observed at 39 that the sensation novel had
become 'a product of industry for which there is now a brisk demand'.

[38] Carnell, *Braddon* ibid, 166.

[39] In correspondence with Lytton, and quoted in Mangham, *Violent Women and Sensation Fiction*
(above n 37) 5.

[40] See Carnell, *Braddon* (above n 37) suggesting at 158 that whilst Braddon was indeed rather more
evasive when compared with authors such as Reade, 'she knew that a hint of real life scandal or crime
could add a little frisson for catching prospective readers', and at 165–66, noting perhaps the most overt
parallel in her novels, between the plot of *The Lady Lisle*, published in 1862, and the famous *Tichborne*
case. In correspondence with Edmund Yates, Braddon confessed that she rather relished the thought
that her critics assumed she had been 'cradled into wrong by magazines'. Carnell, *Braddon* (above n 37)
at 170.

[41] H James, 'Miss Braddon' in *Nation*, 9 November 1865, 594.

[42] In 'Our Female Sensation Novelists' (above n 19) 210. Mansel reached the same conclusion,
observing that: 'The sensation novel, be it mere trash or something worse, is usually a tale of our times.'
Mansel, 'Sensation Novels' (above n 18) at 488–89.

[43] James, 'Miss Braddon' (above n 41) 593–94.

[44] Mansel, 'Sensation Novels' (above n 18) 512. For broader commentaries on the link between the
sensation novel and the sensationalism of the newspapers, see P Brantlinger, 'What is "Sensational"
about the "Sensational Novel"?' (1982) 37 *Nineteenth-Century Fiction*, 2, 5–7, 10; Liddle, 'Anatomy of a
"Nine Days Wonder"' (above n 20) 89; Hughes, *The Maniac in the Cellar* (above n 19) 18–20, 86; and
M Diamond, *Victorian Sensation* (Anthem, 2004) 1–4, 189–94.

everywhere. A 'book without a murder, a divorce, a seduction, or a bigamy', *Fraser's Magazine* observed ruefully, 'is not apparently worth either writing or reading'.[45] Certainly the reader of a Braddon novel could be confident of encountering a least one murder and a fair amount of sinful sex.[46] As Rae observed:

> According to Miss Braddon, crime is not an accident, but it is the business of life. She would lead us to conclude that the chief end of man is to commit murder, and his highest merit is to escape punishment; that women are born to attempt to commit murders, and to succeed in committing bigamy.[47]

The home, as Ruskin rather floridly affirmed, was supposed to be a shelter from the 'hostile society of the outer world', a 'vestal temple, a temple of the hearth watched over by Household Gods'.[48] This was not true of a Braddon novel. The *Saturday Review* adopted an ironic tone, observing that 'it is an amazing relief' in an 'age when everything seems pretty well discovered' to 'know that any unsolved, nay ... an insoluble mystery is standing on one's very hearthrug'.[49] The *Temple Bar* adopted the same imagery:

> It is on our domestic hearths that we are taught to look for the incredible. A mystery sleeps in our cradles; fearful errors lurk in our nuptial couches; fiends sit down with us at table; our innocent-looking garden walks hold the secret of treacherous murders; and our servants take £20 a year from us for the sake of having us at their mercy.[50]

Sensation novelists, the Archbishop of York warned, 'want to persuade people that in almost every one of the well-ordered houses of their neighbours there is a skeleton shut up in some cupboard'.[51] The plots of all sensation novels moved around the unveiling of terrible, and thrilling, secrets; 'those most mysterious of mysteries', as Henry James observed, 'the mysteries that are at our own doors'.[52] As Arnold Bennett noted, no-one unveiled secrets better than Mary Elizabeth Braddon, who was forever inviting her devoted readers to 'lift the edge of the curtain of the past' invariably 'disclosing behind it the monstrous shadow of a crime'.[53]

Fashionable Crimes

And two crimes in particular, the first being murder. Victorians loved murder. 'There is nothing', as Braddon observed, 'that English men and women enjoy

---

[45] Unsigned, 'The Popular Novels of the Year' (1863) 68 *Fraser's Magazine* 262.

[46] See Hughes, *The Maniac in the Cellar* (above n 19) 31–32, and R Helfield, 'Poisonous Plots: Women Sensation Novelists and Murderesses of the Victorian Period' (1995) 21 *Victorian Review* 161.

[47] Rae, 'Miss Braddon' (above n 31) 98.

[48] J Ruskin, 'Of Queen's Gardens' in D Birch (ed) *Selected Writings* (Oxford University Press, 2004) 159.

[49] E Linton, 'Modern Women and What is Said of Them', *Saturday Review*, 25 January 1868, 109.

[50] A Austin, 'Our Novels: The Sensational School' *Temple Bar*, 29 July 1870, 424.

[51] The Archbishop's words were widely quoted by contemporary reviewers, including Rae in 'Miss Braddon' (above n 31) at 203.

[52] James, 'Miss Braddon' (above n 41) 594.

[53] A Bennett, *Fame and Fiction: An Enquiry into Certain Popularities*, (Grant Richard, 1901) 23.

more than the crime which they call "a really good murder!"[54] They liked a particular kind of murder, as Braddon knew and as George Orwell later and famously observed. The Victorian age was the age of the 'good murder', all the better for being 'essentially domestic'.[55] Contemporaries noted the particular interest that women took in the trials of alleged murderesses.[56] Cold statistics suggest that twice as many women as men were convicted of murder in the years 1855 to 1874. However, it was not statistics that excited Victorian England; it was rumour and speculation. In *Aurora Floyd*, the suffering heroine is haunted by newspaper commentaries and 'clever letters' that insinuate her guilt, encouraging gossip amongst servants while also inviting intrusive speculation from outside (396). Early editions of *Aurora Floyd* contained a very pointed allusion to the 'slow agonies' and 'ever-increasing tortures' that had befallen one 'Somersetshire household in which a dreadful deed was done'. The case to which Braddon referred, the 'sensation topic of a conversation in a thousand happy home-circles', was that of Constance Kent, suspected of murdering her little brother in 1860.[57] Allusions to another notorious contemporary case, that of the 'Doncaster poisoner', William Palmer, can be similarly discerned in earlier editions of *Aurora Floyd*.[58] No less notorious

---

[54] Comment in *Beyond These Voices* published in 1910, and quoted in Carnell, *Braddon* (above n 37) at 236.

[55] G Orwell, 'Decline of the English Murder' in *The Penguin Essays of George Orwell* (Penguin, 1968) 351–54.

[56] *Punch* systematically ridiculed what it termed the 'Old Bailey ladies'. See Showalter, *A Literature of Their Own* (above n 24) 168–70, and Diamond, *Victorian Sensation* (above n 44) 4–5 quoting an editorial in the *Pall Mall Gazette* which attacked female spectators at one trial as 'ghoulish women, armed with opera glasses, sherry flasks and sandwich boxes' who 'hang with eager curiosity upon every movement and look of their miserable sister'.

[57] In the absence of compelling material evidence, though strongly suspected by the police, Kent was not charged. The newspapers had been generally sympathetic, finding it hard to believe that a 14-year-old girl could commit such a crime. The fact that her brother had been murdered with a knife was also taken as evidence of Constance's innocence. Women were supposed to use poison. Kent later confessed to the murder, which only enhanced a general sense of bewilderment. The most extensive literary reference to the *Kent* case can be found in Wilkie Collins's *The Moonstone*. The allusion to the *Kent* case was removed from later editions of *Aurora Floyd*, and does not appear in any modern texts. Sibling murder was a subject of especial fascination in Victorian England, often importing the collateral insinuation of incest and adolescent sexual deviance. See Mangham, *Violent Women and Sensation Fiction* (above n 37) 12–13, 63–71, inferring a clear influence of the case in Braddon's sensation novels, especially *Aurora Floyd*. Chapter 2 of *Violent Women* provides an extensive commentary on the *Kent* case. Other commentaries, stressing the particular influence of the case on the novels of Braddon, as well as those of Wilkie Collins and Ellen Wood, can be found in A Trodd, *Domestic Crime in the Victorian Novel* (Macmillan, 1989) 19–26, 109–10; Helfield, 'Poisonous Plots' (above n 46) 163–64, 169, 177–82; and J Sturrock, 'Murder, gender and popular fiction by women in the 1860s: Braddon, Oliphant, Yonge' in A Maunder and G Moore (eds), *Victorian Crime, Madness and Sensation* (Ashgate, 2004) 73–79.

[58] Doncaster is the nearest town to Mellish Park in *Aurora Floyd*, and much of the later action in the novel takes place there. In one passage (291), the narrator observes that people take a 'strange pride' in any association with such notorious cases, confessing to having visited Palmer's Doncaster lodgings. Braddon did precisely this in 1859. Another reference can be found at 241, part of an ironic aside on the wisdom of foresight, and at 298, where the narrator comments on the phrenologists who examined Palmer's head and concluded that he must have been 'utterly deficient in moral perception'. For a commentary on Braddon's interest in Palmer, see Carnell, *Braddon* (above n 37) 165–68, and for a broader discussion of the case, see Diamond, *Victorian Sensation* (above n 44) 166–71.

was the case of Madeline Smith, who was alleged to have poisoned her lover in Glasgow and whose trial kept newspaper readers enraptured throughout much of 1857 and 1858. The affinity of sex and murder in the Smith case was guaranteed to engage particular popular interest, making it, in the words of Henry James, a 'rare work of art'.[59]

Braddon liked to include at least one good murder in each of her novels. Her audience expected it, especially after publication of *Lady Audley's Secret* and it was the reason they bought her novels. There was murder in *Aurora Floyd* too. But unlike the murderous Lady Audley, Aurora Floyd is innocent of murder at least. She is, however, guilty of a different, barely less thrilling, crime. Aurora is a bigamist. Worse still, she is a rather likeable one, as we shall see. The Victorians loved bigamy almost as much as they loved a good murder. By the early 1860s it had become, as Oliphant bemoaned, the most 'fashionable' of literary crimes.[60] Again, the reason was obvious: reports of suitably salacious bigamy cases uncovered in the new Divorce Court had sharpened the appetite of Braddon's readers. Of these, undoubtedly the most notorious was the *Yelverton* case, accounts of which had begun to appear on the breakfast tables of Middle England in the summer of 1858, and continued for a thoroughly satisfying three years as the litigation bounced chaotically around English, Scottish and Irish jurisdictions.[61] If Braddon needed inspiration as she began to contemplate the writing of her 'pair of bigamy novels' she did not have to look far.

The facts of the *Yelverton* case were confused and conflicted though probably not so confused and conflicted as the law of bigamy. Theresa Longworth and Major William Yelverton had met in 1852 and had maintained an amorous correspondence before setting up home together in Scotland six years later. The prospect of a happy ever after was ruined by the revelation that the Major was

---

[59] Quoted in E Gordon and G Nair, *Murder and Morality in Victorian Britain: The Story of Madeleine Smith* (Manchester University Press, 2009) 189. A number of factors intensified public interest, not least the fact that Smith's victim, her fiancé Emile L'Angelier, although hailing from the Channel Islands was deemed to be French and therefore naturally lascivious. Smith's confessed liking for French literature, as well as French fiancés, also chimed with contemporary expectations of lascivious murderesses. Love letters written by Smith and L'Angelier were read out in court, and provided much fodder for newspaper reporters. So apparently depraved were certain passages that the presiding judge decided that they should be withheld. Smith's behaviour, the judge observed, had been that of a 'common prostitute'. In the end, and to the judge's evident disappointment, the jury returned a verdict of not proven. For commentaries on the trial, see Gordon and Nair, *Murder and Morality* (above n 59) 45–46, 53–56, 114, 141–43, and M Hartmann, 'Murder for Respectability: The Case of Madeleine Smith' (1973) 16 *Victorian Studies* 386, 389–91, 397–98, musing on the possibility that Smith was inspired in her *modus operandi* by seeing a performance of *Lucrezia Borgia*.

[60] As Jeanne Fahnestock concludes, the avidity with which they read both factual and fictive accounts confirms that 'in the midst of their devoted families the Victorian husband and wife of the 1860s fantasized on the delights and penalties of having another spouse', J Fahnestock, 'Bigamy: The Rise and Fall of a Convention' (1981) 36 *Nineteenth Century Fiction* 47.

[61] According to Karen Chase and Michael Levenson, the 'bigamy novel was a precipitate of the buzzing divorce conversation conducted through the length and breadth of every genteel breakfast table in Britain'. See K Chase and M Levenson, *The Spectacle of Intimacy: A Public Life for the Victorian Family* (Princeton University Press, 2000) 202. For further comments on the impact of the *Yelverton* case on public consciousness, see Fahnestock, 'Bigamy' (above n 60) 50–51.

already married to a wealthy and conspicuously pregnant widow named Emma Forbes.[62] Theresa initiated proceedings in the Scottish courts alleging bigamy, whilst also seeking the restitution of conjugal rights in the new Divorce Court, alleging that they had exchanged marital vows, sufficient in Scots law to constitute marriage.[63] The Major admitted to sexual intimacy, but no more.[64] Theresa sought to strengthen her case by providing evidence that their nuptials had been celebrated in accordance with the Catholic faith whilst on a trip to Ireland. The Major suggested that the latter was a meaningless bit of flummery which amounted to nothing more than a 'blessing'.[65] More importantly, his lawyers invited the court to deny jurisdiction on the grounds that the Major was Irish and Theresa had no domicile of her own. The court agreed. Theresa then turned her attention to Ireland, persuading a friend to act as a 'stalking horse' litigant, claiming a debt incurred by Theresa from Yelverton on the grounds that he was her husband and accordingly liable for the debt under the doctrine of coverture.[66] In February 1861 the Dublin Court of Common Pleas began consideration of *Thelwell v Yelverton*. It was at this point that the public imagination was properly caught. Journalists jostled for space. The galleries were packed. Many brought picnics.[67]

It was plain to all that bigamy law, across the three jurisdictions, was a mess.[68] Hardwicke's Marriage Act of 1753 was supposed to have addressed the root

---

[62] For a recent account of the facts of the *Yelverton* case, one that, with a perhaps appropriate irony is written as something of a 'matter-of-fact romance' itself, see C Schama, *A Wild Romance: the True Story of a Victorian Romance* (Bloomsbury, 2010) chapters 2 and 3. An earlier and rather less breathless account of the disputed facts can be found in A Erickson and J McCarthy, 'The Yelverton Case: Civil Legislation and Marriage' (1971) 14 *Victorian Studies* 275–78.

[63] They had, Theresa explained, exchanged vows whilst holding copies of the Anglican Book of Common Prayer. If such an exchange took place with the intent of constituting a marriage contract or even as a promise of marriage followed by intercourse, a marriage was deemed in Scots law to have taken place.

[64] Yelverton did not help his case by emphasising, at every opportunity, his sexual prowess. When challenged by Theresa's lawyer in the first trial in Dublin as to why he seemed so cool in giving evidence, the insinuation being that he was unnaturally heartless, the Major replied 'Not in bed'. It was reported that a sound of hissing could be heard around the court. See Schama, *A Wild Romance* (above n 62) 91–92.

[65] The fact that the officiating Irish priest had initially failed to register the marriage in the parish books and only later provided a certificate, in the process forging the names of two witnesses, fatally undercut Theresa's claim as to the validity of this particular ceremony. It also added to the pervasive sense that a matter of such import could not be left to the whimsies of 'Popish priests'.

[66] The reason for pursuing the action in Dublin was that Yelverton was Irish. The friend was a Mr Thelwall with whom Theresa lodged after discovering Yelverton's marriage to Emma Forbes. Thelwall sued Yelverton for the incurred debt of £259 17s 3d.

[67] 'From its very first day', according to Chloe Schama, 'the trial became a public melodrama, indulging in the trademarks of the genre: extremes of emotion, moral polarization, villainy, extravagant expression, and suspense'. Penny pamphlets were legion. Even *The Times* guaranteed to provide its readers with daily accounts of proceedings. The Lord Justice insisted that the galleries were cleared of female spectators whilst details of love letters were being read out. See Schama, *A Wild Romance* (above n 62) at 66, 88, and R Gill 'The Imperial Anxieties of a Nineteenth-Century Bigamy Case' (2004) 57 *History Workshop* 68.

[68] A 'strange jumble' according to the editor of the *Albany Law Journal*. See Schama, *A Wild Romance* (above n 62) 119.

problem in England, which was perceived to lie in the lax regulation of 'clandestine' marriages but it had not done so.[69] As John Boyd Kinnear observed in 1868, despite 'all this intolerable strictness of form, oppressing the honest' the Acts provided not 'the least security against secret or ill-assorted marriages'.[70] Statutory provision, in short, was largely ignored, not least by the courts themselves. Less than 20 per cent of cases of known bigamy were actually prosecuted in court and, whilst conviction rates were high, punishments were notoriously light. This was the case with the unfortunate Mr Hall who had appeared before Mr Justice Maule in 1845.[71] As the *Yelverton* litigation drifted from court to court, the Westminster Parliament enacted a new statute, the 1861 Offences Against the Person Act. Section 57 of the Act was supposed to help clarify the situation regarding bigamy. It confirmed that:

> Whosoever, being married, shall marry any other person during the life of the former husband or wife, whether the second marriage shall have taken place in England or Ireland or elsewhere, shall be guilty of felony, and being convicted thereof shall be liable ... to be kept in penal servitude for any term not exceeding seven years.

The only exceptions permitted in the statute related to a second marriage contracted where a spouse had been absent for seven years or more, or where a first marriage had ended in divorce or had been otherwise 'declared void'.[72] In the former case, any subsequent 'marriage' would be declared void if the first spouse was found to be still alive, a jurisprudence which, as we shall see, haunted Aurora Floyd.[73] None of this helped Theresa Longworth, whose cause was blighted by the problem of jurisdiction, and what the *British Quarterly Review* termed the 'barbarism' of Catholic canon law in the Celtic peripheries.[74] The 1753 provisions did not apply in Ireland, where there were no civil restrictions and where Catholic canon

---

[69] The Act required adherence to the formal prescriptions of matrimonial canon law, including publication of the banns, a licence and public registration. In order to ameliorate the consciences of dissenters, an 1836 Statute had permitted marriage by registrar.

[70] 'Marriage Laws of England and Scotland' 7 *Contemporary Review*, February 1868 at 223, and quoted in Fahnestock, 'Bigamy' (above n 60) at 59.

[71] Part of the reason why prosecution figures were so low was the fact that spouses could not testify against one another which meant that there had to be evidence attested by third parties. The ratio of convictions was approximately 80%. Punishment was only more severe if the presiding judge took exception to what he perceived to be particular mendacity. Male bigamists motivated by financial gain were the most likely to receive a heavier sentence. See G Frost, *Living In Sin: Cohabiting as Husband and Wife in Nineteenth Century England* (Manchester University Press, 2008), 72–76.

[72] The first of these two exceptions had been originally enacted in the 1828 Offences Against the Person Act.

[73] A common law defence of 'reasonable and honest belief' would be affirmed in *R v Tolson* (1889) LR 23 QBD 168.

[74] An anonymous and untitled comment in (1861) 34 *British Quarterly Review* at 140. The comments were made in anticipation of a Royal Commission, eventually established in 1865 and tasked with resolving the jurisdictional problem. The *Review* advised that much the best cause was to follow the 'common sense' lead of the English common law. The Commission by and large agreed, concluding that it was above all imperative that marriages be conducted only by licensed clergymen of whichever established Church, their authority subject to the 'control and surveillance of the State'. Legislation for Ireland and Scotland duly followed, in the form of the 1870 Matrimonial Causes and Marriage Law (Ireland) and the 1878 Marriage Notice (Scotland) Act.

law remained in force, nor in Scotland, where again the Catholic canon, with one or two minor amendments, retained its authority.[75]

Accordingly, for those following the case it was simply a matter of listening to different stories and picking a favourite. If Theresa was to succeed, she and her lawyers had to make her story seem that bit more plausible and that bit more worthy of sympathy than the story presented by the Major and his lawyers. Theresa protested her 'wounded innocence', whilst her lawyers immersed themselves in familiar images of rakish seducers. Yelverton's lawyers countered that Theresa was flighty and deluded, something which was confirmed by the tone of her correspondence and her evident liking for French literature. She was a 'syren', her mind irretrievably 'tainted by books of this description'. Perhaps, but the jury fell for Theresa, young, pretty, blond and evidently a 'lady of superior attainments', and declared both marriages valid.[76] Her supporters composed a celebratory ballad entitled the 'The Grand Triumph of Mrs Yelverton'.[77] The case was, however, far from ended. The following year the Scottish Court of Session agreed to assume jurisdiction, at the request of the Major, and found in his favour; a decision which Theresa was able to have reversed in the Inner Court of Session. Yelverton responded by appealing to the House of Lords, where in July 1864 it reversed the Inner Court's reversal. The House based its decision on the content of Theresa's letters, where they found many intimations of sex but none of marriage, and a visceral distrust of the idea that a good solid Protestant gentleman might be bound by the ritualistic incantations of a 'Popish priest'. *The Times* approved their Lordship's mistrust, praising both the Lords and the Scottish courts for ignoring the distant 'roar of an Irish mob and the claptraps of an Irish court'.[78]

The passage had been rough, but the law had finally run its course;[79] public interest had not. Bigamists, it seemed, were everywhere. In evidence given to the 1865 Royal Commission it was calculated that there were 884 reported cases brought before English courts between 1853 and 1863, and a further 110 in Scotland.[80] Any respectable middle-class woman sat quietly in her drawing room reading the latest Braddon might suddenly discover herself to be 'married' to a bigamist; worse still so might any respectable middle-class 'husband'. Some of these women, perhaps not many, worried about jurisprudential incoherence; a few

---

[75] Marriage in Ireland, accordingly, still followed the provisions of the 1563 decree of *Tametsi*, which described the various ritualistic provisions that had to be certified by an ordained priest.

[76] Such was the feeling running against the Major that it was reported that he was 'obliged to escape from the fury of the mob by running into a shop'. See Erickson and McCarthy, 'The Yelverton Case' (above n 62) 280, and Schama, *A Wild Romance* (above n 62) 69–77, 82–85, 97.

[77] Theresa was carried from the court and down Sullivan Street in a makeshift chariot. It was reported that between 50,000 and 100,000 supporters followed her.

[78] The House of Lords took evidence from the Bishop of Leahy with regard to the intricacies of Catholic marriage law in Ireland. The House was not impressed, and the evidence was 'put aside'. See Gill, 'Anxieties' (above n 67) 70, and Erickson and McCarthy, 'The Yelverton Case' (above n 62) 282–83, 288–89.

[79] Theresa made a couple of unsuccessful attempts to have the case reopened in the Court of Sessions on the basis of new evidence.

[80] Figures given to the 1866 Royal Commission on marriage law reform quoted in Fahnestock, 'Bigamy' (above n 60) 57–58.

more contemplated moral collapse. A spate of anthropological studies of 'heathen' marriage practice appeared.[81] But most simply waited in eager expectation of the next case to appear in the papers, and in the meantime they read novels. Theresa wrote one herself, entitled *Martyrs to Circumstance*.[82] 'Life indeed', she encouraged her readers, 'is a wild romance, if truly written'.[83] In the England of 1862 nothing, not even murder, sold as well as a good bigamy story. Reviewers sniffed their disapproval. Bigamy, Geraldine Jewsbury airily declaimed, was all rather 'hackneyed'.[84] Nevertheless, publishers kept offering contracts and the presses continued to roll. Jewsbury reflected that:

> If in after-times the manners and customs of English life in 1864 were to be judged from the novels of the day, it would naturally be believed that people, in the best regulated families, were in the habit of marrying two wives, or two husbands, as the case might be; and of suppressing the one that proved inconvenient, either by 'painless extinction' or by more forcible methods, 'regardless of the cost' of suffering to the victim.[85]

'This tendency to bigamy in works of fiction', she concluded, 'points to a joint in our social armour. Our marriage laws are confessedly imperfect, and open to hairbreadth escapes, which offer a fascinating complication, not devoid of probability'.[86]

Margaret Oliphant also noted the jurisprudential context, accusing Braddon in particular, of having 'brought in the reign of bigamy as an interesting and fashionable crime', adding 'which no doubt shows a certain deference to the British relish for law and order'. She continued casting a very pointed aspersion:

> It goes against the seventh commandment, no doubt, but does it in a legitimate sort of way, and is an invention which could only have been possible to an Englishwoman knowing the attraction of impropriety, and yet loving the shelter of law.[87]

The suspicion that too many, and particularly too many young women, were not taking bigamy seriously enough was commonly shared. Of course, men were naturally given to seduce; such was the conclusion of popular ballads such as 'Undaunted Mary' and 'The Squire and Milkmaid'.[88] But women, it seemed, were only too eager to be seduced, and the reason for this, it was surmised, lay in what they read. Bigamy had become the subject of 'wild romance' rather than moral

---

[81] Perhaps the most famous of these was John McLennan's *Primitive Marriage* (A and C Black, 1865).

[82] Maria Theresa Longworth, *Martyrs to Circumstance* (Bentley, 1861).

[83] See Schama, *A Wild Romance* (above n 62) xii and 104–107. Theresa's contribution did not help her cause, suggesting that she had been, in sexual terms, rather less innocent than she sought to portray herself. It seems, the *Athenaeum* remarked, that the author was 'hardly the ingénue she had so convincingly presented herself as', Gill, 'Anxieties' (above n 67) at 67.

[84] Private correspondence, quoted in Fahnestock, 'Bigamy' (above n 60) at 56.

[85] From a review of Bentley's *Lord Lynn's Wife*, published in the *Athenaeum*, 3 December 1864, 743–4.

[86] Ibid, 744.

[87] Oliphant, 'Novels' (above n 23) 263.

[88] As one of Yelverton's lawyers declared in his client's defence, 'If any man in this crowded court were driven to review his own past life, when passions were strong, and the influence of youth and warm blood predominated, perhaps he might, if called upon to cast a stone at this gentleman' instead be 'more disposed to slink out of court.' Schama, *A Wild Romance* (above n 62) 97.

chastisement. As a crime it titillated rather than terrified. At one point in Braddon's *Aurora Floyd*, as speculation swirls amongst the servants at Mellish Park, the narrator supposes that one 'pretty housemaid who had seen the thrilling drama of "Susan Hopley" performed' at the local theatre 'would have rather liked to be accused of the crime, and to emerge spotless and triumphant from the judicial ordeal, through the evidence of an idiot, or a magpie, or a ghost, or some other witness common and popular in dramatic courts' (396).[89]

Mrs Mellish's Marriages

The story of Aurora Floyd, 'of murder and violence and treachery' was classically sensationalist (365).[90] As a girl Aurora was pretty and 'horsey', and confident, too confident. She was, to use the contemporary vernacular, 'fast' (21–23). She attracts the interest of Conyers, a groom who happens to be equally handsome, 'horsey' and confident. In due course Aurora is sent to France to 'finishing school'. Conyers follows. They elope and marry. Discovering Conyers's infidelity, she abandons him, and returns to England, confessing all to her father, and pretending that her husband has died in a racing accident (355). Aurora is then courted by the aristocratic Bulstrode, and agrees to his proposal of marriage. Bulstrode, however, a man driven by 'honour' above all else, senses that something is wrong, and when Aurora refuses to divulge her 'secret', he breaks off the engagement (31, 34, 44). Aurora then accepts an alternative proposal from a bluff Yorkshire squire Mellish, and they are married, or at least they go through a marriage ceremony. By the kind of unhappy coincidence so relished by the readers of sensation novels, Mellish then decides to hire a new groom, who turns out to be an all-too-alive Conyers. Blackmailed by Conyers, Aurora agrees to pay him £2,000, which is to be delivered one evening in Mellish Park. Later that night, Conyers is found murdered, and suspicion falls on Aurora who was seen leaving the house earlier in the evening. In the end, the murderer is found to be another of the grooms, the half-witted and thoroughly mendacious 'Softy' Hargraves, and Aurora is exonerated, at least as a prospective murderess. They all, it seems, live happily ever after, except, of course, for Conyers, and Hargreaves who, the reader is reassured, will suffer the full force of a disapproving law.

The author of *Aurora Floyd*, one reviewer observed, was 'evidently acquainted with a very low type of female character'.[91] Certainly, there was plenty of crime.[92]

---

[89] The housemaid is speculating as much about murder as bigamy but the sentiment is no less apposite.
[90] All internal citations are from ME Braddon, *Aurora Floyd* (Oxford University Press, 1996).
[91] Rae, 'Miss Braddon' (above n 31) 190.
[92] See M Tromp, 'The Dangerous Woman: ME Braddon's Sensational (En)gendering of Domestic Law' in Tromp, *Beyond Sensation* (above n 26) 96, referring to the 'Pandora's box' nature of crime and transgression in Braddon's sensation novels.

Whilst the *Medical Critic* tried to salvage a crumb of comfort in the thought that any young woman who came across *Aurora Floyd* might learn 'not to let their fancies run away with them', most were less sanguine.[93] 'We have bigamy, murder, divorce', one seemingly overwhelmed reviewer reported, followed by 'a lady whipping her stableman, criminal trials and horse-racing'.[94] The crime and the cultural transgression, however, served a deeper purpose. Braddon's primary concern in *Aurora Floyd* is with the institution and the law of marriage, and with the human experience of marriage; far more so than was the case in *Lady Audley's Secret*. The character of Aurora Floyd, accordingly, is written to be far more human, more nuanced than that of the confessed 'fiend' Lucy Audley. Aurora is no less beautiful, but she is also 'so frank and fearless, so generous, affectionate and true' (21). Fast or not, 'it was impossible for honest people to know Aurora without loving her' (274). As one contemporary critic observed, there was no surprise in the heroine of a Braddon novel turning out to be a bigamist. The surprise is that Aurora Floyd is such 'an amiable one'.[95] Jewsbury preferred *Aurora Floyd* for precisely this reason. Its protagonist, she observed, 'is a woman not a fiend, nor a maniac, but a warm-hearted, generous, loving woman, with an earnest desire to do what is honourable and just and true'. For this reason, she concluded, 'we cannot help liking her and sympathizing with her, in spite of our better reason and judgement'.[96] Aurora is not an 'angel in the house'. She has 'unfeminine tastes and mysterious propensities' (49). She 'knows', as Henry James famously observed, 'much that ladies are not accustomed to know'.[97] She makes mistakes, serious ones. But that is what people do, real people reading novels and fictional people living in them; for 'if she had been faultless she could not have been the heroine of this story' and, as the narrator wryly observes, alluding to the more 'womanly' wife to whom Bulstrode is eventually married: 'There are so many Lucys but so few Auroras' (48, 393).[98]

Herein lay the challenge. Braddon wanted her readers to empathise, even envy, her 'amiable' Aurora, just as she also wanted them to be unsettled by her. Aurora beats her own servants (138). Beating servants is fine but it is something husbands should do. Aurora, however, is 'imperious', possessed of a 'queenly defiance' and 'haughty insouciance' (33, 74, 138, 293). She barely seems to need one husband, never mind two. Mellish, possessed conversely of a 'tender weakness', too scared to challenge Aurora about her 'secret', is given to staring 'in blank amazement at his mutinous wife', turning 'white with horror' as he watches her whipping his groom in a 'beautiful fury' (139, 143). His friend Bulstrode is just as baffled, constantly 'falling back into that state of bewilderment in which this girl always threw him' (53). He stares 'blankly' at Aurora when she finally tells him her 'secret' (352).

[93] Forbes Winslow, 'Sensation Novels' (1863) 3 *Medical Critic and Psychological Journal* 519.

[94] Unsigned, 13 *Saturday Review*, 31 January 1863, 149.

[95] 'Our Novels', 29 *Temple Bar*, July 1870 (above n 50) 415.

[96] Review of *Aurora Floyd* in *Atheneasum*, 31 January 1863, 144.

[97] James, 'Miss Braddon' (above n 41) 593.

[98] The allusion being, of course, to Aurora's cousin, the angelic Lucy, and not Lucy Audley, the pathological murderess of *Lady Audley's Secret*.

Their incomprehension has a darker tone, one that speaks to another common Braddon theme: the decay of masculinity. The mendacity of Hargraves, and of Conyers, a 'mercenary wretch' and a 'boor', is unsurprising. Both were drawn from the working classes (145–46, 191, 354).[99] But 'gentlemen' are supposed to know better how to treat women, and how to govern them. This is not the case, it seems, in *Aurora Floyd*. The baffled Bulstrode contemplates rape, whilst Mellish, faced with the prospect of Aurora leaving, warns:

> I would rather see your coffin laid in the empty niche besides my mother's in the vault yonder . . . I would rather take you in my arms and plunge you into the pond in the wood; would rather send a bullet into your heart, and see you lying murdered at my feet (197).[100]

The sentiment adds a chilling edge to Mellish's later, supposedly jokey, comment that when Bulstode and his new wife next visit they will be able to see 'whether solemn Talbot beats her in the silence of her matrimonial chamber' (199). The contemplation of marriage in a Braddon novel always invited contemplation of violence. It has been suggested that the role of Bulstrode's 'poor little Lucy', is to give the 'female reader in the text' a spur to contemplating alternative ideals of femininity and marital fortune (159–60, 217).[101] Lucy Bulstrode is a woman of 'purity and goodness', a representative of 'a great many others of precisely the same type of graceful womanhood', the 'highest type, and the holiest and best' (48).[102] Above all, her attitude towards her husband is properly 'reverential' (348). The Bulstrode marriage is stolidly patriarchal. The nature of the Mellish marriage, however, is less easily discerned. Fascinated by the subject of marriage, Braddon was well aware of contemporary debates which argued the merits and demerits of alternative 'companionate' models. Spousal passion may be largely absent in Mellish Park but there is affection, respect, and perhaps even a sense of equal worth. They have 'learned' to love one another (141).[103] Ruminating on his wife's

---

[99] Nevertheless, in the tradition of sensation and Gothic romance, Conyers is also suitably handsome and dashing, the 'very perfection of physical beauty' (184–85).

[100] The scene where Bulstrode 'furiously' rams his shotgun whilst imagining Aurora's violation and death is notorious and clearly supposed to raise images of both rape and murder (60). See Mangham, *Violent Women and Sensation Fiction* (above n 37) 89–92, for a broader commentary on rape allusions in Braddon's sensation novels. Imagined violence is pervasive in the minds of both Bulstrode and Mellish. Driven by jealousy Bulstrode even contemplates murdering Mellish (149–50). Mellish has a 'strong inclination to thrash' various men who come across his path (411).

[101] See K Tatum, 'Bearing Her Secret: Mary Elizabeth Braddon's *Aurora Floyd*' (2007) 40 *Journal of Popular Culture* 512.

[102] In contrast with Aurora, whose mother died whilst she was a baby, Lucy has been 'hemmed in' by goodness since she was in her 'cradle' (48).

[103] As was the case with Aurora's parents, whose marriage is described in the opening chapter. Her mother, Eliza Prodder, is described as having come from a working-class theatrical background, whereas her father, as a wealthy banker, was firmly embedded in the middle classes. Their marriage proved to be happy, despite the mutterings of 'friends' (7–11, 16–17). Of course, the early death of Eliza robs Aurora of a steadying maternal influence. See Schroeder and Schroeder, *From Sensation to Society* (above n 11) 69–72 for a commentary on this marriage as a possible complement to that of Aurora and John Mellish, 86–90 exploring Lucy's marriage to Bulstrode, and 96–99 discussing the 'companionate' marriage of Aurora and Mellish.

first marriage, Mellish suggests that being 'unequal' it was thus a 'sham' (335). Conversely, the fact that Mellish 'had subsumed his very identity into that of the woman he loved' is similarly notable; a very pointed inversion of the legalistic principle of coverture (334). Aurora's reflection on their shared possession of Mellish Park is again suggestive:

> There is something satisfactory, too, in the sense of possession; and Aurora felt, as she looked down the long avenues, and away through distant loopholes in the wood to the wide expanse of park and lawn, and the picturesque, irregular pile of building beyond, half Gothic, half Elizabethan, and so lost in a rich tangle of ivy and bright foliage as to be beautiful at every point she felt, I say, that all the fair picture was her own, or her husband's which was the same thing. (168–69)

It is an oddly ambiguous passage. The final clause accords with the principle of coverture insofar as Aurora's legal personality and possession was subsumed in that of her husband. But the reference to a 'fair picture' which 'was her own' intimates a rather different 'sense of possession'. Until the Matrimonial Property Act 1870 such a 'sense' had little legal substance. But the sentiment would again have resonated with those advocates of companionate marriages who argued the case for legal reform in the late 1850s.

The settlement of property was a critical matter in any middle-class marriage in nineteenth-century England, real or fictional. The marriage of Aurora Floyd is no exception. The Floyds are a wealthy family and Aurora is a wealthy woman, at least in terms of legal interest. As Bulstrode notes, she stands to inherit 'fifty thousand pounds for her fortune' which 'will no doubt be very tightly settled upon herself if she is ever allowed to marry' (30). Combined with her husband's income of 'something between sixteen and seventeen thousand a year', it is clear that the Mellish estate will be considerable (144). Of course, Aurora's prospect is compromised by her first marriage to Conyers. The nature of their elopement precludes an initial settlement, whilst Conyers's death conveniently removes the danger of any future squabble over her financial and legal interests. When Aurora gives Conyers the £2,000 she also warns that if he declines to agree to her terms she will telegraph her father next day 'telling him to alter his will' (206). The threat implies that the money was drawn from the settlement made at the time of her second 'marriage', for which reason, as her father later observes, she would also need her husband's permission to withdraw the money. In fact, Aurora presumes that she can draw the money herself; a presumption which, given that her 'marriage' to Mellish was void in law, may have been justified. But she also knows that both Mellish and her father would probably have discovered the truth, for which reason she approaches her father for the sum anyway. The fact that Aurora appears to appreciate that her settlement is for the benefit of any children, rather than herself, is significant (226–27). Aurora Floyd knows her worth, and the limitations which her father, her husband and the law place on it.

Again, Braddon was not against marriage in the way that John Stuart Mill famously was. Indeed, as we shall see, she was herself desperate to marry. However, she was also acutely aware of its limitations, legal and cultural and for this reason she was keen to advise her female readers that entering the institution of marriage was not a guarantor of happiness. The 'business of real life-drama' does not 'end upon the altar-steps' (163). Much of life remains to be lived, and marriage should not be entered into carelessly. Some marriages are happy; many are not. Aurora may have 'escaped shipwreck for a while, and has landed on a pleasant shore, but the storm may still lower darkly upon the horizon, while the hoarse thunder grumbles threateningly in the distance' (163). Although she may have been the victim of mischance at various times in the narrative, Aurora is in the end lucky; certainly luckier than Isabel Carlyle and, insofar as her second marriage proves to be genuinely happy, also luckier than Clara Highgate. Her second husband proves to be as forgiving as he is doting. However, she had not been so fortunate in her first marriage, which was hasty and ill-conceived. If a woman makes a mistake, the law of marriage is not written to facilitate an easy redress. Matrimonial law is written by men for men, and the law of bigamy is part of that jurisprudence.

According to Aurora's uncle, Captain Prodder, the 'law of the British dominions' is a 'complication of inscrutable enigmas, only to be spoken of and thought of in a spirit of reverence, and wonder' (381). The irony or this view betrays an unsettling truth. The law may be inscrutable and awe-inspiring. But that is all it is. In the prosaic matter of uncovering criminal responsibility and effecting justice, neither the institutions nor the officers of law are useful in *Aurora Floyd*. The inquest into Conyers's death is predictably inconclusive.[104] Hargraves's later trial is reported briefly at the close of the final chapter, with the observation that a plea of insanity was rejected by a 'set of matter-of-fact jurymen' even though the accused was plainly 'half-witted' (457–58). As for the officers, the 'minions of the law', the collective 'Dogberries of Doncaster' who are first called to the scene, are hopelessly out of their depth (377, 436). In time, following the receipt of two anonymous letters sent by a conniving housekeeper, a London detective named Grimstone arrives at the Park (413). Grimstone is more capable but he is far from welcome, and it comes as no surprise to discover that Grimstone is motivated less by a sense of justice than by the lure of financial reward (436).[105] As is invariably the case in a Braddon novel, the mystery is finally resolved by a gentleman amateur.[106] A gentleman knows that there is more to solving murders than simply identifying murderers. Bulstrode is such a gentleman, for he appreciates the greater 'perils' which afflict such affairs, those of scandal and speculation:

---

[104] Returning an interim verdict of 'wilful murder against some person or persons unknown' (317–18).

[105] Grimstone's presence in the text speaks to contemporary concerns regarding the novelty of professional detectives, generally drawn from the working class who, as representatives of the state, earned their living by prying into the private lives of middle-class Victorians, a subject upon which Fitzjames Stephen mused in his influential essay 'Detectives in Fiction and Real Life'. Stephen was particularly contemptuous of the police employed in the *Palmer* case. See Fitzjames Stephen, 'Detectives in Fiction and Real Life' in Trodd, *Domestic Crime* (above n 57) 24–26, 29–30, 42–43, 156, and D Miller, *The Novel and the Police* (California University Press, 1988) 3–6.

[106] Whilst Grimstone might have pieced together a few critical clues, as the narrator affirms in the final paragraph of the novel, it is Bulstrode who caught Hargraves in an incriminating position (459).

> Different persons set up different theories; one man writes to a newspaper to declare
> that, in his opinion, the crime was committed by some person within the house; another
> man writes as positively to another paper, asserting that the murderer was undoubtedly
> a stranger. Each man brings forward a mass of supposititious evidence in favour of his
> own argument, and each thinks a great deal more of proving his own cleverness than of
> furthering the ends of justice. (417)

In this matter the law cannot help.[107] The law is not, in truth, really wanted. The
suggestion, vouched in a 'clever letter' sent to a newspaper, that a 'cordon be
drawn around the house, and every creature living in it be held under the surveillance of the law' until the 'case' is finally resolved, is intended to send a shudder
through every right-minded Victorian reader (383, 396).

However, the most striking jurisprudential absence in *Aurora Floyd* is the heroine's decision not to pursue legal redress against her first husband. *Aurora Floyd*
was written as the new Divorce Court opened its doors. Aurora first discovers her
husband's infidelity in the summer of 1857. The narrator notes:

> Had she, upon the discovery of her first husband's infidelity, called the law to her aid she
> was rich enough to command its utmost help – she might have freed herself from the
> hateful chains so foolishly linked together, and might have defied this dead man to tor-
> ment or assail her. (393)

This may be true, but it was not so straightforward. First, in the early years there
was much uncertainty as to whether the new court would countenance evidence
of prior infidelity and be sympathetic to supplicant wives. Moreover, for reasons
of the notorious 'double-standard' written into the 1857 Act, Aurora would have
needed to allege more than mere infidelity, as indeed she seemed to appreciate,
later recalling to Bulstrode that on discovering her husband's infidelity she had
written to him 'telling him I had discovered that which, coupled with his brutality
to me on more than one occasion, gave me the right to call upon the law to release
me from him' (354–55). It is perhaps significant that the allusion to spousal abuse
was not present in the first serialised version of *Aurora Floyd*. Evidently Braddon
only subsequently realised that the new legislation required female petitioners to
evidence not just adultery but also at least one of the crimes of bigamy, desertion
or spousal violence. However, perhaps the greatest impediment was fear. Pursuit
of legal remedy could only invite that most dreaded of consequences, 'shame' and
'horrible degradation' (326, 334). The Floyds might have found themselves the
subject of salacious accounts in *The Times*; Aurora herself might have been the
subject of whisperings.[108]

Reflecting once again on her failure to seek legal redress, Aurora admits that
hers was a failure of courage. She had not been 'brave enough' (418). Instead, she
had chosen to 'follow the counsel of expediency, and it had led her into thorny and

---

[107] Mellish is reduced to speculating, characteristically, on the 'thrashing' he might give to any editor
who crosses his path (446).

[108] The opening chapter, in which Aurora's parents' marriage is described, emphasises the potentially
corrosive effect of mendacious gossip and rumour, and as stories of Conyers's murder are published in
various newspapers, this fate inevitably befalls their daughter too.

crooked ways', committing the 'crimes' of desertion and bigamy and succumbing to blackmail (393). It was, the narrator sagely advises, a mistake but it was an understandable, even forgivable, mistake. If Aurora is lucky in her second husband, it might reasonably be thought that she was decidedly unlucky in the mischance of the first husband returning. This may be so but she is also guilty, not just of committing the crime of bigamy and succumbing to blackmail, but of keeping secrets. From the start, it is evident that Aurora has a 'skeleton in some quiet corner', a secret, 'my secret' which she refuses to 'tell' (103, 118, 315). By the third chapter she is being approached in the street by shadowy strangers demanding money (28–30). There is no escape. Mellish Park is not a sanctuary, but a house in which dissimulation and distrust is rife, where 'household spies' gossip 'feverishly' about 'the doings and sayings, the joys and sorrows', of those who employ them (177).[109] There is, as Aurora comes to appreciate, danger 'without' the estate, and danger 'within', the latter 'nursing discontent and hatred within the holy circle of the domestic hearth' (141).

Mellish uses the same imagery as he ponders his wife's secret, wondering 'how people felt who had no social mystery brooding upon their hearth; no domestic skeleton cowering in their homely cupboard' (289). The irony is a necessary one for it is, of course, his fate to be the subject of speculation, in the novel and in the minds of those who turned its pages. Indeed, speculation is all-consuming at Mellish Park. Everyone is a spectator; everyone watches everyone else. In the absence of legal regulation, disciplinary surveillance has become habitual, even addictive. No-one is surveyed with a greater intensity than Aurora, and no-one is more conscious of being surveyed.[110] Too fearful to press his new wife as to the meaning of her 'secret', Mellish instead undertakes a strategy of intense, besotted, surveillance. He stares silently at 'her masses of ebon hair uncoiled and falling about her shoulders in serpentine tresses that looked like shining blue-black snakes released from poor Medusa's head' (271). The imagery is that of seduction and sorcery, of the kind we will encounter in chapter four, when we contemplate the pre-Raphaelite poetics of sexuality and prostitution. Aurora is a 'dark-haired goddess' (42).[111] As the narrator confirms: 'Her beauty was of that luxuriant and splendid order which has almost always most effect upon the masses, and the fascination of her manner was almost akin to sorcery in its power over simple people.' (132) Aurora enchants. Bulstode is immediately 'bewitched', whilst Mellish Park is

[109] See Trodd, *Domestic Crime* (above n 57) 61, suggesting that the novel 'offers a comprehensive description of the Victorian home as a state of war in which the domestic staff are primarily engaged in espionage, and only secondarily with their domestic duties'.

[110] Aurora is particularly conscious of others at the Park, including the housekeeper and servants, constantly 'watching' her (276). See J Curtis, 'The Espaliered Girl: Pruning the Docile Body in *Aurora Floyd*' in Tromp, *Beyond Sensation* (above n 26) 79–81, and Tatum, 'Bearing Her Secret' (above n 101) 504, suggesting that in Braddon's novels, as in so many others of the time, 'men posit women as mysteries to be deciphered, and they do this in order to establish their masculine identity in proportion to unravelling women's "riddles"'.

[111] Cultural imagery presumed that seductresses were dark-haired. No-one trusted a dark-haired beauty, and equally no-one expected a fair-haired one to be a serial murderer. Lucy Audley was fair-haired, an anomaly that contemporary critics noted.

turned upside down, subject to 'pettycoat government', its master the 'slave' of a 'despotic and capricious sovereign' who accepts his 'devotion with a Sultana-like grace' (47, 63, 129, 141–43, 288). The oriental imagery compounds the sense of transgression, cultural and sexual. Aurora is Semiramide and Hecate, a 'Cleopatra-like bride' (67, 131, 213, 217, 277).

The enchantment which Aurora casts can only be broken when her secret is discovered. And it is so discovered. Aurora, it transpires, wants to conform, to be 'true' to her husband (142).[112] That is her secret. As soon as she confesses her 'sin' of 'disobedience' she is rewarded with Bulstrode's sympathy and assistance (352–25). Her punishment will be redemptive. She will suffer, for a while: 'Heaven only knows the bitterness of the silent battle' (118). She will contemplate the prospect of losing the love of an adoring husband, and with it her comfortable estate. In terms that would have resonated with those who had only recently contemplated the sorry demise of Isabel Carlyle, Braddon's narrator duly cautions:

> Ah careless wives! Who think it a small thing, perhaps, that your husbands are honest and generous, constant and true . . . stop and think of this wretched girl, who in this hour of desolation recalled a thousand little wrongs she had done to her husband, and would have laid herself under his feet to be walked over by him could she have thus atoned for her petty tyrannies, her pretty caprices! Think of her in her loneliness, with her heart yearning to go back to the man she loved. (345)

Aurora will be forgiven. Chastened she will first defer to what Bulstrode, 'a wise judge, to whose sentence she would be willing to submit', advises (360). Thereafter she will await a future which is no longer hers to 'dispose of', but which 'belongs' to her husband (362). The men, altogether more comfortable in dealing with problems to be resolved and women who want to conform, assume responsibility for ensuring a happy ending. Bulstrode advises Mellish that he and Aurora must obtain a special licence from Doctors' Commons so that they can immediately marry 'for the second time' (374).[113] This they do quietly in an 'out-of-the-way church in the City' (359, 374–75). It has been suggested that the final scene, where 'we leave Aurora, a little changed, a shade less defiantly bright, perhaps, but unspeakably beautiful and tender, bending over the cradle of her first-born' should be read ironically (459). Such a reading avoids the sense that Aurora's final redemption is not just a matter of conformity, but of subjugation.[114] Certainly Aurora's performance will be different. She will assume the life of the respectable middle-class woman enjoying a marriage founded on a relation of mutual love and respect, 'happy in the calm security of her home'; the life, as we shall see, so ear-

---

[112] As do, in the end, so many heroines of sensation novels. See Maunder, 'Mapping the Victorian Sensation Novel' (above n 23) 17; Pykett, *The Improper Feminine* (above n 34) 88; and Chase and Levenson, *The Spectacle of Intimacy* (above n 61) 211.

[113] For once Braddon here appears in error. Doctors' Commons was dissolved in 1857.

[114] See Schroeder and Schroeder, *From Sensation to Society* (above n 11) 101–105; J Schipper, *Becoming Frauds: Unconventional Heroines in Mary Elizabeth Braddon's Sensational Fiction* (Writers Club Press, 2002), 72–74; and Curtis, 'The Espaliered Girl' (above n 110) 78, referring to this as 'another kind of violence', the 'reshaping of the temptress Aurora into a Madonna figure'.

nestly craved by her creator (142). Aurora Floyd will be fine; after all, as the narrator noted at the start, she has inherited a 'taint of the play-acting' (20).

The Shame of Miss Braddon

Trollope, as we noted, famously identified 'a great division' between 'sensational novels' and 'anti-sensational novels', the latter passing into critical memory as realist or 'domestic' novels. However, it was, as he shrewdly observed, a distinction essentially created by critics. A 'good novel should be both' sensational and realist.[115] Recent critics have tended to agree.[116] Indeed, it has become fashionable to suggest that novels such as *Aurora Floyd* belong to a genre that can be more closely defined as 'domestic sensationalism', a description that is very commonly, and perhaps most comfortably, applied to Ellen Wood's *East Lynne*. Nevertheless, with the possible exception of *Lady Audley's Secret*, it can be fairly claimed that the sensation novel remains in the shadows of nineteenth-century literary criticism, only very recently aspiring to some greater measure of critical respectability.[117]

Yet, as much as any other genre, perhaps more, the sensation novel of the 1860s raised the 'good spirit' that Dickens invoked in *Dombey and Son*, so that readers could better discern the 'dark shapes' that might lie within. As Braddon concurred:

> But it is good sometimes to see the 'night-side' of things to have laid bare our social scourges both of the moral and material kind, in order that we may with one heart and mind unite in striving to rectify those evils which madden peoples and hurry nations to premature decay.[118]

When the reader of a Braddon novel contemplated what was happening within the superficially idyllic homes of women such as Aurora Floyd, they encountered presentiments of just such evil and decay in the form of frustrated sexuality, crime, the harbouring of secrets, and families riddled with suspicion and mistrust, where men and women desperately tear away veils of mutual dissimulation, sometime

[115] Trollope, *An Autobiography* (above n 17) 146. The distinction was not, of course, solely Trollope's, as Hughes notes in *The Maniac in the Cellar* (above n 19) at 53–56.
[116] See Brantlinger, 'What is "Sensational"' (above n 44) 1, suggesting that the sensation novel incorporated much that was familiar in contemporary 'domestic realism', and also (9) stressing the particular affinities between sensation and late Gothic novels. The same argument is made in M Knight, 'Figuring Out the Fascination: Recent Trends in Criticism on Victorian Sensation and Crime Fiction' (2009) 37 *Victorian Literature and Culture* 323.
[117] See Brantlinger, 'What is "Sensational"' (above n 44) 1, and Maunder, 'Mapping the Victorian Sensation Novel' (above n 23) 2–3, 7, stressing the determination of early twentieth-century critics to ensure that the sensation novel remained marginalised. Mark Knight has more recently argued that the 'sensation' novel has finally attained a greater degree of critical respectability. See Knight, 'Figuring Out the Fascination' 323.
[118] Quoted in Phegley, 'Literary Valuation' (above n 23) at 163.

imaginary, more often not.[119] Blackmail, a common affliction of Braddon's heroines is, of course, the classic crime of secrecy, and the 'exposure of secrecy' is the defining characteristic of the sensation novel.[120] This was Braddon's greatest crime, to invite her readers to peer inside the homes of her variously dysfunctional families and uncover their darker secrets.

It was for this reason that critics were so troubled by the sensational novelist in general and Braddon in particular. Braddon was commonly identified as the most culpable of the sensationalists by Oliphant, Rae and Mansel.[121] As we have already noted, it was generally assumed that Braddon had become too enamoured of French literature, by writers such as Flaubert; a suspicion which the publication of *The Doctor's Wife* seemed only to confirm.[122] At least Ellen Wood's novels, as the *Spectator* later observed, were 'English', even if they too were crammed full of adulteresses and bigamists. Wood prescribed 'murder and mutton'. Braddon created murders and 'French verse' with 'scraps of art criticism'.[123] Unsurprisingly, *Lady Audley's Secret*, with its stunning portrait of a young woman who, chapter by chapter, changed from careless bigamist to cold-blooded murderess, attracted venomous criticism. It was, the *North British Review* advised, 'one of the most noxious books of modern times'.[124] *Lady Audley's Secret* has retained its place in the Victorian canon, perhaps in large part for precisely this reason. *Aurora Floyd*, in comparison, has not.[125] To contemporaries, however, the story of Aurora Mellish was every bit as concerning. She may not have cut as evil or as degenerate a figure as Lucy Audley but she was barely less culpable. There was too much in the novel that was simply too troubling: too many 'fashionable' crimes, too many 'things', as the Irish novelist Mrs Humphries later recalled her aunt commenting, 'that little girls have no business to know anything about'.[126]

In defence of his friend, Augustus Sala argued that 'we shall take no great harm by reading realistic novels of human passion, weakness and error'.[127] It was an opinion which Margaret Oliphant pointedly did not share, observing of Braddon:

> It is a shame to women so to write; and it is a shame to the women who read and accept as a true representation of themselves and their ways the equivocal talk and fleshly inclination herein attributed to them. It may be done in carelessness. It may be done in that

[119] See Pykett, *The Improper Feminine* (above n 35) 111, and Trodd, *Domestic Crime* (above n 57) 1, the sensation novel, more than perhaps any other genre, concentrated on the 'uneasy relations between respectability, privacy and surveillance' in the Victorian home.

[120] E Showalter, 'Family Secrets and Domestic Subversion: Rebellion in the Novels of the Eighteen-Sixties' in A Wohl (ed), *The Victorian Family: Structure and Stresses* (Croom Helm, 1978) 104.

[121] Altogether 'coarser' than fellow sensationalist Ellen Wood, Oliphant added, 'in sum the 'chief purveyor' of immorality. See Hughes, *The Maniac in the Cellar* (above n 19) 107–10.

[122] See Wolff, *Sensational Victorian* (above n 15) 128–29, 137 quoting her admission to Edmund Yates, that 'the Balzac-morbid-anatomy school is my especial delight'.

[123] *Spectator*, 17 October 1874, 133–34. Ellen Wood's *East Lynne*, the plot of which moves around the consequences of adultery, was equally famous, or more accurately notorious, as Braddon's trilogy.

[124] Rae, 'Sensation Novelists' (above n 31) 96.

[125] In relative terms 'cast into the shadows', according to Chase and Levenson, *The Spectacle of Intimacy* (above n 61) 208.

[126] Wolff, *Sensational Victorian* (above n 15) at 10.

[127] Carnell, *Braddon* (above n 37) at 165. Sala was editor of *Temple Bar* and a close personal friend.

mere desire for something startling which the monotony of ordinary life is apt to produce; but it is debasing to everybody concerned.[128]

The repercussions of the offence have lingered. For a short while around the turn of the twentieth century Braddon's reputation seemed to recover. Writing in 1901 Arnold Bennett praised a writer who had 'woven herself' into being 'part of England', so much so that 'without her it would be different'.[129] A few years later, no less a figure than Arthur Quiller-Couch suggested that Braddon's novels would 'be studied one day as respectfully as people now study the more sensational Elizabethans'.[130] This prediction was too bold. For much of the last century Braddon, like the genre with which she was so readily identified, has remained at the margins of nineteenth-century literary criticism.[131] In recent years, however, Braddon has attracted greater critical attention as a chronicler, perhaps even a catalyst, of an 'insurgent femininity'.[132] Braddon, it is contended, wrote about bigamy for a reason, because in so doing she touched upon the particular experiences and frustrations of her target audience. Cases such as those of Theresa Longworth helped to fashion this audience, allowing Braddon to exploit latent feelings of empathy in her readers.[133] Here, the sensation novel in general and the novels of Braddon in particular represent an exemplar of the 'improper' literary feminine, the 'domestic ideal's dangerous other' and it is for this precise reason that the genre has remained neglected and is still dismissed as a species of 'low art'.[134] The 'narrative trajectory' in Braddon's sensation novels, as Lyn Pykett affirms, is invariably 'directed towards the proper feminisation of the heroine'.[135] There is a resonance here with Nancy Armstrong's broader observation that in its shaping of 'communities' of women readers, the mid-Victorian novel acted as an empowering 'agent' of nineteenth-century feminisation.[136] As to the more particular community of sensation novel readers, the very popularity of the genre suggests

---

[128] Oliphant, 'Novels' (above n 23) 264.

[129] Indeed, Bennett went so far as to suggest that her reputation, nationally and internationally, exceeded that of Hardy, Ibsen or Kipling. See Wolff, *Sensational Victorian* (above n 15) at 2.

[130] Carnell, *Braddon* (above n 37) 1.

[131] See Pykett, *The Improper Feminine* (above n 35) at 3; Woolf, *Sensational Victorian* (above n 15) 3, 15 noting that Braddon's novels barely raise a critical 'flicker' a century on even amongst Victorian specialists; and Hughes, *The Maniac in the Cellar* (above n 19) suggesting that the sensation genre as a whole has been 'consigned' to critical 'oblivion'.

[132] See Schipper, *Frauds* (above n 114) 7; Pykett, *The Improper Feminine* (above n 35) 5; Maunder, 'Mapping the Victorian Sensation Novel' (above n 23) 3–4, 11–18; and M Tromp, *The Private Rod: Marital Violence, Sensation and the Law in Victorian Britain*, (University Press of Virginia, 2000), 4–12. Ann Cvetkovich is more ambivalent, wondering if the 'affective' presentation of the female protagonist in a number of sensation novels is both transgressive and regressive. See Cvetkovich, *Mixed Feelings* (above n 37) 6–7, 13, 38–44.

[133] See M Hartman, 'Crime and the Respectable Woman: Toward a Pattern of Middle-Class Female Criminality in Nineteenth-Century France and England' (1974) 2 *Feminist Studies* 44–45.

[134] Pykett, *The Improper Feminine* (above n 35) 24, 199–202.

[135] Ibid, 85.

[136] N Armstrong, *Desire and Domestic Fiction: A Political History of the Novel* (Oxford University Press, 1987) 42–48, and Flint, *The Woman Reader* (above n 9) 43, 190, 286–87, suggesting that *Aurora Floyd* can be read as an especially good example of a novel which was intended to fashion a particular 'community' of female readers.

that many women 'readers recognised themselves in their outspoken heroines'.[137] More recently, it has been argued that the 'sensation' novel should be read as an alternative species of realism, one which was peculiarly suited to articulating both the experience of domestic violence and the failure of the law to address it.[138] The collateral thought that Braddon, like Thackeray and perhaps also Dickens, was seeking to recommend the particular virtues of 'companionate' as opposed to patriarchal models of marriage, is intriguing.[139]

Of course, the idea that the sensation novel represented a peculiarly vital medium with which to raise the 'muted feminine voice' was appreciated by a number of Braddon's contemporaries.[140] In 1862, the *Christian Remembrancer* ruminated on the possibility that in reading a sensation novel such as *Aurora Floyd* women might 'open out a picture of life free from all the perhaps irksome checks of their own existence'.[141] Novels about sex and crime necessarily challenged the increasingly fragile defences of the Englishman's castle, and in writing about this threat Braddon had few peers. The threat imported in the presentation of attractive and intelligent female criminals carried an added charge, particularly when designed to evince the sympathy of a female readership. The real crime of novels such as *Aurora Floyd* was not just the depiction of murder or blackmail or bigamy. It was the insinuation that their heroines were driven to criminality because the institution of marriage so often causes pain, and the law of marriage is unable, and unwilling, to provide relief. Braddon was not, of course, the first to cast this aspersion. Dickens and Thackeray did the same, as did Ellen Wood and Braddon's mentor, Bulwer Lytton, who had earlier, and rather more sensationally, suggested in his 1846 novel *Lucretia* that there might be a 'household epidemic' of criminal wives.[142] Cases like that of Aurora Floyd seemed to realise the prophecy. As the disapproving Rae observed:

> There is nothing more violently opposed to our moral sense, in all the contradictions to custom which they present us, than the utter unrestraint in which heroines of this order are allowed to expiate and develop their impulsive, stormy, passionate characters. We believe it is one chief among their many dangers to youthful readers.[143]

It seemed that Braddon's 'women are born to attempt to commit murders, and to succeed in committing bigamy'.[144] Oliphant put the problem succinctly. Rather than reading about all the 'charming girls' found in Trollope, young Victorian

---

[137] See Showalter, *A Literature of Their Own* (above n 24) 160–61 and 163 suggesting that *Lady Audley's Secret* can be read as a 'carefully controlled female fantasy'.

[138] Tromp, *The Private Rod* (above n 132) 14. For a similar conclusion, see Schipper, *Frauds* (above n 124) 2–3.

[139] As suggested in Schroeder and Schroeder, *From Sensation to Society* (above n 11) at 20–21.

[140] See Pykett, *The Improper Feminine* (above n 35) 206.

[141] 'Our Female Sensation Novelists' (above n 19) 209–10.

[142] Trodd, *Domestic Crime* (above n 57) 97.

[143] F Rae, 'Our Female Sensation Novelists' (1863) 78 *Living Age* 353.

[144] Rae, 'Miss Braddon' (above n 31) 202–204.

women were entranced by all 'the Aurora Floyds'.[145] No good could be expected to come of it.

As we have already noted, contemporary reviewers were certainly sensitive to the particular implications of a genre in which women, as writers and readers and, of course, as protagonists, were peculiarly conspicuous. Commenting on the publication of Florence Marryat's *Women Against Women*, written in 1866, another reviewer remarked:

> It is curious that the most questionable novels of the day should be written by women. To judge from their books, the ideas of women on points of morals and ethics seem in a state of transition, and consequently, in confusion.[146]

The suggestion that women writers were confused, and also ignorant, was commonly articulated. They could not, as WR Greg confirmed in his 1859 essay 'The False Morality of Lady Novelists', be otherwise, their experience of life being so 'partial' and 'superficial'.[147] 'No man would have dared to write and publish such books as these are: no man could have written such delineations of female passion' the Reverend Paget declared two years later:

> No! They are women, who by their writings have been doing the work of the enemy of souls, glossing over vice, making profligacy attractive, dealing with licentious minuteness the workings of unbridled passions, encouraging vanity, extravagance, wilfulness, selfishness in their worse forms ... Women have done this, have thus abused their power and prostituted their gifts, who might have been bright and shining lights in their generation.[148]

Paget sensed a conspiracy; he was not alone. Charles Reade, in one of his more neurotic moments, opined that circulating libraries would now 'only take in ladies novels', for 'these are their gods'.[149] It was indeed 'the age of the lady novelists'.[150]

Again, as we have already noted, the idea that fiction played a vital role in the nurturing of an emergent female consciousness in nineteenth-century England has become a critical commonplace. Regardless of their many other differences, in this at least there is an undeniable affinity between the sensation novel, the domestic realist novel and indeed the late Gothic romances of writers such as Charlotte Bronte. Each was intended to be read by women and to be discussed by women. Braddon was certainly conscious of the capacity of print to help fashion such a consciousness. The editorial policy of her *Belgravia* magazine moved around precisely this aspiration.[151] In this, moreover, she saw herself as writing within a

---

[145] M Oliphant, 'Novels' (1867) 102 *Blackwoods* 260.

[146] Carnell, *Braddon* (above n 37) 152.

[147] W Greg, 'The False Morality of Lady Novelists' (1859) 7 *National Review* 149. Pykett quotes a 1860 essay in *Fraser's* in which it was likewise argued that women's literary facility was necessarily limited by the fact that they 'can describe, or rather transcribe with success only those scenes and characters which come under the observation', Pykett, *The Improper Feminine* (above n 35) at 26.

[148] Paget, *Lucretia* (above n 21) 305.

[149] Carnell, *Braddon* (above n 37) 169. He had a point. Mudie's Circulating Library purchased 600 copies of each Braddon novel published.

[150] ES Dallas in his review of *Aurora Floyd* in the *The Times*, 18 November 1862, 4.

[151] See Phegley, 'Literary Valuation' (above n 23) 153.

distinctively confessional tradition which, like so many of her contemporaries, she traced back to the publication of *Jane Eyre*.[152] There is certainly an echo of the young Jane in Braddon's later reflection: 'What does surprise me is that every girl who is well educated and endowed with imagination does not long to express herself with the pen.'[153]

In this context, there is a further, necessarily personal, irony to be considered in any critical reading of *Aurora Floyd*. There is no surprise in Braddon being familiar with bigamy. She read newspapers. She even played bigamists, and wronged wives, during her earlier years as an aspiring actress. But perhaps most importantly, she was also a kind of bigamist herself. Reade was typically succinct. The author who had made bigamy such a 'fashionable crime' was 'the wife of a man, who had got a wife and children'.[154] In much the same way as Theresa Longworth moved in with the Major only to find out that he was already married, so Braddon moved in with the publisher John Maxwell only to discover, a couple of months later, that he already had a wife, consigned to an asylum on the outskirts of Dublin.[155] Braddon, however, did not seek recourse to the law. She settled instead for 'some form of marriage' ceremony.[156] For the following decade, like Aurora, she played the role of wife, forever conscious that her precarious 'secret' might be uncovered at any time.[157] The craving for respectability proved to be more a bane than a virtue. When Maxwell placed a notice in the press announcing that 'Miss Braddon, the novelist, was recently married to Mr Maxwell, the publisher', instead of dampening speculation, it prompted Mrs Maxwell's brother to place a contradictory notice accusing Braddon of being nothing more than a live-in mistress.[158] When Mrs Maxwell died in 1874, the same brother had ostentatious obituary notices published; one of which prompted the London correspondent of *The New York Times* to inform his readers that: 'A curious incident and, I may almost say, char-

[152] A novel in which, of course, a bigamous marriage is only narrowly averted. According to Braddon, Charlotte Bronte was the 'only genius the weaker sex can point to in literature'. The inspiration was inevitably decried by Braddon's fiercest and most consistent critic, Margaret Oliphant. Novels such as *Lady Audley's Secret* and *Aurora Floyd*, Oliphant advised, were precisely the sort of thing that disciples of *Jane Eyre* were all too given to producing. See Wolff, *Sensational Victorian* (above n 15) 201, 234; Carnell, *Braddon* (above n 37) 90; and Showalter, *A Literature of Their Own* (above n 24) 154.

[153] Carnell, *Braddon* (above n 37) 87.

[154] Private diary entry on 1874, quoted in Wolff, *Sensational Victorian* (above n 15) at 80.

[155] Maxwell, of Irish origins, bought and sold a multitude of magazines during the 1860s and 1870s, including *Robin Goodfellow*, in which the early instalments of *Lady Audley* appeared, the *Halfpenny Journal*, and the later *Belgravia*, of which Braddon would become editor. Reade termed him Braddon's 'task-master'. A former maid confirmed that Braddon was quickly appraised of the fact that Maxwell was already married. When challenged in later years about his first wife, Maxwell would stolidly reply that she was not dead but 'defunct'.

[156] As Ginger Frost has recently confirmed, such 'marriages' were not at all uncommon, particularly amongst the middle classes demonstrating the extent to which parties were keen to appear to conform as much as possible to the contemporary expectations of 'respectability'. See Frost, *Sin* (above n 71) 83–84, 118, 225–26.

[157] For this reason, as she confided to her old friend Bulwer Lytton, she could only occasionally sign herself, in private correspondence, as Mary Maxwell. Such a signature on any formal documents would necessarily render them void in law. It was for this reason that she continued to publish as Mary Braddon. See Wolff, *Sensational Victorian* (above n 15) 107.

[158] Ibid, 104–105.

acteristic incident has happened to Miss Braddon, the novelist. Having like so many of her heroines committed a species of bigamy, she has been found out.'[159] Miss Braddon had been shamed, to the barely concealed glee of her more disapproving critics. Within months, in October 1874, Braddon and Maxwell were married; their impulse to conform, like that of John and Aurora Mellish, was gratified quietly and out of public sight.

---

[159] Carnell, *Braddon* (above n 37) 182.

3

Unnatural Mothers

On Tuesday 16th March 1802, Mary Voce was executed on Nottingham gallows. She had been convicted of child-murder. It was, according to one contemporary broadsheet account, a 'happy' death; presumably, at least, rather happier than Mary's life. It was happy because Mary had experienced a religious conversion two days earlier. Finally confessing her guilt in the early hours of the Saturday she had 'manifested real penitence and earnestly sought the Lord'. She had then, the reporter confirmed, wobbled a bit. But after being joined in prayer by assorted concerned evangelicals, Mary had recovered her spirits, declaring that 'peace and resignation' had 'flowed into her happy soul' once more. All present agreed that those 'few hours' were 'some of the happiest of our lives', so 'delivered from every fear' Mary appeared to be, and so 'lost in wonder, love and praise'. Mary 'not only forgave but loved her enemies', who presumably included the father of her child whose identity she refused to disclose and who it appears was less keen to repent of anything much. Mary awaited the 'pardoning love of God' with eager anticipation. She was then carried in a cart to the gallows, where she was strung up to suffer an agonising death whilst interested spectators stood gawping in the morning drizzle. Mary, it can be reasonably supposed with the benefit of hindsight, had lost her reason; pretty much at the same time, it seems, as she had found her God. Later that evening, the resident Methodist minister at the Halifax Lane Chapel preached, predictably enough, on the cherished evangelical text 'Is not this a brand plucked from the fire?'[1]

One of those who attended Mary, and who prayed with her in her final days and hours, was George Eliot's Aunt Elizabeth Samuel. Writing in her journal in November 1858, Eliot recalled a visit by her aunt 'probably in 1839 or 40', during which she recounted the 'anecdote' of Mary Voce's conversion. The 'story', Eliot recorded, 'told by my aunt with great feeling, affected me deeply and I never lost the impression of that afternoon and our talk together'. Twenty years later, Aunt Samuel's recollection of a 'very ignorant girl who had murdered her child' provided the 'germ' of the story of Hetty Sorrel.[2] Prompted by GH Lewes, Eliot had originally conceived a simple recitation, provisionally entitled 'My Aunt's Story',

---

[1] Zechariah 3:2. The broadsheet account is given in G Eliot, *Adam Bede* (Penguin, 1980) at 544–57. All internal citations are taken from this edition.

[2] Eliot's entry is reprinted in the Penguin edition of *Adam Bede*, at 540–43. Aunt Samuel was a Methodist lay preacher, as was Hetty's confessor, Dinah, in *Adam Bede*. For the likely influence of Aunt Samuel on the young Eliot, see R Ashton, *George Eliot: A Life* (Hamish Hamilton, 1996) 20.

and intended for publication as one of her ongoing 'scenes of clerical life'. In time, however, the name and the scope of the story changed. It was not the first time that Eliot had decided to furnish the narrative of a wronged woman with a conspicuously male title, and it would not be the last. The 'happy' death of Mary Voce filtered through Aunt Samuel and recast in the case of Hetty Sorrel became the narrative of *Adam Bede*; the novel which according to an admiring Jane Welsh Carlyle, restored her faith in 'the whole human race'.[3]

The case of Mary Voce matters to us for the obvious reason that it is a confirmed source for Eliot's *Adam Bede*. It is not, as we shall see, the only source but it is a significant one, as Eliot confirmed in her journal entry. There was nothing, of course, particularly unusual in novelists gaining inspiration from real cases. The *Norton* case, as we have already noted, proved to be a peculiarly fertile literary source for a number of novelists of the period, whilst sensationalists such as Braddon assiduously scoured the morning papers in order to discover cases of murder, adultery or bigamy. The real case was the lifeblood of 'sensation' and 'anti-sensation' novelist alike. For a 'realist' author such as Eliot, moreover, the invocation of a real case reinforced the aspiration to somehow convey a 'truth' about the human condition, one that could be verified by history and experience. As we will see, *Adam Bede* has assumed a particular authority as one of the defining texts in mid-Victorian realist fiction for precisely this reason. It is, moreover, about a very ordinary fallen woman. Gone are the beautiful if errant aristocrats who populate East Lynne or Mellish Park. Hetty is a simple girl, too simple, and she lives simply too. There is nothing romantic about Hetty's life, just as there was nothing romantic about Mary Voce's.

Nor is there anything romantic about the life of Mary Furley. The case of Mary Furley, who in desperation had flung herself and her baby into the Thames in 1844, attracted the attention of Charles Dickens just as he was sketching his Christmas story of that year, *The Chimes*. Mary's sorry life was inscribed, as was her crime 'so terrible', so 'unnatural and cruel', and so common and so horribly familiar.[4] Dickens, as we have already noted, and as we shall see again in chapter four, was fascinated by all kinds of fallen women. When he was not attending the trials of adulterous aristocratic wives, he was attending those of allegedly murderous unmarried mothers.[5] In January 1850, one of the newer contributors to his magazine *Household Words* wrote seeking advice in regard to one particular fallen woman whose case she had come across whilst supporting her husband's ministry in Manchester. Elizabeth Gaskell recounted the sad life of Pasley, the daughter of a deceased Irish clergyman who had been orphaned and then, with the same kind

---

[3] See M Jones, 'The Usual Sad Catastrophe: From the Street to the Parlor in *Adam Bede*' (2004) *Victorian Literature and Culture* 317, and J McDonagh, 'Child-Murder Narratives in George Eliot's *Adam Bede*: Embedded Histories and Fictional Representation' (2001) 56 *Nineteenth Century Literature* 255–57.

[4] C Dickens, *The Christmas Books* vol 1 (Penguin, 1985) 195–96.

[5] Claire Tomalin opens her recent biography of Dickens with a description of his attendance at an inquest into the death of a child allegedly killed by its mother in 1840. See C Tomalin, *Charles Dickens: A Life* (Penguin, 2011) xxxix–xlii.

of sad familiarity, ended up on the streets. Gaskell wondered if a place might be found at Dickens's Urania Cottage.[6] It could not. But Dickens replied with a long letter of advice on what Gaskell might do.[7] One of the short stories which Gaskell had recently contributed to *Household Words*, and which Dickens most admired, was *Lizzie Leigh*. It related the descent of a prostitute lost on the streets of Manchester. It would have been extraordinary if Gaskell did not have Pasley in mind when she wrote *Lizzie Leigh*. She certainly did a year later when she began to contemplate what turned out to be perhaps her most controversial full-length novel, *Ruth*.[8]

Ruth Hilton does not fall quite so far as Hetty Sorrel but it is again a very different fall from that of Isabel Carlyle. Clara Newcome or Aurora Floyd. Ruth, like Hetty, is a simple girl, living an ordinary life in ordinary surroundings. It is an ordinariness which facilitates a great empathy. Like Hetty, Ruth is not married; for which reason the jurisprudential focus also switches. The closer concern is no longer with the consequences of adultery, but with illegitimacy and in the more extreme case, infanticide. It is no longer simply a question of how to regulate prospectively errant wives, but of what to do with women who become mothers outside of marriage. The 'cult' of motherhood was as closely regulated, culturally and legally, as any of the other aligned familial fetishes before which middle-class Victorians paid obeisance: the 'separate' spheres, the 'angel in the house', and the 'womanly' wife. When it came to deciding which 'fallen' women might be saved, perceived abilities to fulfil the expectations of the 'natural' mother could play a critical part in refining authorial imaginations and shaping reader expectations. It certainly described the very different fates of Hetty and Ruth. Both die, but only one dies redeemed.

The Precious Quality of Truthfulness

In the Preface to the second edition of her novel *The Tenant of Wildfell Hall*, Anne Bronte asserted:

> My object in writing the following pages, was not simply to amuse the Reader, neither was it to gratify my own taste, nor yet to ingratiate myself with the Press and the Public.

[6] Pasley's first name remains unknown, though it has been hazarded that it might have been Ruth. See J Hartley, *Charles Dickens and the House of Fallen Women* (Methuen, 2008) 49, and J Uglow, *Elizabeth Gaskell* (Faber and Faber, 1993) 246.

[7] At the time, Dickens was struggling to find places on ships for those women who had completed the requisite period at the Cottage. As we shall see in the next chapter, the purpose of Urania Cottage was to prepare all its inmates for voyages overseas in order to start fresh lives. In the end, following Dickens's advice, Gaskell appears to have found Pasley a place on a ship to the Cape; though there is no evidence as to whether she ever boarded it. See Uglow, *Elizabeth Gaskell* (above n 6) 246–47, and Hartley, *Charles Dickens* (above n 6) 49–50.

[8] See Uglow, *Elizabeth Gaskell* (above n 6) 246–47. For commentaries on Gaskell's interest in prostitution, and the depiction of prostitutes in her novels, see D D'Albertis, *Dissembling Fictions: Elizabeth Gaskell and the Victorian Social Text* (Macmillan, 1997) 47–56.

I wished to tell the truth, for truth always conveys its own moral to those who are able to receive it . . . Is it better to reveal the snares and pitfalls of life to the young and thoughtless traveller, or to cover them with branches and flowers?[9]

Trollope would undoubtedly have approved the aspiration, to please and to teach. Certainly there was little in *The Tenant* that was calculated to ingratiate its author with the critics; with its myriad instances of sexual and moral corruption, adultery, insinuations of rape, spousal violence, child abuse, gambling and alcoholism. Whilst Charles Kingsley admired the author's determination to expose the 'foul and accursed undercurrents' which lay beneath 'smug, respectable, whitewashed English society', the overwhelming majority shared the unalloyed horror of the reviewer in the *North American Review* who declared it a 'disgusting' novel, in which the author seemed incapable of resisting the temptation to 'degrade passion into appetite'.[10] The subject matter appeared to reinforce the author's prefatory aspiration, for which reason it might be supposed that *The Tenant* was one of those novels which Trollope would have termed, with some confidence, 'anti-sensational'. But it was also one of those which, as Trollope further advised, defy easy categorisation. A devotee of Braddon would have found much that was familiar in Anne Bronte's breathless tale of sexual corruption amongst the English aristocracy, and much to enjoy.

If they had come across her sister Charlotte's *Shirley* they would have found something rather different. But they would also have found the same kind of prefatory admonition:

If you think, from this prelude, that anything like a romance is preparing for you, reader, you were never more mistaken. Do you anticipate sentiment, and poetry, and reverie? Do you expect passion, and stimulus, and melodrama? Calm your expectations; reduce to them to a lowly standard. Something real, cool, and solid, lies before you; something unromantic as Monday morning, when all who have work wake with the consciousness that they must rise and betake themselves thereto.[11]

There is a defensive tone here as there was to so many similar admonitions. *Shirley* may have been a fiction, but it was supposed to be read as something more. The same is true of *The Tenant of Wildfell Hall*, and, as we shall see in chapter four, the same was true of *Oliver Twist*, or at least so its author claimed. In making these claims to representational truth, Dickens and the two Bronte sisters were seeking to establish themselves as realists. Definitions of the realist novel, of course, tend to be as slippery as definitions of the sensationalist, as Trollope wryly observed. Emile Zola suggested that a realist was driven to present an 'exact reproduction of life', something which necessitated the 'absence of all novelistic elements'.[12] There is, of course, an obvious paradox in deploying literature to better access something

---

[9] A Bronte, *The Tenant of Wildfell Hall* (Oxford University Press, 1993) 3–4.

[10] See I Ward, *Law and the Brontes* (Palgrave, 2012) 43–45.

[11] C Bronte, *Shirley* (Oxford University Press, 2007) 5.

[12] E Langdon, *Dirt for Art's Sake: Books on Trial from Madame Bovary to Lolita* (Cornell University Press, 2007) 24.

that might be termed the truth; one which finds famous expression in the renowned
defence of realism with which Eliot opens the second book of *Adam Bede*:

> So I am content to tell my simple story, without trying to make things seem better than
> they were; dreading nothing, indeed, but falsity, which, in spite of one's best efforts,
> there is reason to dread. Falsehood is so easy, truth so difficult . . . Examine your words
> well, and you will find that even when you have no motive to be false, it is a very hard
> thing to say the exact truth, even about your own immediate feelings much harder than
> to say something fine about them which is *not* the exact truth. (178–79)

As she contemplated embarking on *Adam Bede*, Eliot confided that she wanted
above all to represent the 'working-day business of the world'.[13] Alongside the
representation of 'this rare, precious quality of truthfulness', the realist novel commonly made claim to experiential veracity (179). 'I know that such characters do
exist', Anne Bronte urged in the Preface to the *Tenant*, making an undoubtedly
painful allusion to the disgrace of brother Branwell.[14] It was similarly implicit in
Eliot's account of the origins of *Adam Bede*, seeded in the 'suggestions of experience wrought up into new combinations' (541).[15] It was also explicit in her defence
of realism: 'I aspire to give no more than a faithful account of men and things as
they have mirrored themselves in my mind.' (177) According to Eliot, 'art' in all
its forms 'is the nearest thing to life; it is a mode of amplifying experience'.[16]

Eliot has long been critically associated with the realist novel; texts such as *Felix
Holt* and *Middlemarch* being taken to represent contributions as definitive to the
'industrial' sub-genre as the various *Scenes of Clerical Life* and *Adam Bede* are to
the 'pastoral'.[17] The latter seems, at first glance, to be rather lighter and rather more
nostalgic, full of pretty dairymaids strolling down country lanes in the dappled
sunlight; 'gilded by a sort of' ever-present 'autumn haze' as Henry James famously
put it.[18] The former, conversely, is dark and dangerous and modern, its streets
populated by heartless industrialists and seething mobs. On closer inspection,
however, they have rather more in common. Neither England is a happy England.[19]

---

[13] Ashton, *George Eliot* (above n 2) at 163.

[14] Bronte, *The Tenant of Wildfell Hall* (above n 9) 3–4.

[15] Rosemary Ashton has suggested that the *Tenant* was an immediate influence on some of Eliot's
early writings, both in terms of its realist aspiration and its subject matter, in the latter case most
obviously in regard to spousal violence. See Ashton, *George Eliot* (above n 2) 179.

[16] In 'The Natural History of German Life', published in the *Westminster Review* in July 1856, and
reprinted in G Eliot, *Selected Essays, Poems and Other Writings* (Penguin, 1990) at 110. For a comment
on Eliot's writing from 'experience', see G Beer, *George Eliot* (Harvester, 1986) 17.

[17] 'Whatever traps for the unwary lie in the term "realism"', suggests Ian Adam, 'few would quarrel
over its appropriateness for *Adam Bede*'. See his 'The Structure of Realisms in *Adam Bede*', (1975) 30
Nineteenth Century Fiction 127. On the particular place of *Adam Bede* at the centre of the 'pastoral'
realist genre, see L Berry, *The Child, the State and the Victorian Novel* (Virginia University Press, 1999)
137–40, and T Winnifrith, *Fallen Women in the Nineteenth Century Novel* (St Martin's Press, 1994) 54.

[18] H James, 'George Eliot's Life' (1885) 55 *Atlantic Monthly Magazine* 674. FR Leavis famously
concluded that Eliot's earlier pastoral novels were her 'classics', after which she merely set about
translating into fictive form her 'intellectual' preferences. See FR Leavis, *The Great Tradition* (Chatto
and Windus, 1948) 33–34.

[19] As Rosemary Ashton suggests, speaking in particular of *Adam Bede*, it is apparent that 'Rural life is
not all scenic beauty and happy families. Eden has its serpent'. See Ashton, *George Eliot* (above n 2) 201.

Moreover, both are violent; the further and important difference being that the violence in the 'pastoral' England is more likely to take place behind closed doors than out in the streets.

In correspondence with her publisher Blackwood, a young Eliot confirmed that in her opinion:

> Art must be either real or concrete, or ideal and eclectic. Both are good and true in their way, but my stories are of the former kind. I undertake to exhibit nothing as it should be; I only try to exhibit some things as they have been or are, seen through such a medium as my own nature gives me.[20]

The observation was made as Eliot defended the depiction of spousal violence in her third 'scene' of clerical life, *Janet's Repentance*. When Eliot's publisher ventured that the subject matter of *Janet's Repentance* was a bit 'Thackerayan', and that she might have been better advised to present a 'pleasanter picture', he was curtly informed that there 'is nothing to be done with the story, but either to let Dempster and Janet and the rest be as I *see* them, or to renounce it as too painful'.[21] Indeed, Eliot observed:

> Everything is softened from fact, so far as art is permitted to soften and yet to remain essentially true. The real town was more vicious than my Milby; the real Dempster was more disgusting than mine; the real Janet alas! had a far sadder end than mine, who will melt away from the reader's sight in purity, happiness and beauty.[22]

Blackwood backed off, diplomatically acknowledging that 'still it is true to nature'.[23] The readers of *Janet's Repentance* were left to contemplate one of the most resonant depictions of marital violence in nineteenth-century English literature.[24] Raising the image of Janet's mother looking down from a 'portrait' which is 'hanging over the mantelpiece' above where her daughter is being assaulted, Eliot invited her readers to wonder:

> Surely the aged eyes take on a look of anguish as they see Janet not trembling, no! it would be better if she trembled standing stupidly unmoved in her great beauty, while the heavy arm is lifted to strike her. The blow falls another and another. Surely the mother hears the cry 'O Robert! Pity! Pity!'
>
> Poor grey-haired woman! Was it for this you suffered a mother's pangs in your lone widowhood five-and-thirty years ago? Was it for this you kept the little worn morocco

---

[20] G Haight, *Letters of George Eliot* (Yale University Press, 1954/1978) 2.362.

[21] Correspondence reprinted in D Carroll (ed), *George Eliot: The Critical Heritage* (Routledge, 1971) 57–58.

[22] Ibid, 58. Dempster was based on a Nuneaton lawyer named James Buchanan. The young Marian Evans attended a school run by one of Buchanan's daughters. The same daughter was also known by one of Marian's earliest friends, Maria Lewis, from whom she learned all the grim details of the Buchanans' married life.

[23] However, Eliot, ever sensitive to criticism, never forgot his initial 'want of sympathy' for the first two parts of *Janet's Repentance*. See her journal entry reprinted in *Scenes of Clerical Life* (Penguin, 1973) at 231. For Blackwood's concession, see Carroll, *George Eliot* (above n 21) 57.

[24] For a commentary on the significance of this particular scene, see L Surridge, *Bleak Houses: Marital Violence in Victorian Fiction* (Ohio University Press, 2005) 106–109, 118.

shoes Janet had first run in, and kissed them day by day when she was away from you, a tall girl at school? Was it for this you looked proudly at her when she came back to you in her rich pale beauty, like a tall white arum that has just unfolded its grand pure curves to the sun?

The mother lies sleepless and praying in her lonely house, weeping the difficult tears of age, because she dreads this may be a cruel night for her child.

She too has a picture over her mantelpiece, drawn in chalk by Janet long years ago. She looked at it before she went to bed. It is a head bowed beneath a cross, and wearing a crown of thorns. (285)

When Eliot proclaimed that a novelist must write with 'purpose', this was the kind of purpose she had in mind; to present a realistic account of injustice and brutality which a reader could recognise and with which far too many mothers might empathise.[25] All Janet's mother can do is 'read her Bible' and worry (291). Janet, meanwhile, refuses to leave her husband, concluding that it were 'Better this misery than the blank that lay for her outside her married home' (335). Eventually, however, after months of 'blank listlessness and despair', she is thrown out of the house (333, 341–43). As she goes she carries the same stigma as Florence Dombey, and so many of her contemporaries, fictional or otherwise; a 'dark bruise on her shoulder, which ached as she dressed herself' (333).[26]

Janet Dempster was not a 'fallen' woman in the familiar sense. She did not commit adultery, but she did fall. The break-up of the marriage, the incidence of spousal violence and ultimately Janet's expulsion from the house, can all be traced to alcoholism. Dempster's 'drunken fits' are regularly reported, and it is when drunk that he assaults his wife (257, 273, 335). The supposition that alcohol was a primary cause of marital violence, especially amongst the working classes, was strongly urged by evangelists and temperance campaigners. In her 1881 essay 'Temperance in the Home', Ellen Webb suggested that it was the particular responsibility of the wife to 'purify' her home from the 'blighting' influence of drink.[27] Not only does Janet fail to purify her home, but she turns in despair to drink herself, even in recovery fearing that she might slip back into the 'paroxysm of temptation' (396).[28] Only a renewed devotion to God, it was commonly agreed,

[25] Although the 'scene' is set 60 years previously, the commentary is written in the present tense and intended to be read in the context of contemporary debates regarding the incidence of spousal violence in the England of the 1850s. The novelty of *Janet's Repentance*, like that of the violence alluded to in Anne Bronte's *The Tenant of Wildfell Hall*, lying in the fact that the abuse takes place in a middle-class home. Eliot continued to maintain that on these terms she 'had done nothing better than the writing in many parts of "Janet"'. Haight, *Letters of George Eliot* (above n 20) 3.267.

[26] It was not the only depiction of spousal violence in Eliot's fiction. There would be intimations in *Middlemarch* and then more obviously in Eliot's final novel, *Daniel Deronda*. In the latter, which clearly owed much to the influence of later sensationalist novels, most particularly those of Wilkie Collins, the abuse would be more obviously mental than physical, and no less terrifying for that. See A Dowling, 'The Other Side of Silence: Matrimonial Conflict and the Divorce Court in George Eliot's Fiction' (1995) 50 *Nineteenth Century Literature* 323–24, 331–33, and M Tromp, 'Gwendolen's Madness' in (2000) *Victorian Literature and Culture* 451–63.

[27] E Webb, 'Temperance in the Home' in S Jeffreys (ed), *The Sexuality Debates* (Routledge, 1987) 256, 258.

[28] For a commentary on the depiction of female alcoholism in *Janet's Repentance*, concluding that it 'seems almost a generic portrait' of the disease, not least in the allied presentation of drink and violence,

could save such a sinner. It saves Janet; along with the industry of Reverend Tryan, the rather more prosaic incidence of her husband dying conveniently in a riding accident, and the 'loving' embrace of an adoptive family (412).

This closing image, of Janet 'in her old age' pottering around the garden with 'children about her knees', gestures to a second thing which Janet is not; a 'natural' mother. The Victorians were fascinated with the 'cult' of motherhood, a much favoured subject of the 'domestic' novel. As we shall see, most Victorians preferred a strict, essentially jurisprudential, determination of what made a mother 'natural'. A 'natural' mother gave birth to the legitimate children of her husband. An 'unnatural' mother gave birth to other necessarily 'unnatural' kinds of children, bastards. It was, of course, a broad prejudice and there were exceptions. As we shall shortly see, readers of Elizabeth Gaskell's *Ruth* were invited to consider an alternative; that the naturalness of a mother was better adjudged in terms of the quality of her devotion, and an appreciation of her maternal responsibilities. It is this quality which makes Ruth Hilton a 'natural' mother, despite all appearances to the contrary. Indeed, it is this which saves her.

Hardwicke's Children

In 1753, Lord Chancellor Hardwicke secured the passage of his cherished Marriage Act. It was intended to address rising concerns about the apparent propensity of 'clandestine' or 'irregular' marriages; the former being marriages conducted by licensed clergy but which did not subscribe to the formal requirements written into canon law, and the latter being marriages conducted by persons who were not ordained members of the Church of England. Hardwicke's concern was primarily in regard to the former species of marriage, and was moreover essentially proprietary. As Samuel Johnson bluntly confirmed, the chastity of a woman was 'of the utmost importance, as all property depends upon it'.[29] The Act was written less to protect young lovers from themselves than to protect fathers from unwanted sons or daughters-in-law. Parental consent had always been a nominal requirement in canon law, as were the reading of banns, the licensing of clergy and the presence of witnesses. But ecclesiastical courts had long exercised its discretion to support marriages contracted *per verba de praesenti*, where despite certain formal 'irregularities', words of 'present assent' might alone be taken as sufficient evidence of matrimonial intent.[30] The 1753 Act simply confirmed that such marriages would have no force in common law.

see S Demetrakopoulos, 'George Eliot's *Janet's Repentance*: The First Literary Portrait of a Woman Addict and Her Recovery' (1993) 35 *Midwest Quarterly* 96.

[29] A Macfarlane, 'Illegitimacy and Illegitimates in English History' in P Laslett, K Oosterveen and M Smith (eds), *Bastardy and its Comparative History* (Arnold, 1980) 75.
[30] Ecclesiastical courts continued to support marriages *per verba de praesenti* in the early nineteenth century. See, for example, *Dalrymple v Dalrymple* (1811) 2 Hag.Con 54; 161 ER 665.

In such manner therefore the 1753 Act served only to increase the number of 'unlawful' marriages. The extent to which customary marriages were actually prevalent in mid and late eighteenth-century England remains a matter of dispute. However, even if the number of women wandering the shires mistakenly thinking themselves to be legally married was rather more limited than contemporaries might have supposed, the number of them wandering through the pages of the English novel was not. The case of Beatrice Brooke, the heroine of Caroline Norton's 1863 novel *Lost and Saved*, is just one of these women. Beatrice is 'lost' when she elopes with her lover Montagu Treherne to Egypt in order to get married. Though initially wary of Montagu's proposal, cautioning that they should 'do nothing wrong and rash and passionate', Beatrice is persuaded to elope (1.146, 149).[31] Arriving in Alexandria, Montagu produces a consular 'chaplain' who conducts the ceremony (1.166, 173–75, 196). Shortly afterwards, Beatrice discovers she is pregnant. On returning to England, Montagu confesses that the person who 'read the marriage ceremony' was 'not even in holy orders' (1.167). When Beatrice protests, Montagu confesses himself to be 'amazed' adding that, given the obvious inadequacies of the 'sort of ceremony' they went through, including the absence of witnesses, he had reasonably presumed that Beatrice was unconcerned that they were not, in strictly legal terms, actually married (1.267–68).[32]

Beatrice, however, stubbornly prefers to believe that she is still 'married', initially allowing herself to be deluded by 'two cheerful lies' which Montagu spins, both of which engage the kind of customary jurisprudence against which the 1753 Act was enacted.[33] The first is the thought that, despite their marriage being not 'strictly legal it seems', they were still 'as much married in the sight of Heaven' (2.67). The second is the collateral notion that theirs is one of 'hundreds of

---

[31] All internal citations are taken from C Norton, *Lost and Saved* (Hurst and Blackett, 1863).

[32] Montagu resorts to duplicity because he wishes to inherit the Treherne estates. The Treherne family settlement, however, precludes the possibility of his marrying outside a narrow kinship circle limited to full cousins. Beatrice is a half-cousin. It is a 'wilful will', as the narrator puns, set up by the 'old' Earl of Caerlaverock who, having failed to produce a son, 'in vain endeavoured to set matters right by a confused and intricate will, limiting descent of the fortune as far as he could, to any male heir who should marry out of the stock of female heirs' (1.24–25). It is written 'with every entanglement of legal terms and legal suppositions' (1.151–52). The present Earl, the brother of the 'old' Earl, has also failed to produce any sons. Thus Montagu, son the eldest of the Earl's sisters, stands to inherit both the Earldom and the estate. He will inherit the former as of right, but the latter only if he accedes to the terms of the settlement. In practice, this means that Montagu must chose from one of the five daughters of one of the other sisters, Lady Eudocia. The stipulation of such a condition in a will was not barred in common law, and nor was it uncommon. A court would only consider voiding a 'condition subsequent' written into a settlement if it was intended to prevent marriage at all, or conversely intended to encourage divorce or separation. For this reason a condition that operated to divest property on marriage could be voided in court for reason of public policy. However, conditions that simply limited prospective spouses were never declared void. See, for example, the 1807 case of *Perrin v Lyon*, which concerned a will that sought to prevent a beneficiary marrying someone born in Scotland or of Scottish parents. For a commentary on the closer legal aspects of the settlement, see I Ward, 'The Case of Beatrice Brooke: Fictions of Law and Marriage in Caroline Norton's *Lost and Saved*' (2012) 17 *Journal of Victorian Culture* 211–14.

[33] For this reason she refuses to consider marrying anyone else until Montagu is dead. As she tells her later husband: 'I believed I was his wife, as firmly as I believe there is a God! While he lives, I never can become, I never ought to become, the wife of any other man.' (3.212–13)

instances of secret marriages', the purpose of which is to sanctify before God a relationship that by reason of strict legal formality cannot as yet be observed in 'public' (2.67). The first lie engages the jurisprudence of *per verba* marriages, whilst the second introduces a clear instance of an 'irregular' marriage proscribed by the 1753 Act.[34] Beatrice's marriage is clearly in breach of the common law. As Montagu's aunt observes with disdain, she is nothing more than a 'mistress', her prospective child merely a bastard (1.292–93).

Cases of failed marriages such as Beatrice's were, of course, entirely predictable after 1753, and far from unfamiliar to eighteenth- or nineteenth-century novel readers;[35] so too were illegitimate children. For a while Beatrice thought that her child might be legitimated by some kind of after-marriage. This could not happen. Hardwicke's Act was written precisely to ensure that the sanguinary integrity of families such as the Trehernes, and the jurisprudential integrity of their settlements, could be protected from the likes of Beatrice Brooke. The consequences of this patent 'injustice', legal, moral and financial, were however dire (3.126, 177). Scripture advised that the illegitimate child would be born 'wild' and should be 'cast out'.[36] The common law did its best to oblige. Illegitimate children, as Blackstone's *Commentaries* confirmed, were declared *filius nullius* in regard to property law. They could 'inherit nothing, being looked upon as the son of nobody . . . incapable even of a gift from parents'.[37] However, it was the financial consequences that were most significant. Bastards needed feeding, as did their mothers.[38] Moreover, the situation, as any Malthusian would have known, was only going to get worse. Joseph Townsend had brought the scriptural and the utilitarian proscription into an unlikely affinity in 1783, when he concluded that 'no human efforts' would be able to improve the lot of the poor. Only starvation could induce 'sobriety, diligence and fidelity'.[39]

At the beginning of the nineteenth century, financial provision for the 'evils' of bastardy was still defined by Elizabethan common law which placed responsibility for bastard children with fathers, who could be either compelled to marry the mother of his child, or alternatively, to pay maintenance for a period of seven years. Critics had long argued the case for reform, suggesting that the law represented a charter for scheming young women to seduce gullible young men into

---

[34] The 1823 Marriage Act confirmed that if any party acted 'knowingly and wilfully' in breach of the 1753 Act, the marriage was automatically rendered void. Montagu was only too knowing and wilful.

[35] See L Zunshine, *Bastards and Foundlings: Illegitimacy in Eighteenth Century England* (Ohio State University Press, 2005) 8–9, referring to their 'casual ubiquity' in the literature of the period.

[36] Genesis 16:12 and Galatians 4:21–31. The prohibition was reinforced in Deuteronomy 23:2, 'No bastard shall enter the assembly of the Lord'. For a commentary on the scriptural proscription, see J Witte, 'Ishmael's bane: the sin and crime of illegitimacy reconsidered' (2003) 5 *Punishment and Society* 329–31.

[37] W Blackstone, *Commentaries* vol 1 (London, 1828) 434.

[38] The extent to which illegitimacy rates were rising remains somewhat uncertain. For conflicting views, see L Cody, 'The Politics of Illegitimacy in an Age of Reform: Women, Reproduction, and Political Economy in England's New Poor Law of 1834' (2000) 11 *Journal of Women's History* 136, suggesting a 'noticeable rise', and G Frost, 'The Black Lamb of the Black Sheep: Illegitimacy in the English Working Class' (2003) 37 *Journal of Social History* 295, arguing to the contrary.

[39] A Briggs, *The Age of Improvement* (Longmans, 1959) 16, 279–80.

agreeing to punitive maintenance arrangements or even marriage. A Royal Commission, appointed in 1833 to consider the case for reform, agreed, concluding that existing provision served only to encourage 'immoral' habits, inciting perjury, promoting improvident marriages, and above all doing nothing to 'prevent' the excesses of rampant female sexuality.[40] Lewd women were the 'pests of society', for which reason the law should be written to reflect the injunctions of scripture, for a bastard is 'what Providence appears to have ordained that it should be, a burthen on its mother, and, where she cannot maintain it, on her parents'.[41]

The result was the enactment in 1834 of a new Poor Law, praised by Edwin Chadwick as the 'first great piece of legislation based upon scientific or economical principles'.[42] It repealed existing statutory provision which authorised magistrates to levy maintenance against fathers, and enacted new 'bastardy clauses' which shifted financial responsibility to mothers who, if they could not support themselves and their children, must seek recourse to newly established Boards of Guardians now empowered to regulate admittance to the union workhouse. The enactment was intended to ensure efficiency savings, to extend the supervisory reach of government officials and with a bit of luck prevent illicit sex. In practice, of course, it was as likely to encourage promiscuous men as discourage promiscuous women. The new law quickly attracted renewed criticism: from many Tories who saw the imposition of deputy Commissioners as an affront to local autonomy; from a fair number of utilitarians who worried that the new system was proving to be no less expensive than the one it replaced; and from a few higher-minded critics such as Cobbett and Dickens who suggested that it was simply wrong. In 1844 the so-called 'little' Poor Law moved procedural responsibility once again, this time to the civil courts, whilst also enabling mothers to apply to Petty Sessions for maintenance orders against named fathers.[43]

Just a year earlier in 1843, a heavily pregnant Jessie Phillips sought admittance to the Deepbrook Union Poorhouse. Jessie was the eponymous heroine of Frances Trollope's *Jessie Phillips*, another poetic angel whose fall was precipitated by a mistaken belief that she was legally married, at least in the 'eyes of God'.[44] The scenario is familiar. Jessie is 'passionately' in love with Frederic Dalton, the son of the local squire. Any possibility of marriage, however, is precluded by the terms of the

---

[40] Introducing the new Bill in the House of Lords, Lord Althorp preferred to think of it as a matter of protecting women against the 'frailty' of their sex, against indeed their 'own passions'. See Cody, 'Politics of Illegitimacy' (above n 38) 133 and 139, and U Henriques, 'Bastardy and the New Poor Law' (1967) 37 *Past and Present* 106–107, commenting on the conclusions of the Report.

[41] *Report from Her Majesty's Commissioners for Inquiring into the Administration and Practical Operation of the Poor Laws* (Fellowes, 1834) 530. For a commentary, see Cody, 'Politics of Illegitimacy' (above n 38) 132, quoting the evidence of Edward Tregaskis as regards the 'pests of society' in the Appendix to the *Report*.

[42] Chadwick was Secretary to the Commission.

[43] Provided there was corroborative evidence of paternal identity. Maintenance was limited to 10 shillings for the midwife, and 2 shillings and 6 pence a week until the child was 13 years of age.

[44] See K Kalsem, *In Contempt: Nineteenth Century Women, Law and Literature* (Ohio University Press, 2012) 52–53 suggesting that Jessie is 'the embodiment' of the kind of young woman whose 'haunting presence' is raised by the 1753 Act.

Dalton family settlement which would disinherit Frederic if he fails to secure parental approval for his marriage (109, 112).[45] Jessie, a humble needlewoman, does not question whether she might have secured such approval but she agrees to sexual intercourse, and predictably enough becomes pregnant. At this point, with an equal predictability, Frederic loses interest in her. Jessie is left to console herself with the thought that

> she was not in reality degraded; for truly did the deluded girl believe that the vows she had exchanged with Frederic Dalton were as sacred in his eyes as in her own, and that she was in spirit and in truth his wedded wife, although the ceremony which was to proclaim their union to the world was delayed till it could take place without injury to the interests of her betrothed husband. (199)

Jessie Phillips is another of Hardwicke's jurisprudential progeny, as is her bastard child. Like Beatrice Brooke, Jessie was seduced into thinking that she was properly 'affianced' in the eyes of God, if not the eyes of the law, only slowly coming to realise that she is, instead, a 'fallen' woman (252).[46] It is only when Frederic confirms that he has no intention of honouring their 'conditional promise' and instead offers her ten pounds that the prostituted Jessie realises that she has been 'deluded' (267, 276). She has no greater claim to his support. The precariousness of her situation was confirmed by the complementary statutory jurisprudence of 1753 and 1834. Prior to 1834 she would have been able to name Frederic as the father and make a claim for maintenance. But this is no longer the case as Frederic gleefully notes, 'thanks to our noble law-givers there is no more swearing away a gentleman's incognito now'. It is 'just one of my little bits of good luck that this blessed law should be passed precisely when it was likely to be more beneficial to me' (108). The law was written to protect men like Frederic Dalton; just as it was written to condemn women like Jessie Phillips.[47]

This view is confirmed by the local solicitor, Lewis, when Frederic seeks to thwart Jessie's threat to expose him. The 'admirable' new bastardy clause exists, Lewis reassures him, 'exactly to render such attempts utterly harmless and abortive' (394).[48] He observes that the law is as strong as that 'which awards hanging for murder' (394–95). When Jessie arrives shortly afterwards, she is left in no doubt of her powerlessness:

[45] Frances Trollope, *Jessie Phillips*, (Nonsuch, 2006), Frederic has reason to be concerned, knowing that his grandfather would anyway prefer to re-assign the settlement in favour of his sister Ellen (30). There is no evidence that Norton drew on the plotline of *Jessie Phillips* when she came to devise the Treherne settlement in *Lost and Saved*. The function of the respective settlements, in terms of limiting matrimonial options, is nevertheless striking.

[46] Her realisation is reinforced when she is obviously pregnant and the local ladies decide not to give her any more work mending dresses. It is at this point that Jessie realises that she has indeed 'fallen' into an 'abyss' (256).

[47] For a commentary on Trollope's indictment of the 'bastardy clauses', see H Heineman, 'Frances Trollope's *Jessie Phillips*: Sexual Politics and the New Poor Law' (1978) 1 *International Journal of Women's Studies* 99–101.

[48] Lewis repeats the advice in very similar terms to the Reverend Rimmington. The 'incalculable benefit of the clause' is precisely to 'prevent this sort of damsel from picking and choosing a papa for her precious offspring from amongst all the lords of creation, from the prince to the peasant' (453).

It does seem pretty nearly impossible, to be sure, that, after all the pains taken by the government to make the law as plain as plain can be, that anybody should *really* misunderstand it. However, whether the ignorance is make-believe or not makes no difference in my readiness to speak out upon the subject, and I, therefore, tell you, my girl, that you may stand all day swearing that one man or another man is the father of your child, and no more notice will be taken of it than if you whistled. (396)

Jessie is a 'hussy' who 'snapped her fingers at the law' (449) but the law offers her nothing so it makes no difference whether the 'father be a king or a cobbler' (397). Even so, the law can only protect Frederic up to a point. It cannot secure him against the risk of public humiliation or the loss of a prospective attractive match. Frederic hopes that his next conquest will be the altogether richer and more suitable Martha Maxwell. Martha, however, is well aware of Frederic's history and his failings, and under the pretence of agreeing to elope, she persuades him to sign a blank 'written promise' to marry, with the intention of inscribing his name and that of Jessie (246).[49] The document has no legal force but Frederic becomes increasingly troubled by Martha's apparent unwillingness to return the 'pledge' and by the prospective consequences of public exposure (272). Critics were appalled by Martha's 'scheming'; far more, predictably enough, than they were by Frederic's.[50]

The broader purpose of Trollope's novel was to critique the 1834 Poor Law; for which reason critics have long read *Jessie Phillips* as a contribution to the 'condition of England' genre. In an early exchange, the Deepbrook Board wonder if the best strategy for mitigating the effects of a 'law so infernally bad' is to simply 'evade it' (86–87). The loudest protest is made, unsurprisingly, by Mr Lewis, a very 'positive' lawyer (90). It does not matter whether the law is good or bad although Lewis, needless to say, thinks the 1834 Act a thoroughly good thing. It is simply 'the LAW sir', and the 'law is law', for which reason it is best left to lawyers to 'reason' (129, 181–82).[51] Similarly, large tracts of *Jessie Phillips* are given over to impressing just how grim life in the poorhouse 'prison' might be (37).[52] Governed by men but populated almost exclusively by women, the poorhouse will punish Jessie, shame her and imprison her precisely because she is a woman. It will make her wear the 'hateful livery of crime' (293). It will cut her hair. It will discipline her. It will scrutinise her regulation and prescribe the terms of her reformation, if not

[49] It is to Martha that a desperate Jessie first relates the circumstances of her 'painful narrative' though Martha had already suspected the truth (266–68). Ultimately, Martha wants to 'terrify' Frederic into 'providing' for Jessie (314). She succeeds in terrifying him, but the offer of provision extends only so far as the casual tossing of another sovereign (387).

[50] The reviewer in the *Athenaeum* took especial exception to the 'scheming' Martha. See Kalsem, *In Contempt* (above n 44) 57.

[51] Adding that as one of the 'most complex and difficult' laws 'ever framed' it is not susceptible to the 'common usage and common sense' of 'every man' (182). The observation rather undercuts Lewis's later berating of Jessie for not understanding bastardy law provisions.

[52] It was intended to be like a prison. The Royal Commission accepted the 'penitential' principle that the best way of encouraging people to leave and find work was for life inside the poorhouse to be more grim than life outside.

her redemption. When she first appears before the Board, Jessie is subject to a 'silent examination' before falling quite literally 'prostrate upon the floor' (289). Ultimately, Jessie is 'doomed', broken by the law of 1834 just as her fall was caused by the law of 1753.

Unsurprisingly, contemporary critics were appalled by *Jessie Phillips*. Whilst the *New Monthly Magazine* grudgingly admitted that 'Mrs Trollope' was possessed of a 'bold and unflinching hand', the *Spectator* disparaged an 'appeal to the vulgar prejudices and vulgar cant which animate the ignorant and narrow-minded of every grade'.[53] The reviewer in *John Bull* was of a similar opinion, concluding that *Jessie Phillips* 'sinned grievously against good taste and decorum'.[54] The reviewer in the *Athenaeum* took the opportunity to make a broader swipe at the presumptions of writers who believed that their business was 'truth-telling'.[55] Certainly, Trollope was another author motivated by a desire to 'tell the truth'. The story of Jessie Phillips, as the final passages confirmed, was written to illustrate the particular iniquity of a law which was plainly 'deficient in legislative morality' (541). The extent to which it was successful must remain a matter of conjecture. But Rosina Bulwer was in no doubt. When the 1834 Act was repealed a few months after the publication of *Jessie Phillips* she proclaimed her friend to be a 'pioneer of feminism'.[56]

R v Sorrel

Jessie Phillips is not only concerned with the legal construction, and exclusion, of fallen women and their illegitimate progeny. The plot is twisted further by the murder of Jessie's baby and her subsequent prosecution for infanticide. Infanticide was commonly perceived to be the most 'unnatural' of the many crimes written into the narrative of the fallen woman. *Jessie Phillips* is clearly intended to question that assumption; intimating that it is hardly surprising that such women might contemplate killing their children, and hardly surprising that her neighbours can be persuaded that she has.[57] The owner of the barn in which the baby's body is found immediately assumes that the 'horrid deed' must have been committed by its 'unnatural mother' (446).[58] The affinity may indeed be troubling, but it 'has

---

[53] (1843) 19 *New Monthly Magazine* 282, and 16 *Spectator*, 1843, 17–18.

[54] *John Bull*, 18 November 1843, no 23, 732.

[55] *Athenaeum*, 28 October 1843, 956.

[56] See Heineman, 'Sexual Politics' (above n 47) at 102 and 105, and K.Kelsem, *In Contempt: Women, Law and Literature* (Ohio State University Press, 2012), 65.

[57] An insinuation commonly cast in contemporary reform literature. See G Behlmer, 'Deadly Motherhood: Infanticide and Medical Opinion in Mid-Victorian England' (1979) 34 *Journal of the History of Medicine and Allied Sciences* 417–19.

[58] For this reason she will not 'escape a hanging' (415). The 'case of murder', according to the governor of Deepbrook workhouse is as 'clear as a pikestaff' (419). Thomas Carlyle, in typically obtuse tones, invited readers to contemplate the inevitability of desperate mothers killing their newborn children in his essay on the notorious *Sandys* case in 1843, which questioned what else starving parents

enough of truth and practical wisdom' to be placed before readers 'honest enough' to appreciate its veracity (326).

In time Jessie is discovered to be innocent, but not before she has been tried and condemned. Here, accordingly, alongside the Acts of 1753 and 1834, Trollope insinuates the engendered injustice of a third statute, Lord Ellenborough's Act of 1803. The 1803 Act repealed the provision in the 1623 Infanticide Act, which held that if a 'lewd' woman:

> Be delivered of any issue of her body, male or female, which being born alive, should by the laws of this realm be a bastard, and that she endeavour privately, either by drowning or secret burying thereof, or any other way, either by herself or the procuring of others, so to conceal the death thereof, as that it may not come to light, whether it were born alive or not, but be concealed; in every such case the said mother so offending shall suffer death as in the case of murther, except such mother make proof by one witness at least, that the child (whose death was by her so intended to be concealed) was born dead.[59]

Lord Ellenborough's Act was intended to address the fact that juries had become increasingly reluctant to send young women to the gallows on the basis of this provision. There were simply too many variables.[60] The 1803 Act, accordingly, introduced a new offence, again specific to unmarried mothers, of concealment of birth.[61] However it had little effect. Between 1840 and 1860 there were 60 concealment prosecutions at the Old Bailey. Each one ended in acquittal. Writing in the *Saturday Review* in 1856, the Reverend William Scott bemoaned the fact that juries 'will not convict under any circumstances'. Using the particular example of Celestine Sumner, prosecuted and acquitted at Dorchester Assizes earlier that year, Scott reported that the verdict had been met with a round of applause, whilst young females who had attended court in support were heard to go out into the street boasting that 'now they may do what they liked'.[62] On the rare occasion that a woman was convicted of concealment, her sentence was more likely to be counted in months than in years.[63] Similarly, in the exceptional event of a woman

were supposed to do with the children they could not feed. See J Flanders, *The Invention of Murder* (Harper Press, 2011) 231.

[59] 21 James 1, c.27, 1623.

[60] The most common difficulties were in regard to proving premeditation and intent, uncertainty as to the verification of 'live-birth', and disputed claims to accidental death, particularly in cases of possible umbilical strangulation.

[61] 43 Geo III, c.58. The law was amended in 1826 so as to permit separate concealment prosecutions, and then two years later, in the Offences Against the Person Act of 1828, in order to extend criminal liability to all mothers, whether or not married. The 1861 Offences Against the Person Act developed the law further to extend the offence of concealment to any person involved in the act.

[62] C Krueger, *Reading for the Law: British Literary History and Gender Advocacy* (Virginia University Press, 2010) 221–22.

[63] See M Arnot, 'Understanding women committing newborn child murder in Victorian England' in S D'Cruze (ed), *Everyday Violence in Britain 1850–1950: Gender and Class* (Pearson, 2000) 56–57, and A Higginbotham, 'Sin of the Age: Infanticide and Illegitimacy in Victorian London' (1989) 32 *Victorian Studies* 327–28, quoting one Scottish judge who commented that the new concealment charge merely served as a means of 'bringing within the reach of the criminal law a few women who have improperly escaped the graver charge of intentionally killing the child'.

being convicted of murder, customary recommendations for mercy invariably secured a reprieve from the Home Secretary. Between 1849 and 1864 all 31 women convicted of child-murder in England were reprieved on the basis of temporary insanity; something which led William Acton to muse doubtfully on the merit of such a 'merciful legal fiction'.[64]

As the century progressed, infanticide 'scares' jostled for space alongside the myriad other scares of the period. There was, Parliament was informed, a public perception that 'child murder was going on to a frightful, to an enormous, a perfectly incredible extent'.[65] In late 1860, the Middlesex coroner, Edwin Lankester, advised the Home Secretary that the incidence of child-murder had increased fourfold over the previous 12 months, and suggested that in excess of 12,000 children had been killed in London alone in recent years.[66] The medical profession was vocal in its anxiety; implicitly critical of the apparent inability of the law to address the incidence of infanticide. An editorial in *The Lancet* concluded that the mortality rate in England in 1858 'out Herods Herod'.[67] Chadwick, writing in 1860, suggested that the 'infantile death rate' was the 'best single test of the sanitary condition' of any 'place or population'.[68] By this measure mid-Victorian England was in a sorry state indeed. Something, it was generally agreed, had to be done. The 1866 Royal Commission on Capital Punishment suggested that there should be a separate crime of infanticide which, whilst a type of murder, would not carry a capital conviction. Fitzjames Stephens approved, observing that 'the crime itself is less serious than other kinds of murder', adding in bluntly utilitarian terms: 'You cannot estimate the loss to the child itself, you know nothing about it.'[69] A little later the *Pall Mall Gazette* agreed that infanticide was not 'quite' murder.[70]

Popular anxiety was not, however, readily assuaged by jurisprudential contemplation. The *Morning Star* concluded that infanticide had become a 'national institution' and the *Daily Telegraph* agreed that it had become the 'absolute custom among English society of the present day'.[71] Not to be outdone, the *Saturday Review* suggested that it heralded the collapse of 'society', whilst the *Pall Mall Gazette* took particular exception to the thought that foreigners were stigmatising the English as a 'nation of infanticides'.[72] Popular newspapers meanwhile seized on

---

[64] Behlmer, 'Deadly Motherhood' (above n 57) 413.

[65] Evidence given in Parliament in 1844. Lankester and his predecessor, Thomas Wakley, were at the forefront of campaigns designed to awaken Londoners to the apparent prevalence of infanticide particularly amongst the working classes. See Behlmer, 'Deadly Motherhood' (above n 57) 407–10.

[66] Ibid, 404, and Higginbotham, 'Sin of the Age' (above n 63) 319.

[67] The editorial concluded that the reason lay in an 'injurious excess' of wet-nursing, a lack of cow's milk and a more general ignorance of proper infant feeding. See Behlmer, 'Deadly Motherhood' (above n 57) 403, and Krueger, *Reading for the Law* (above n 62) 228–31.

[68] E Chadwick, 'Address on public health' in *Transactions of the National Association for the Promotion of Social Science* (1860) at 580, quoted in Behlmer, 'Deadly Motherhood' (above n 57) 403.

[69] Evidence to the Royal Commission, quoted in Higginbotham, 'Sin of the Age' (above n 63) 351.

[70] Quoted in Flanders, *The Invention of Murder* (above n 58) 224.

[71] See T Ward, 'Legislating for human nature: legal responses to infanticide 1860–1938' in M Jackson (ed), *Infanticide: Historical Perspectives on Child Murder and Concealment 1550–2000* (Ashgate, 2002) 253, and Behlmer, 'Deadly Motherhood' (above n 57) 405 and 422–25.

[72] See Behlmer, 'Deadly Motherhood' (above n 57) 406.

the subject, titillating their readers with increasingly gruesome accounts of alleged child-murders, invariably casting the aspersion that infanticide was a crime prevalent amongst unmarried working-class mothers. In his 1862 study 'Infanticide' Dr Burke Ryan invoked 'the feeble wail of murdered childhood', inviting his readers to take a grimly evocative tour of their neighbourhood, and their neighbour's homes:

> But turn where we may, still we are met by the evidence of a wide spread crime. In the quiet of the bedroom we raise the box-lid, and the skeletons are there. In the calm evening walk we see in the distance a suspicious-looking bundle, the mangled infant within. By the canal side, or in the water, we find the dead child. In the solitude of the wood we are horrified by the ghastly sight; and if we betake ourselves to the rapid rail in order to escape the pollution, we find at our journey's end that the smouldering remains of a murdered innocent have been our travelling companion; and that the odour from that unsuspected parcel truly indicates what may be found within.[73]

Unsurprisingly, literary narratives of infanticide became increasingly popular. *Jessie Phillips* was one; Sir Walter Scott's *The Heart of Midlothian*, published a couple of decades earlier in 1818, another. The most influential, however, and certainly the most widely-read was *Adam Bede*. It is evident that Scott's novel was in Eliot's mind as she composed *Adam Bede*. It is possible that Trollope's novel was too. Wordsworth's poem 'The Thorn' was another very obvious influence, Eliot choosing the same 'pastoral' setting for Hetty Sorrel so that she too might gesture to the allied images of nature and innocence, and corruption. Other obvious literary influences include Elizabeth Barrett Browning's *Aurora Leigh*, which Eliot had just finished reading as she began to sketch out *Adam Bede*, and very probably Gaskell's *Ruth*, against which it is often suggested Eliot perceived herself to be writing. As the story of Hetty Sorrel began to take shape in her mind, Eliot also re-read Southey's admired *Life of Wesley*. This does not, of course, preclude the possibility that Eliot drew on contemporary accounts of infanticide cases, or diminish the impact of Aunt Samuel's hearthside chat. The story of Hetty Sorrel owes something to each of these.

As we have already noted, *Adam Bede* was originally conceived as the fourth 'clerical tale'. It quickly assumed greater proportions, but it remained, in many ways, a clerical tale. Scriptural allusions are common, while tensions between Anglican, evangelical and dissenting theology would have had, for Eliot's readers at least, a certain familiarity.[74] There is also the figure of the saintly Dinah, a Methodist lay-preacher. It is Dinah who hears Hetty's confession. The eponymous Adam, thinking himself to be in love, has long supposed that he would marry the 'distractingly pretty' Hetty (84). However, Hetty, possessed of a 'foolish' heart,

---

[73] W Ryan, 'Infanticide: the law, prevalence, prevention and history' (John Churchill, 1862) 45–46. See McDonagh, 'Child-Murder Narratives' (above n 3) 233 on the 'Gothic' nature of Ryan's account, and Berry, *The Child* (above n 17) 131, arguing that it is best read as a piece of 'sensation' fiction.

[74] See W McKelvey, *The English Cult of Literature: Devoted Readers 1774–1880* (Virginia University Press, 2007) 225–27, venturing the thought that it was with *Adam Bede* that Eliot summoned up the courage to put into literary form her emergent idea of an alternative 'religion of humanity'.

agrees to a series of trysts in the Chase and is, with a due sense of inevitability, seduced by the 'good natured' but irresolute Arthur Donnithorne, son of the local squire (97, 124, 128–30).With a like inevitability, Hetty finds herself pregnant and alone. In 'great dread' she runs after Arthur who has joined the army, only to find that he has gone to Ireland. Terrified of having to enter a workhouse, Hetty 'must wander on and on', eventually giving birth to a child whom she then abandons at the roadside (364, 391). The body of the baby is discovered, and so in time is Hetty, who is accused of infanticide, tried and convicted, and sentenced to be hanged. Finally, Arthur partially redeems himself by securing Hetty's reprieve, which arrives just as she is about to mount the gallows.[75]

The setting of the novel in 1799 is significant insofar as Hetty would have been tried for infanticide under the provisions of the 1623 Act. If it had been after 1803, she might have been prosecuted instead for concealment. Under the 1623 Act, the burden of proof lies with Hetty. She must prove that she did not kill her baby. It is for this reason that her lawyer summons a witness to testify to the fact that Hetty had been seen walking away from her baby whilst it was still crying. Unfortunately, the image of Hetty abandoning a baby who was evidently not stillborn creates a negative impression in the mind of the jury. Her lawyer might have sought recourse to the strategy adopted by Jessie Phillips's lawyer; to plead 'moral' insanity. It was commonly recommended and commonly successful. Yet Hetty's lawyer prefers 'quarrelling with the other lawyers' and neglects to adopt the same strategy (429). At first glance it might be thought that the facts of Hetty's case did not anyway lend themselves to an insanity defence. There is no evidence that Hetty was particularly disturbed when she walked away from her baby. There was certainly no momentary loss of the senses. Her behaviour appears to be entirely within character. Yet her behaviour was also a reaction consistent with emergent medical opinion in regard to puerperal insanity; the 'impulse to destroy' which according to the noted physician James Reid in 1848 was in constant conflict with 'maternal tenderness'.[76] The abandonment of babies, as the eminent psychiatrist Thomas Clouston confirmed a little later, was again entirely consonant with the depressive 'antipathy' which could easily overcome new mothers, especially those who felt isolated and abandoned.[77]

The broader thesis, that new mothers were particularly susceptible to associated pregnancy trauma, might also have served to explain Hetty's attitude in court. The appearance of defendants, particularly female ones, could easily prejudice a nineteenth-century court in the same way as it could prejudice a nineteenth-

---

[75] See Jones, 'The Usual Sad Catastrophe' (above n 3) 312, noting the incongruity of such a melodramatic scene in a novel which was otherwise determinedly realist. As we have already noted, it would have been extraordinary if Hetty had not secured a reprieve.

[76] Quoted in H Marland, 'Getting away with murder? Puerperal insanity, infanticide and the defence plea' in M Jackson (ed), *Infanticide: Historical Perspectives on Child Murder and Concealment* (Ashgate, 2002) 175–76, who concludes at 189, that by the mid-eighteenth century most psychiatrists and childbirth specialists viewed puerperal insanity as a 'normal side-effect of giving birth'.

[77] Ibid, 176.

century novel reader.[78] When Hetty stands trial for infanticide, it is clear that she is condemned as much for what she does not do as for what it is thought that she probably did. Hetty does not emote, at least not enough, merely hiding 'her face in her hands' and remaining in 'obstinate' denial of ever having given birth; an attitude which can only 'make against her with the jury' (429–30). The 'sympathy of the court', the narrator confirms, 'was not with the prisoner: the unnaturalness of her crime stood out the more harshly by the side of her hard immovability and obstinate silence' (438). It is for this reason that the jury decides exceptionally not to make a recommendation for mercy, leaving Arthur to redeem himself, at least modestly, by pleading Hetty's case in London.

By the middle of the century it was recognised that women such as Hetty may have failed to respond to accusations of infanticide because they were in a state of trauma-induced denial.[79] In such a circumstance legal proceedings would have barely registered; at least until the dramatic moment when sentence is passed. At this point Hetty, like Jessie Phillips, shrieks before collapsing to the floor. The ritual of sentencing was, of course, intended to serve precisely this purpose. Women convicted of child-murder, as we have already noted, were never actually executed but it was at least satisfying to terrify them out of their wits. Eliot does not impugn the judgement of the court, perfunctory though it seems, but her depiction of its proceedings does not flatter. The court is 'dusty', its rituals pompous, its lawyers pedantic and indifferent (432, 437). There is little prospect here of accessing some deeper truth as regards the nature or extent of Hetty's criminal responsibility, and no real ambition to do so either.[80] Hetty is reduced to the incidental in her own trial, listening to lawyers and witnesses fashion alternative narratives of her crime, whilst 'foolish women in their fine clothes' gossip in the gallery (429). When she fails to enter a plea, the court enters one for her. It is a dramatic event in which the lead character has no lines.

Hetty's silence, of course, serves a larger poetic purpose; one that is hardly unfamiliar in Eliot's work. Janet Dempster is silenced too, as is Gwendolen Grandcourt, the similarly abused wife in *Daniel Deronda*. It is only after the trial is completed that Hetty finds a voice, confessing all to Dinah in much the same way as Mary Voce confessed to Aunt Samuel and her companions. Even then, the confession is decidedly ambiguous, Hetty admitting in terms which to many readers might have served only to validate the court's decision, that the baby felt 'like a heavy weight round my neck', before confirming that 'I seemed to hate it' (453–54).[81] Once again, however, a medical reader might have reached a different conclusion.

[78] See L Zedner, *Women, Crime and Custody in Victorian England* (Oxford University Press, 1991) at 30, arguing that 'descriptions of women's crime, frequently referred to past conduct, marital status, protestations of regret, or shamelessness, and even to the woman's physical appearance'.

[79] Arnot, 'Understanding women' (above n 63) 62, and Marland, 'Puerperal insanity' (above n 76) 172, quoting Robert Gooch, an early expert on puerperal insanity, arguing in 1829 that 'there is no time' in the process of child-birth and its immediate aftermath, 'at which the mind may not become disordered'.

[80] The jury takes 'hardly more than a quarter of an hour' to reach its verdict (437).

[81] See J Schramm, *Testimony and Advocacy in Victorian Law, Literature and Theology* (Cambridge University Press 2000) 138.

Where the law saw an 'unnatural' mother slaying her child without compunction, the psychiatrist might recognise an isolated and depressed, and more often than not impoverished, young woman disassociating herself from the source of her distress.[82] Dinah sees this and for this reason it is tempting to think that Eliot might also have done so. There again, it is clear that Eliot did not much like Hetty, still less the excessive sexuality to which she fell prey.

Eliot did like *Adam Bede* though, declaring, perhaps mindful of the rather mixed reviews which attended the publication of her *Scenes of Clerical Life*, 'I love it very much and am deeply thankful to have written it, whatever the public may say of it' (543). As the plot took shape, Blackwood had voiced the hope that things would 'not come to the usual sad catastrophe', seduction, illegitimacy and infanticide.[83] When they did, Eliot defended herself in the same way as she had in the case of *Janet's Repentance*. 'What girl of twelve', she inquired by return, 'was ever injured by the *Heart of Midlothian*?'[84] In fact, there was no reason to worry. Dickens was quick to attest his admiration, particularly for the 'extraordinarily subtle and true' characterisation of Hetty.[85] Even Queen Victoria expressed her approval of such a 'clever' book, commissioning Edward Henry Corbould to paint two of her favourite scenes; rather incongruously scenes of Dinah preaching and Hetty making butter.[86]

More importantly, the literary reviews approved. They liked the Wordsworthian resonance, and accepted the claim to experiential veracity. The *Athenaeum*, always one of the toughest nuts to crack, admired a 'story' that is 'not a story but a true account of a place and people who have really lived'. That 'everything happened as here set down', its reviewer concluded, 'we have no doubt in the world'.[87] According to *Bentley's Quarterly Review*, the story of Hetty Sorrel will seem to 'readers who welcome it as the voice of their own experience in sense no other book has ever been'.[88] 'There can be no mistake about *Adam Bede*', ES Dallas concluded in *The Times*: 'It is a first-rate novel, and its author takes rank at once among the masters of the art.'[89] Whilst a few chafed at the insinuations of illicit sex in the Chase, they appreciated the didactic tone and the injunctions to 'preserve' the reader from 'being the beginners of such misery' (391).[90] They liked the Reverend Irwine

---

[82] On the ready affinity in the medical literature between isolation, depression and poverty, see Marland, 'Puerperal insanity' (above n 76) 183–84.

[83] L Rodensky, *The Crime in Mind: Criminal Responsibility and the Victorian Novel* (Oxford University Press, 2003) 124.

[84] The reference was, of course, to the case of Effie Deans written into Scott's *Heart of Midlothian*. Blackwood remained squeamish, and as a consequence decided against serialisation. Instead, Eliot accepted an offer of £800 for four years copyright and the novel appeared in volume form.

[85] He also urged Eliot to contribute to *Household Words*. Letter reprinted in Carroll, *George Eliot* (above n 21) 84–85.

[86] See Ashton, *George Eliot* (above n 2) 213.

[87] G Jewsbury, *Athenaeum*, 26 February 1859, 284.

[88] *Bentley's Quarterly Review*, July 1859, i.433–56. The reviewer was Anne Mozley.

[89] *The Times*, 12 April 1859, 5. Dallas was not alone in preferring to make a favourable comparison with Thackeray. Where Thackeray liked to impute that all his countrymen and women had an 'evil corner', the author of *Adam Bede* was 'good enough to tell us that we all have a remnant of Eden in us'.

[90] There were one or two exceptions, most notably the *Saturday Review* which regretted a lack of

reminding Arthur of the 'terrible consequences' that might flow from unchecked passion; even if his advice went unheeded (171). They even approved his later jurisprudential caution as to those consequences, and the imputation in regard to Arthur's culpability:

> It is not for us men to apportion the shares of moral guilt and retribution . . . The evil consequences that may lie folded in a single act of selfish indulgence, is a thought so awful that it ought surely to awaken some feeling less presumptuous than a rash desire to punish. (424–25)

The critics liked *Adam Bede* for the same reason that they would welcome *East Lynne* a few months later. In summary, they admired its purpose, accepted its premise, and they applauded its resolution.[91] The narrative of Hetty Sorrel lost none of its currency either. The subject of infanticide remained a matter of concern throughout much of the nineteenth century; a contributory reason, perhaps, for its enduring commercial success.[92] *Adam Bede* sold well throughout the 1860s, by which time the original infanticide 'scare' had transmuted into an adjacent baby-farming 'scare'; the belief, generated by a handful of eagerly reported legal cases, that vast numbers of unmarried mothers were paying baby-farmers to take their children on the pretence of having them adopted, but in the knowledge that they would be strangled, placed in card-boxes and dumped in a nearby river.[93]

The Lost and the Saved

The demise of Hetty Sorrel, a thorough 'little villain' according to Blackwood, did not stir much critical sympathy, any more perhaps than it did the sympathy of her

---

depth in the character of Hetty, and the 'sham legal excitement' that the author thought fit to include. *Saturday Review*, 26 February 1859, 250–51. However, they were exceptions. See K Flint, *The Woman Reader 1837–1914* (Oxford University Press, 1993) 146, suggesting that the presentation of Hetty was deemed to be at a sufficient 'social distance' to be perceived as unthreatening.

[91] They also expended considerable critical energy, and ink, on trying to guess the gender of the author. Dickens immediately 'nailed' his 'colours to the mast' and declared it to be a woman. ES Dallas was equally sure; others were less so. See Beer, *George Eliot* (above n 16) 59–60.

[92] In commercial terms, *Adam Bede* was Eliot's most successful novel. Mudie's Library, critically, decided to adopt the title, ordering 500 copies at 10% discount. Three thousand copies were sold in the first three months, 15,000 by the end of the year.

[93] The most notorious of these cases were those involving Charlotte Winsor in 1865 and Margaret Waters in 1870. In the later case, the coroner's inquiry initially brought in a verdict of manslaughter, but following agitation in the press, Waters was prosecuted for murder in the Crown Court, convicted and hanged. According to an editorial in *The Times*, 'manslaughter' was far too 'mild' an 'expression' for such a crime. Following the *Waters* case, Parliament passed the Infant Life Protection Act in 1872, which required the registration of all births and deaths, and the registration and supervision of all 'lying-in' houses and baby-farms. It did not, however, provide any credible means of supervising the supervision; for this reason the Act is generally viewed as having been yet another failed legal intervention. For a comprehensive commentary on the baby-farming 'scare', including the *Waters* case and the 1872 Act, see M Arnot, 'Infant death, child care and the state: the baby-farming scandal and the first infant life protection legislation of 1872' (1994) 9 *Continuity and Change* 271–311.

creator.[94] Critics have long mused on the reason for Eliot's determination to deny Hetty redemption; saved from the gallows but transported to the further reaches of both empire and novel. Eliot, like Braddon, was herself a 'fallen' woman; unable to marry her long-time partner GH Lewes because, having 'condoned' his wife's adultery, he was unable to cite grounds for divorce. She was, accordingly, peculiarly sensitive to the cultural imputation that all 'fallen' women were the same. Eliot, as she was keen to advise friends, was engaged in a relationship of 'mutual faithfulness and mutual devotion', in a tone oddly reminiscent of the deluded Jessie Phillips and Beatrice Brooke affirming that whilst her 'marriage is not a legal one' strictly speaking 'it is regarded by us both as a sacred bond'.[95] Hetty was different, a silly girl, too easily deluded, her fall as miserable as it was ordinary. In her otherwise laudatory review in the *Athenaeum*, Geraldine Jewsbury wondered if the 'brutal facts' of Hetty's case might not have been 'softened to fit them for their place in a work of Art'.[96] However, Eliot was rarely inclined to soften, no matter how nicely her publisher asked. Her reason was simple. If a reader of *Adam Bede* had chanced upon an infanticide trial in the England of 1859, or indeed 1799 when the novel was set, they were likely to come across as silly a woman as Hetty Sorrel, and as sordid a crime.

Hetty's crime was beyond redemption, her confession too compromised by self-pity. However, if Hetty could not be saved others, it appeared, could be. In fact, it quickly becomes apparent that fictive Victorian fallen women might expect to experience a variety of consequences: moral, legal and indeed corporeal. Trials were occasional; accounts as extensive as that which Eliot writes into *Adam Bede* were more rare. More typically, Trollope deemed it 'needless' to detain her readers with 'any detailed account' of the trial of Jessie Phillips (534–35). Death was much more common. Jessie dies moments after the jury's verdict. Isabel Carlyle dies too, almost as dramatically if not quite so obviously redeemed; so too, as we will see, does Nancy Sikes. Dickensian 'fallen' women tended to fare badly. Others, again like Hetty, tend to drift away. Edith Dombey drifts away as does Lady Clara Highgate. Middle-class women like Edith and Clara tend to fare better, though few end their days so obviously forgiven as Aurora Mellish.

Beatrice Brooke is another example of a woman who enjoys forgiveness. At the end of the book she is left basking in the Tuscan sun, 'passionate, strong and defying', and not remotely persuaded to confess anything (1.198). Critics were quick to voice their doubts as to whether Beatrice should have been 'saved' at all. 'No woman', Fitzjames Stephen observed, at least none of 'proper feeling of self-respect and decency would have eloped with her lover in the middle of the night, at half an hour's warning, whether or not she was promised marriage'.[97] The reviewer in the *Cornhill Magazine* adopted a similar tone. 'No girl of good feeling' would have

---

[94] 'Introduction' to *Adam Bede* x.

[95] See Beer, *George Eliot* (above n 16) 24; Ashton, *George Eliot* (above n 2) 183; and Winnifrith, *Fallen Women* (above n 17) 49–51.

[96] G Jewsbury, *Athenaeum*, 26 February 1859, 284.

[97] R Craig, *The Narratives of Caroline Norton* (Palgrave, 2009) 55–56.

thought of marrying without first ensuring they had the blessing of their parents. Beatrice 'clearly did wrong; and not only wrong, but very wrong indeed, and richly deserved to be punished'.[98] Norton had anticipated such a response, deploying her narrator to mount a pre-emptive bid for the empathetic support of her readers. After all, how many of them had not at one time 'loved untowardly, rashly' (1.248). 'Nothing is so fallible as human judgment, but nothing is so pitiless' she added (2.64). As for the fact that Beatrice falls foul of the provisions written into English matrimonial law:

> If my readers think it positively ridiculous to suppose that an educated girl of seventeen would either have believed herself married by the simple ceremony of a clergyman reading the service without witnesses . . . let them ascertain what the ideas of law on these simple points might be, among very young ladies brought up in retirement, in this country where Gretna Green has only just ceased to be a Hymeneal temple in this country, the only in Europe I believe, where the innocent suffer for the guilty, and an after-marriage does not redeem the destiny of the children. (2.69–70)[99]

Beatrice is not sorry. After all, as she protests to her father, despite all appearances she has in fact 'no sin to reproach to myself' (1.245). Norton felt the same and pointedly observed, responding to her critics in *The Times*, that she had written about extramarital sex because it was 'unquestionably the favourite amusement of the English aristocracy'.[100]

Aside from class and authorial inclination, there is one other factor which plays a significant role in determining the respective consequences of fictive fallen women: their qualities as mothers. Hetty Sorrel is, of course, the epitome of the 'unnatural' mother, unmarried and murderous.[101] Beatrice Brooke, conversely, is reported as raising a 'dark-eyed robust babe', as well as serving as a step-mother to the children of her new husband (2.289). The 'repentance' of Janet Dempster is finally confirmed by her adoption of a daughter. While she never has the opportunity to test her maternal metal, Jessie Phillips is left in no doubt as to the surest way of securing her redemption: 'When your child is born, Jessie, your heart will tell you that nothing whatever, whether it is hate, or whether it is love, can compare with the duty of doing the best you can for it' (367). A case could be credibly made for Jessie's creator being the most radically feminist writer of the mid-Victorian period but there was nothing radical here.

---

[98] 'Anti-Respectability' 8 *Cornhill Magazine* September 1863, 283–84.

[99] Interestingly, two contemporary reviewers did note the jurisprudential critique written into *Lost and Saved* but neither were concerned by matrimonial law. The reviewer in *Chamber's Journal* surmised that the Treherne estate might have been in breach of the equitable rule against perpetuities, whilst the reviewer in the *Saturday Review* mused on what the new Divorce Court might have made of a marriage conducted overseas, but allegedly on consular soil. See 516 *Chamber's Journal*, November 1863, 335–36 and *Saturday Review*, 25 July 1863, 112–13.

[100] A Chedzoy, *A Scandalous Woman* (Allison and Busby, 1992) 276.

[101] See D Kreisel, 'Incognito, Intervention, and Dismemberment in *Adam Bede*' (2003) 70 *ELH*, 561–62, 567–69, suggesting that Eliot may have intended her readers to infer that Hetty dismembered her baby's body; something that would have added to the heinous nature of her 'unnatural' offence.

The 'cult' of motherhood, as we have already noted, was cherished by the Victorians, and was a common subject of the literature they preferred to read. Most 'angels in the house' were mothers, or at least were supposed to be, their principle duty lying in the proper education of their children so that they too, in time, could be 'natural' parents. 'Mighty is the force of motherhood', the narrator in *Janet's Repentance* confirms, stilling 'all anxiety into calm content' (334); a view that would certainly have earned Lewes's approval, given the tenor of his comments in reviewing Charlotte Bronte's *Shirley*:

> The grand function of woman, it must always be recollected is, and ever must be, *Maternity*: and this we regard not only as her distinctive characteristic, and most endearing charm, but as a high and holy office the prolific source, not only of the best affections and virtues of which our nature is capable, but also of the wisest thoughtfulness, and most useful habits of observations, by which that nature can be elevated and adorned.[102]

It was this kind of sentiment which could be read into Ruskin's 'Of Queen's Gardens' and countless similar tracts. According to the secretary of the National Home Reading Union, 'motherhood' was the 'most difficult and noble of all life's responsibilities', for which reason there was nothing more important than mothers staying at home and reading to their children, provided of course they read the right books.[103] It was a sentiment impressed with increasing urgency as the mid-century decades progressed and ever larger numbers of women were perceived to be abandoning home and children in order to seek employment inside the factories or outside on the streets. Harriet Martineau was not alone in suggesting that there would soon need to be 'schools' for mothers who could no longer 'boil potatoes, nor mend stockings'.[104] Elizabeth Lynn Linton suggested that maternal neglect was the 'saddest part' of what she termed the 'Modern Revolt' of women.[105]

Discussions of motherhood could be found scattered across the literary genres. Beatrice is certainly not the only mother found wandering the pages of a sensation novel, still less the only unmarried one. Readers of Eliot's late contribution to the genre, *Daniel Deronda*, would encounter Lydia Glasher and her illegitimate son. They would encounter a bitter and unhappy woman. They would also encounter a resourceful and determined mother, and a child who will one day inherit his father's vast estate. Isabel Carlyle, as we have already noted, was condemned as much for the abandonment of her child as the abandonment of her husband. Yet this did not make her an 'unnatural' mother. Unnatural mothers, as the law confirmed, were mothers who had children out of wedlock. Isabel was thus both a 'natural' mother in regard to her son William, and an 'unnatural' mother in regard

---

[102] *Edinburgh Review*, January 1850, 155.

[103] Flint, *Reader*, 108–109.

[104] Writing in 1859, Martineau suspected that 'no less than half' of the women in Britain aged 20 or over were 'industrial in the mode of life'. H Martineau, 'Female Industry' *Edinburgh Review*, April 1859, reprinted in S Hamilton (ed), *Criminals, Idiots, Women, and Minors: Victorian Writing by Women on Women* (Broadview, 1995) 58.

[105] E Linton, 'The Modern Revolt' *Macmillan's Magazine*, December 1870, reprinted in Hamilton, *Criminals*, ibid, 179.

to her child by Levison. Helen Huntingdon is a natural mother too, even if in escaping the family home with her child, she was also a deeply troubling one. The pejorative 'unnatural', rooted in centuries of scriptural and jurisprudential proscription, was reserved not for those who were not good at being mothers, but for those who had sex at the wrong time with the wrong man.

Unsurprisingly, motherhood was a particularly favoured subject in 'domestic' novels, of the kind perhaps most commonly associated with Elizabeth Gaskell.[106] Gaskell did not, of course, write about mothers just to entertain. She also wrote to inform and to educate, possessed of the same burning desire to depict the 'truth'.[107] She would later confirm that she took 'heart' from the fact that her *Ruth* had 'made' people 'talk and think a little on a subject which is so painful'.[108] She was a mother herself, by all accounts a doting if slightly frantic one; much like, she could reasonably assume, a good number of her readers. 'She was much prouder of ruling her household well', an approving George Smith observed in his obituary to Gaskell, 'than of all she did in those writings'.[109] In this, Gaskell's view was again entirely conservative. A good mother does not deposit her children with baby-farmers. She stays at home and nurtures them for 'home duties are always paramount' as Gaskell observed of her own maternal responsibilities.[110] Gaskell was, of course, peculiar in being able to both work and stay at home. Few of her contemporaries, certainly few of her poorer ones, were so lucky. Gaskell's canon is replete with mothers happy at home, doing the baking, cleaning the house and raising their children. There was little doubt as to what Gaskell thought a good mother should do.

There was, however, room for doubt as to how Gaskell thought a 'natural' mother might be defined; and this was nowhere more obviously, and controversially, questioned than in *Ruth*. Ruth Hilton is another of Hardwicke's 'fallen' progeny; her demise in part inspired, as we have already noted, by that of the unfortunate Pasley on whose behalf Gaskell had written to Dickens. Ruth is an orphan and a seamstress; misfortunes equally familiar to the devotee of the 'fallen' woman novel. The absence of a maternal influence is noted from the start with Ruth 'crying' in her sleep as she dreams of her dead mother (9).[111] Accordingly, Ruth grows up in ignorance, denied the 'cautions or words of advice respecting *the*

[106] According to Elaine Showalter, Gaskell 'became the heroine of a new school of motherly fiction'. See E Showalter, *A Literature of Their Own: British Women Novelists from Bronte to Lessing* (Princeton University Press, 1977) 69–71; in like terms P Stoneman, *Elizabeth Gaskell* (Manchester University Press, 2006), 33; and D'Albertis, *Dissembling Fictions* (above n 8) 7–8 and 155–56 suggesting that in her final, uncompleted novel, *Wives and Daughters*, Gaskell realised a long-held ambition to write a necessarily fictive 'history of English Domestic Life'.

[107] George Sand famously observed of Gaskell that she had 'done what neither I nor other female authors in France can accomplish she has written novels which excite the deepest interest in men of the world and yet which every girl will be the better for reading'. Quoted in D'Albertis, *Dissembling Fictions* (above n 8) 16–17.

[108] J Chapple and A Pollard (eds), *The Letters of Mrs Gaskell* (Manchester University Press, 1997) 227.

[109] G Smith, 'Mrs Gaskell and Her Novels' (1874) 29 *Cornhill Magazine* 192.

[110] Uglow, *Elizabeth Gaskell* (above n 6) 45.

[111] Internal references are to E Gaskell, *Ruth* (Oxford University Press, 1998).

subject of a woman's life' (44).[112] She is 'young, and innocent, and motherless' (56). She is also gullible and thus she is all too easily seduced by Henry Bellingham believing, like Jessie Phillips, Hetty Sorrel, Beatrice Brooke and so many others, that she is somehow married at least in the eyes of God. Henry, however, is another cad, like Frederic Dalton, Arthur Donnithorne and Montagu Treherne. Ruth is 'degraded', abandoned and pregnant (90, 321). However, she does not leave her child by the roadside like Hetty, nor does she fall asleep in a barn only to awaken and find her baby missing like Jessie. Ruth becomes a doting mother to little Leonard, so doting that by virtue of her experience as a mother she is able to secure her own redemption. She is helped in this by the Reverend Benson who invites her into his home in the sure belief that she can indeed be redeemed.[113] Benson becomes the surrogate parent that Ruth deserves. Ruth's progress will be painful at times. It 'will require some time, and much Christian love' (120). However, her redemption is assured.

As the novel progresses Ruth's redemption is measured by her resistance to future temptation, most obviously in the form of Bellingham's reappearance and offer of marriage.[114] It finds final expression when Ruth volunteers for work in a local hospital during a typhoid epidemic. It is here that she encounters Bellingham once again, this time ravaged by disease.[115] Ruth nurses him back to health, but having been long haunted by the 'shadow of death', contracts the disease herself and dies as a ministering angel and martyr (99).[116] These successive sacrifices are all the more worthy given Ruth's mistaken concern that Bellingham might try to take Leonard away from her; something to which she could never 'consent' (302).[117] As an unmarried mother, her position in regard to legal custody was stronger than if she had been married; a paradox noted by custody law reformers such as Caroline Norton.[118] Bellingham has 'no right, legal or otherwise, over the child' (454). However, Ruth does not know this and she has to resist the obvious

[112] See S Jansson, 'Elizabeth Gaskell: Writing Against the Angel in the House' (1996) 10 *Gaskell Society Journal* 68–69, and H Schor, 'The Plot of the Beautiful Ignoramus: *Ruth* and the Traditions of the Fallen Woman' in R Barreca (ed), *Sex and Death in Victorian Literature* (Macmillan, 1990) 158–60.

[113] Ruth had earlier helped Benson when he fell and injured himself; an early intimation of her skills as a nurse (97–98).

[114] A sort of 'pilgrim's progress' as Jansson suggests in 'Elizabeth Gaskell' (above n 112) 73. Gaskell was, for obvious reasons of personal faith, comfortable with the Bunyanesque idiom.

[115] Interestingly, Gaskell later defended this apparently incredible coincidence in terms not dissimilar from those adopted by Eliot. She had, she informed Dickens, heard an account of precisely such a coincidence, wherein a doctor who had seduced a girl then found himself treating her for an illness in prison. When the two 'came thus suddenly face to face', the prison matron had told Gaskell, the girl 'just fainted dead away'. Chapple and Pollard, *The Letters of Mrs Gaskell* (above n 108) 100.

[116] Ruth dies 'gloriously crucified', according to Deirdre D'Albertis, in *Dissembling Fictions* (above n 8) at 99. On Ruth's 'martyrdom', see P Parker, 'The Power of Giving: Elizabeth Gaskell's *Ruth* and the Politics of Benevolence' (1999) 13 *Gaskell Society Journal* 65–66.

[117] See A Holmes, 'Fallen mothers: Maternal adultery and child custody in England 1886–1925' in C Nelson and A Holmes (eds), *Maternal Instincts: Visions of Motherhood and Sexuality in Britain 1875–1925* (St Martin's Press, 1997) 49.

[118] Norton and Gaskell were on friendly terms, and it is reasonable to suppose that the latter was familiar with the former's writings on child custody and other areas of Victorian matrimonial law. Gaskell revisited the issue of child custody outside marriage in her later novel *Sylvia's Lovers*.

temptation first to marry Bellingham, in order to make Leonard 'legitimate', and then later to allow him to die (303).

It is the depth of her maternal love which sustains Ruth through all these temptations and moments of despair. Her 'whole heart was in her boy' (209). Motherhood is a gift from God, as Benson repeatedly urges. Ruth must 'strengthen her child to look to God' (121). She does so. Ruth may be an 'unnatural' mother in the eyes of popular prejudice and legal proscription, but she is a good one. Reports of Leonard's development are glowing; he is obedient, intelligent and loving, unlike the reports which recount the adventures of the younger Bradshaws to whom Ruth briefly serves as a governess.[119] The Bradshaws pretend to be God-fearing, but Ruth actually is God-fearing.[120] She has been 'entered' by a 'spirit of maternity' (163).[121] It is, of course, a distinctively evangelical spirituality, one with which the dissenting Gaskells were perhaps rather more comfortable than some of Elizabeth's readers.[122] Nevertheless, that was, ultimately, the challenge that Gaskell set: the saving of Ruth through the grace of God, in disregard of ancient scripture and legal proscription. Gaskell was not alone in casting aspersions at the law, and more especially at the idea that the purpose of law might be to somehow enforce moral prejudice. As one senior medical officer observed in an 1864 article, the proper 'teaching' of maternal skills and more particularly the nurturing of 'maternal love' could never 'be enforced by the law'.[123]

However, she was still taking a risk in suggesting that her heroine, even as she veers metaphorically towards prostitution, is deserving of being saved.[124] Gaskell herself feared the worst.[125] Critical reviews were, in fact, mixed. Some were predictably troubled by the seduction of Ruth Hilton, an 'unfit subject for fiction', and even more so by her saving. No 'woman who has violated the laws of purity', thundered the *Christian Observer*, is 'entitled to occupy precisely the same position as one who has never thus offended'.[126] Bell's Library ostentatiously removed copies from its shelves, whilst *Sharpe's London Magazine* warned that it may not be suited for the 'hearth'.[127] Every bit as susceptible to criticism as Eliot, Gaskell com-

---

[119] Ruth is dismissed when Mr Bradshaw is made aware of her earlier transgression. It has been suggested that Leonard became the son that Gaskell never had. Gaskell had two sons. One died in childbirth, the other of scarlet fever aged just nine months. .

[120] Mr Bradshaw's sins are many, not least is his attempt to seduce Ruth whilst she works as the family governess. Ruth's rejection is another marker of her redemption.

[121] The metaphor is obviously loaded. Jansson refers to Ruth as an 'immaculate' mother. See 'Elizabeth Gaskell' (above n 112) 72.

[122] As Unitarians the Gaskells would have rejected the Old Testament notion of original sin. See Stoneman, *Gaskell* (above n 107) 66.

[123] Quoted in Arnot, 'Infant death' (above n 94) 296.

[124] See D'Albertis, *Dissembling Fictions* (above n 8) 79–90 for an extensive commentary on intimations of prostitution in the fall of Ruth Hilton, and Schor 'The Plot of the Beautiful Ignoramus' (above n 112) 168, referring to her 'aesthetic prostitution'. The prostitution insinuation recurs throughout the novel, most obviously in the attempts of Bellingham and his mother to pay Ruth off (127).

[125] She expressed a concern that 'many may refuse to read any book of that kind'. See Uglow, *Elizabeth Gaskell* (above n 6) 322, 338.

[126] Ibid, 338.

[127] Ibid, 338.

pared herself to 'St Sebastian tied to a tree to be shot at with arrows'.[128] She was particularly disturbed by reports that copies of *Ruth* were being 'burnt' because its contents were 'so *very* bad'.[129] Other critics, however, were reconciled, in much the same way as they would be in the later cases of Eliot's *Adam Bede* and Wood's *East Lynne*, by the perceived didacticism written into *Ruth*. Greg praised Gaskell for challenging the assumption that all fallen women must be cast out like lepers.[130] Lewes in the *Westminster Review* concluded that:

> If women are to have their lives rehabilitated, it must be through the means of women, who, noble and pure in their own lives, can speak with authority, and tell them that in this world no action is final; and that, to set the seal of despair and reprobation upon any individual during any point of his career, is to blot out the inner life by which we live.[131]

The fall of Ruth Hilton might have been a little distasteful, but it was hardly unfamiliar, whilst her redemption could be just easily read as a confirmation of conservative family values. If ever a fallen angel proved to truly angelic it is Ruth Hilton. Gaskell made her readers fall in love with Ruth and despair at her fate. On finishing *Ruth*, Charlotte Bronte immediately wrote to Gaskell complaining 'Why should she die? Why are we to shut up the book weeping?[132] Elizabeth Barrett Browning expressed the same misgivings.[133] The irony, of course, is that far from painting too romantic a picture in Ruth's martyrdom, Gaskell was in fact painting an all too realistic one. Hospitals depended upon unmarried women for nursing services and when typhus epidemics raged their casualty rates were high. Ruth Hilton probably would have gone to work in a typhoid ward, and she would probably have died as a result.

No-one felt so moved to tears by the fate of Hetty Sorrel. Indeed, it is clear that Hetty's rather more prosaic demise was inscribed, in large part, as a response to that of the beatific Ruth Hilton.[134] Eliot was an admirer of both novel and author, but doubted whether there was much to be gained from idealising 'fallen' women, still less martyring them. The fact that her Hetty should be comparatively undeserving of sympathy does not imply that Eliot was somehow disengaged with the 'question' of women; quite the reverse, as Leslie Stephen attested in his obituary published in the *Cornhill Magazine* in 1881.[135] In the *Atlantic Monthly*, Henry James likewise suggested that those 'for whom the development of women is the

[128] Chapple and Pollard, *The Letters of Mrs Gaskell* (above n 108) 148.
[129] Ibid, 222–23.
[130] Stoneman, *Gaskell* (above n 106) 65.
[131] G Lewes, 'Ruth and Villette' (1853) 59 *Westminster Review* 483.
[132] She added that the 'slaying' of Ruth marked Gaskell as a 'stern priestess'. Uglow, *Elizabeth Gaskell* (above n 6) 323–24.
[133] While also expressing her admiration for the novel's 'purity'. See ibid, 340.
[134] The thesis is strongly pressed in Beer, *George Eliot* (above n 16) 70–71, suggesting that *Ruth's* romanticism was 'implicitly corrected' in *Adam Bede*. According to Craik, 'without *Ruth* one feels there would have been no Hetty (or a very different one)' nor indeed would there have been a Tess Durbeyfield or Esther Waters. See W Craik, *Elizabeth Gaskell and the Provincial Novel* (Methuen, 1975) 49.
[135] Jenny Uglow has more recently affirmed this view although Eliot 'always drew back from active involvement' in contemporary feminist agitation. See her Uglow, *George Eliot* (above n 6) 9–11, 86–89. For Stephen's review see *Cornhill Magazine*, February 1881, 152–68.

hope of the future ought to erect a monument to George Eliot'.[136] Eliot was thoroughly engaged in the 'question', even if there was, as she attested, 'no subject on which I am more inclined to hold my peace and learn'.[137] She was committed to the writing of a literature that made a 'calm plea for the removal of unjust laws and artificial restrictions' so that the 'possibilities' of the female 'nature may have room for full development'.[138] However, she was not inclined to agitate, any more than she was prepared to 'soften' the stories of women such as Hetty Sorrel. The invocation of sympathy for the plight of women did not justify a retreat into 'silly' romance.

Accordingly until recently, critics have liked to see here a sharp distinction between an Eliot who remained hardened to whimsy and a Gaskell who seemed only too happy, following *Ruth*, to retire into a more 'serene' fictive domesticity.[139] David Cecil, writing in 1935, identified Gaskell as the high-priestess of the cult of motherhood and the epitome of the Victorian female author, 'domestic, tactful, unintellectual', possessed of a 'serene satisfaction'.[140] Nevertheless, just as critics have begun to wonder if Eliot's nostalgic 'pastoral' does not invite a more conservative reading, so too has it become fashionable to discern a more 'subversive' and a more 'dissembling' Gaskell; the Gaskell who wrote *Ruth* being perhaps the most subversive and dissembling of all.[141] On reading a novel such as *Ruth*, it is suggested, or the supposedly more 'serene' *Cranford* or *Wives and Daughters*, it becomes apparent that whilst the idylls of domesticity are not to be doubted, neither is the darker reality. Small wonder perhaps that Dickens was such a fan. Her anger may have been more subdued, but it was none the less intense, fired by

---

[136] See H James, *Atlantic Monthly*, May 1885, 668–78.

[137] Uglow, *George Eliot* (above n 6) 238–39.

[138] In a review of Margaret Fuller and Mary Wollstonecraft, published in the *Leader* in October 1855 and reprinted in G Eliot, *Selected Essays, Poems and Other Writings*, (Penguin, 1990) 332–38.

[139] Uglow suggests that Gaskell's next novel, *North and South*, was written to be 'conciliatory rather than confrontational' as a direct result of the perceived hostility with which *Ruth* was met in some critical circles. See Uglow, *Elizabeth Gaskell* (above n 6) 343. The place of *Ruth* within Gaskell's canon, moreover, has continued to trouble modern critics. Craik assumed a common stance in suggesting that it was just an odd fit, Gaskell's 'problem novel', the 'least read and the least successful', though he was also quick to acknowledge the originality of its treatment of unmarried motherhood. See Craik, *Elizabeth Gaskell and the Provincial Novel* (above n 134) 47–48.

[140] D Cecil, *Victorian Novelists: Essays in Revaluation* (Chicago University Press, 1958) 184. The impression was shared by Judith Lowder Newton, in her *Women. Power and Subversion: Social Strategies in British Fiction 1778–1860*, (Methuen, 1985) 164. In the 1985 edition of her *Gaskell*, Patsy Stoneman suggested that Gaskell was 'almost ignored by feminists'. By 2006 she was prepared to concede that the problem of neglect had been overcome; but not the supposition that Gaskell was an essentially conservative writer. See Newton, *Gaskell* (above n 107) 1–4 reviewing the 'floral school' of Gaskell criticism, and 136–71 assessing the extent to which critical perception of Gaskell has or has not changed. For a similar conclusion in regard to recent critical approaches to Gaskell, see D'Albertis, *Dissembling Fictions* (above n 8) 8–12.

[141] The idea of a 'subversive' Gaskell has been perhaps most forcefully urged by Patsy Stoneman in her *Gaskell* (above n 106), citing *Ruth* as an exemplar at 65–77. For a complementary assessment of the 'subversive' Gaskell, see D Davis, 'Feminist Critics and Literary Mothers: Daughters Reading Elizabeth Gaskell', (1992) 17 *Signs* 517–21. The idea of a 'dissembling' Gaskell finds expression in Deirdre D'Albertis's *Dissembling Fictions* (above n 8) at 3–8, at 73–102 in the particular context of *Ruth*, and then again at 161–65 referring alternatively to Gaskell's 'poetics of dissimulation'.

an urgent need to redress the 'silencing of women' and the injustices which afflicted the lives of those such as Pasley and Ruth, and Hetty, Beatrice and Jessie.[142]

The modern reader is left to contemplate the extent to which Eliot or Gaskell, or indeed Frances Trollope, Norton or Anne Bronte, might or might not be termed radical, or feminist. Each was drawn to the aligned images of the 'fallen' woman and the 'unnatural' mother and, however tangentially, the legal consequences which attended their mistakes and misfortunes. It was what their readers expected. Illegitimate children and murderous mothers were a staple of the mid-nineteenth-century novel, realist and sensational. The fact that their respective protagonists, and their fates, should be so very different is merely a testament to the fluidity of contemporary presumptions and prejudices. As was the case with adultery, divorce and bigamy, the readers of novels such as *Ruth*, *Adam Bede* and *Jessie Phillips* might be expected to share a common appreciation that there was something amiss in regard to illegitimacy and infanticide, and the various, often conflicting, rarely complementary array of statutes intended to proscribe, or where necessary punish, their incidence. It was a reading of *Ruth* which inspired Josephine Butler to dedicate her life to defending the rights of prostitutes against another such expression of statutory misogyny, to which we will now turn: the Contagious Diseases Act.[143] It might be thought to be a nice coincidence; except, of course, that it was not really a coincidence at all.

---

[142] Uglow, *Elizabeth Gaskell* (above n 6) 620.

[143] Butler later defended *Ruth* as having a 'very wholesome tendency' and clearly modelled her own novel, *Rebecca Jarrett*, published in 1886, on Gaskell's. See D'Albertis, *Dissembling Fictions* (above n 8) 81–82.

4

Fallen Angels

In October 1847 Urania Cottage opened its doors to eight carefully selected girls who wished to repent of their former vocation and start a new life in a pleasant and leafy area of Shepherd's Bush. It is unlikely that they had read the published *Appeal to Fallen Women* which had invited their application themselves, but someone must have read it to them, or perhaps the word had spread. The *Appeal* was addressed to a 'very young woman still who was born to be happy, and has lived miserably'. It invited her to imagine her 'present situation', to contemplate the 'vices practiced' on the streets she were forced to walk, and then to imagine an alternative 'home' where she and her fellow inmates might be 'taught all household work that would be useful to them', including cookery, sewing and gardening, where 'they will be treated with the greatest kindness', and where they can then 'begin life afresh, and be able to win a good name and character' albeit in a 'distant country'. Such a woman could be saved the *Appeal* concluded soberly, but only if she enters 'this Home' with 'constant resolutions'.[1] The *Appeal* was written by Charles Dickens.

It was Dickens who had persuaded Angela Burdett Coutts, by popular reputation the richest heiress in 'all England', to part with £500 in order to establish Urania Cottage.[2] In his essay 'Prostitution', the noted social commentator WS Greg recommended publicly-funded rescues.[3] Few others made this recommendation, for reasons of expense as much as propriety. Rescuing prostitutes remained a matter of private philanthropy for women such as Burdett Coutts and men such as Dickens and William Gladstone, for whom prostitution was 'the chief burden of my soul', and who always regarded his work on the streets as being more effective than the many hours he spent pontificating on the subject in Parliament.[4] Dickens also liked to walk the streets, often inviting friends to join him in his strolls; becoming, to use Baudelaire's terminology, *flaneurs*. An alternative term might be stalker; men wandering about looking for and at prostitutes, trying to

---

[1] The *Appeal* is reprinted in J Hartley, *Charles Dickens and the House of Fallen Women* (Methuen, 2008) at 253–55.

[2] Burdett Coutts's reputation was sealed when it transpired that she had personally lent money to Queen Victoria. The family fortune was based on the success of the Coutts Bank.

[3] W Greg, 'Prostitution' (1850) 53 *Westminster Review* 501.

[4] Quoted in J Walkowitz, *Prostitution and Victorian Society: Women, Class and the State* (Cambridge University Press, 1982) 32.

imagine what they might or might not do for other gentlemen who were prepared to toss them a guinea.[5]

Magdalen hospitals and other species of 'rescue' could take various forms, many modelling themselves as penitentiaries, most betraying a strong evangelical impulse. The poet Christina Rossetti volunteered at St Mary Magdalene Penitentiary in Highgate, regularly turning up in her black habit to teach Bible studies and pray alongside the 'penitents'. They assumed, reasonably, that she was training to be a nun.[6] Urania Cottage was perhaps unusual in trying to espouse a more liberal regime. Dickens wanted to create a 'cheerful family' as opposed to a 'kind of Nunnery'.[7] It was for this reason that he insisted on the girls being allowed to wear bright clothing; one of the very few points of disagreement with Burdett Coutts.[8] Dickens maintained a close interest in the management of Urania Cottage for over a decade. There is, of course, an immediate irony in the fact that his relationship with Burdett Coutts deteriorated from the moment that rumours about his relationship with Ellen Ternan began to surface. When Ellen fell so did Urania Cottage which finally shut its doors in 1862. By now, as his marriage had collapsed, the ever-restless Dickens was casting about for another hobby.

He did not have to look far. Dickens had always been fascinated with the theatre. 'Every writer of fiction', he once declaimed, 'writes, in effect, for the stage'.[9] An enthusiastic amateur dramatist, Dickens had been giving occasional 'readings' of his work from as early as 1853. Now he conceived large nationwide tours. Readings for these first tours in 1858 to 1859 and 1861 to 1863 included 'The Memorable Trial of Bardell v Pickwick' and the death of little Paul in *Dombey and Son*, together with re-cast episodes from *Nicholas Nickleby* and *David Copperfield*, as well as his ever-popular Christmas Stories.[10] For his 'farewell' tour of 1868, however, there was a new reading. It was entitled 'Sikes and Nancy'. Dickens had long contemplated the possibility of including this reading. In 1863, he had admitted to friends that: 'I have been trying, alone by myself, the Oliver Twist murder, but have got something so horrible out of it that I am afraid to try it out in public.'[11] The idea stayed in his mind, as did the uncertainty. Accordingly, in the weeks before the 1868 tour was scheduled to begin, Dickens decided to give a 'Trial Reading'. The effect, as he described it to a friend, was electric:

---

[5] See Hartley, *House of Fallen Women* (above n 1) 67 for the allusion to 'benevolent' stalking, and C Tomalin, *Charles Dickens* (Penguin, 2011) 203.

[6] For an account of Christina's work at the Penitentiary, see F Thomas, *Christina Rossetti: A Biography* (Virago, 1994) 180–91.

[7] Quoted in Hartley, *House of Fallen Women* (above n 1) 16.

[8] Another point of disagreement was in regard to unmarried mothers. On this point Burdett Coutts had her way and such women were banned.

[9] Quoted in S Zemka, 'The Death of Nancy Sikes, 1838–1912' (2010) 110 *Representations* 30. For other commentaries on Dickens's love of the theatre, see Tomalin, *Charles Dickens* (above n 5) 46–60, 169–70, and S Callow, *Charles Dickens and the Great Theatre of the World* (Harper, 2012) 163–67, 351.

[10] Dickens would typically give around 18 readings in an evening, taking up to three hours. It was a matter of pride that he could give them from memory and without notes. Over the years the performances became ever more dramatic, with Dickens assuming particular accents and supposed mannerisms of his characters. For an account see Callow, *Great Theatre of the World* (above n 9) 279–83.

[11] Quoted in P Collins, *Dickens and Crime* (Macmillan, 1994) 265.

Now you must know that all this company were . . . unmistakably pale, and had horror-stricken faces. Next morning Harness writing to me about it, and saying it was 'a most amazing and terrific thing', added, 'but I am bound to tell you that I had an almost irresistible impulse to *scream*, and that, if anyone had cried out, I am certain I should have followed'. He had no idea that, on the night, Priestley, the great ladies' doctor, had taken me aside and said: 'My dear Dickens, you may rely upon it that if only one woman cries out when you murder the girl, there will be a contagion of hysteria all over the place.' It is impossible to soften it without spoiling it, and you may suppose that I am rather anxious to discover how it goes on the Fifth of January!!! We are afraid to announce it elsewhere, without knowing, except that I have thought it pretty safe to put it up once in Dublin. I asked Mrs Keeley, the famous actress, who was at the experiment: 'What do *you* say? Do it or not?' 'Why, of course, do it' she replied, 'Having got at such an affect as that, it must be done. But,' rolling her large black eyes very slowly, and speaking distinctly, 'the public have been looking out for a sensation these last fifty years or so, and by Heaven they have got it!' With which words, and a lost breath and a long stare, she became speechless. Again, you may suppose I am a little anxious![12]

Anxious perhaps, but 'Sikes and Nancy' was included and the effect was pretty much as anticipated. On one occasion, Dickens recorded 'we had a contagion of fainting. And yet the place was not hot. I should think we had from a dozen to twenty ladies borne out, stiff and rigid, at various times. It became quite ridiculous.' On another, he reported, with evident relish:

I don't think a hand moved while I was doing it last night, or an eye looked away. And there was a fixed expression and horror of me, all over the theatre, which could not have been surpassed if I had been going to be hanged to that red velvet table. It is quite a new sensation to be execrated with that unanimity; and I hope it will remain so![13]

Nancy 'Sikes' had of course died on stage many times before.[14] Within 10 days of the first three-volume publication of *Oliver Twist*, which appeared in November 1838, Nancy had been beaten to death on the stage of the Surrey Theatre.[15] By the time she was dying nightly in New York in February 1839, she had already met her fate on stages in Sheffield, Bristol, Boston and Philadelphia, and the Lord Chamberlain had taken steps to ban some of the more gruesome adaptations from London stages.[16] Nancy's demise had always been violent. When he had first read the scene from the draft chapter of *Oliver Twist* to his wife, Dickens recorded that she was 'in an unspeakable state, from which and my own impression I augur

---

[12] Ibid, 267.

[13] On the audience reception, see Collins, *Dickens and Crime* (above n 11) 268, and Tomalin, *Charles Dickens* (above n 5) 374–75.

[14] She was not, of course, married to Bill. But theatre managers preferred to think that she was; an incongruous gesture to propriety given the circumstances.

[15] This production, cobbled together by George Almar, would remain the most popular stage version for the rest of the century. See Zemka, 'The Death of Nancy Sikes' (above n 9) 29, and R Barreca, 'The Mimic Life of the Theatre: The 1838 Adaptation of *Oliver Twist*' in C Mackay (ed), *Dramatic Dickens*, (Macmillan, 1989) 87, surmising that Dickens was far from impressed.

[16] See Zemka, 'The Death of Nancy Sikes' (above n 9) 34.

well'.[17] It was written to thrill but, as we shall see, it was also written with textual nuance; 'Sikes and Nancy' was not. Dickens reacted strongly when reviewers of the novel, including Thackeray, had supposed that *Oliver Twist* was a species of Newgate or sensation fiction. By 1868, however, sensation novels had become, if not exactly respectable, then at least more familiar, and undoubtedly lucrative. Shades of grey were banished from 'Sikes and Nancy', as was Oliver. The thrilling murder of a common prostitute replaced the rather dreary 'progress' of a poor 'parish boy'. Dickens the social commentator, it was insinuated by some, had become Dickens the pornographer as well as Dickens the *flaneur*.

The purpose of 'Sikes and Nancy', as Dickens confessed, was simple. It was to 'perfectly petrify an audience'. The handwritten stage directions which Dickens wrote to himself read: 'Beckon down. Point. Shudder. Look Round In Terror. Murder Coming. Mystery. *Terror Through to the End*'.[18] Its purpose was also to make money. It succeeded on both counts. The sacrifice of Nancy Sikes made Dickens's fortune again. It also killed him, as his friend Wilkie Collins later observed.[19] His doctor had warned Dickens that it might, advising him that an elevated pulse rate, which rose from a rest of 72 to approximately 112, even on occasion 124, was dangerous for a man of his age and already indifferent health. Dickens admitted that after a reading it 'takes me ten or twelve minutes to get my wind back at all; I being in the meantime like the man who has lost the fight'.[20] His friend Forster warned him to be careful, but Dickens was as addicted to his audience as the audience was to Nancy.[21] 'I shall', he whispered as he walked on to the stage for the very last reading of 'Sikes and Nancy', 'tear myself to pieces'.[22] Nancy may have died many times before, but she never died as well as she did when Dickens killed her, and himself.

Walking the Streets

Of the many social problems which faced England, Greg advised readers of the *Westminster Review* in early 1850, 'the darkest, the knottiest, and the saddest' was that of prostitution.[23] All women who had sex outside of marriage were deemed to have fallen, but prostitutes, it was commonly supposed, had fallen the furthest.

---

[17] Quoted in P Horne, 'Introduction' to *Oliver Twist* (Penguin, 2002) xxviii.

[18] See Callow, *Great Theatre of the World* (above n 9) 324.

[19] The reading, Collins opined, 'did more to kill Dickens than all his other work put together'. See Collins, *Dickens and Crime* (above n 11) 271.

[20] Ibid, 270.

[21] When his manager, George Dolby, suggested that he might like to vary the repertoire a bit, and perhaps give Nancy a night off, Dickens flew into an uncharacteristic ill-temper, smashing a dinner plate to 'atoms' and bursting into tears. He was quick to apologise but the point was made and the suggestion that Nancy might be given a rest was never repeated. Collins, *Dickens and Crime* (above n 11) 270.

[22] Ibid, 270.

[23] Greg, *Prostitution* (above n 3) 448.

There was no more 'revolting' species of 'sexual irregularity'.[24] There was, for obvious reasons, a recurrent moral anxiety attached to prostitution; one which found itself commonly described in theological tones. It was, as Greg again opined, a 'sin against nature, a 'profanation'.[25] It was described in an uncompromising statement in Ralph Wardlaw's 1842 *Lectures on Female Prostitution* as a species of 'unnaturalness' contrary to the 'terms of holy writ'.[26]

However, the discourse of prostitution was not shaped solely by perceptions of sin and immorality. It was also shaped by economics and by utility, and as the century progressed, increasingly by medical science. Eventually, as we shall see, it was even shaped, a bit, by the law. The medico-economic discourse found famous expression in William Acton's *Prostitution Considered in its Moral, Social and Sanitary Aspects*, which advised that prostitution, simply understood, was the 'artificial supply of a natural demand'.[27] A few pages later Acton delved a little deeper, and wrote a little more floridly:

> What is a prostitute? She is a woman who gives for money that which she ought to give only for love; who ministers to passion and lust alone, to the exclusion and extinction of all the higher qualities . . . She is a woman with half a woman gone, and that half containing all that elevates her nature, leaving her a mere instrument of impurity; degraded and fallen she extracts from the sin of others the means of living, corrupt and dependent on corruption, and therefore interested directly in the increase of immorality.[28]

Prostitutes were distinguished from other 'fallen' women in that they entered a marketplace; the 'conversion of soulless lust', as Elizabeth Blackwell put it, 'into a business traffic'.[29] Annie Besant was similarly succinct: 'Men are immoral for their amusement; women are immoral for bread'.[30] For many, it was simply a matter of 'hard necessity'; a nominal and, given the lack of alternatives, a 'rational' choice.[31] The numerous accounts found in Mayhew's letters to the *Morning Chronicle* time

---

[24] W Acton, *Prostitution Considered in its Moral, Social and Sanitary Aspects* (London, 1870) 449.

[25] Greg, *Prostitution* (above n 3) 450.

[26] R Wardlaw, *Lectures on Female Prostitution* (Glasgow, 1842) 70.

[27] Acton, *Prostitution Considered* (above n 24) 161–62. Acton's research focussed on the incidence of spermatorrhoea, which he attributed to excessive masturbation, and various species of venereal disease, most especially syphilis. In his *Functions and Disorders of the Reproductive Organs*, published in 1857, Acton made the famous claim that 'the majority of women (happily for them) are not very much troubled with sexual feeling of any kind'. See W Acton *Functions and Disorders of the Reproductive Organs* (London, 1857) 112. On Acton's influence, see S Marcus, *The Other Victorians* (Transaction, 2009) xix, suggesting that his were 'the official views of sexuality held by Victorian society'. A revisionist account, arguing that there were greater contemporary doubts, can be found in I Crozier, 'William Acton and the history of sexuality: the medical and professional context' (2000) 5 *Journal of Victorian Culture* 1–27.

[28] Acton, *Prostitution Considered* (above n 24) 166.

[29] E Blackwell, 'Rescue Work in Relation to Prostitution and Disease' (1881) in S Jeffreys (ed), *The Sexuality Debates* (Routledge, 1987) 101.

[30] A Besant, 'The Legalization of Female Slavery in England' in Jeffreys, *The Sexuality Debates* ibid, 98.

[31] Greg, *Prostitution* (above n 3) 457–58, 460–61 observing: 'We shall not take much pains in proving that poverty is the chief determining cause which drives women into prostitution.'

and again stressed the prevalence of poverty in driving women into prostitution.[32] Once they had fallen, women kept falling or at least so it seemed to Wardlaw who sagely advised his readers that 'rising is a thing unknown . . . it is all descent'.[33]

There were, however, other motivations. Too many, Greg suggested, 'fall from pure unknowingness'; women like Jessie Phillips and Beatrice Brooke who were 'deceived by unreal marriages' and who listened to their lovers rather than read Hardwicke's Marriage Act.[34] Besant identified a different statute, the 1857 Divorce Act, as being equally culpable for failing to allow unhappily married couples to divorce more easily. A 'reasonable marriage law' would not leave sexually frustrated men with little alternative but to wander the streets looking for prostitutes.[35] Others, as WT Stead confirmed in his provocative accounts of child prostitution published in the *Pall Mall Gazette* in 1885, decided that it was a sacrifice worth making in order to be able to buy 'clothes' and other 'things which money can bring'.[36] Greg also worried about the 'snares of vanity', as did Acton.[37] Along with shopping sprees, reading was also a concern. Bracebridge Hemyng supposed that exposure to 'penny and halfpenny romances' had turned too many young female heads, making all kinds of criminal and sexual activity seem not merely acceptable, but also rather exciting.[38]

No-one really knew how many prostitutes there were in London, or anywhere else; figures for the metropolis ranged between 8,000 and 80,000. The whimsy of self-proclaimed experts contributed to the uncertainty.[39] Much could also be attributed to the fact that whilst some prostitutes were easy enough to spot, others rather worryingly were not. So-called 'dollymops' were a particular concern; women who operated in an essentially part-time capacity, occasionally offering their services in order to supplement an otherwise meagre income.[40] Whilst there might be something thrilling about your neighbour's wife being an adulteress or a bigamist, there was nothing so enticing about your scullery-maid turning out to be a 'dollymop' particularly if you were a suspicious wife.[41] Acton's suggestion that for many women prostitution was not only a part-time occupation but also a

[32] Mayhew's letters mostly published in 1849 and 1850 formed the substance of his *London Labour and the London Poor*, published serially in 1851–52. Greg used Mayhew's letters extensively in his *Prostitution* (above n 3).

[33] Hartley, *House of Fallen Women* (above n 1) 31.

[34] Greg, *Prostitution* (above n 3) 459.

[35] Besant, *The Legalization of Female Slavery* (above n 30) 99.

[36] Republished as W Stead, *A Maiden Tribute: the Report of the Pall Mall Gazette's Secret Commission* (London, 1885) 8.

[37] Greg, *Prostitution* (above n 3) 458.

[38] H Mayhew, *London Labour and the London Poor* (Penguin, 1985) 477.

[39] As Bracebridge Hemyng inferred in his contribution to Mayhew's *London Labour*, ibid, at 473–76.

[40] In his report *Prostitution in London*, written as a contribution to Mayhew's *London Labour*, Bracebridge Hemyng adopted a tripartite schema: common prostitutes living in brothels; common prostitutes walking the streets, either part or full time; and women 'kept' by men of 'independent means'. The latter would normally expect to either marry well, or at the other extreme as they aged, find themselves downgraded to street walker or brothel worker. See Mayhew, *London Labour* (above n 38) 476, and 486 commenting more closely on 'dollymops'.

[41] About 90% of prostitutes were thought to be working class. See Walkowitz, *Prostitution and Victorian Society* (above n 4) 15–19, discussing the social background of the Victorian prostitute.

'transitory' one hardly settled the nerves. Most prostitutes, Acton surmised, 'fell' aged about 16, and then spent a couple of years drifting on and off the streets until they could find a husband. The related ideas that 'once a harlot, always a harlot', and that a 'harlot's progress' was inevitably 'short and rapid' and only went one way, downward, were accordingly two of the 'vulgar errors' which pervaded contemporary misperceptions of prostitution.[42] A few gentlemen might wittingly marry a prostitute; as George Gissing famously did a little later in the century, but rather too many, Acton insinuated, might subsequently discover that they had married one unwittingly. Though they might have fallen further, it seemed that there was nothing in the end to stop a prostitute rising again, and without trace.

A gentleman might not only find himself married to a prostitute, but might find himself infected by one. Sex disease 'scares' added to the ever-growing list of things the mid-Victorians worried about. Medical journals hazarded all kinds of statistics in order to emphasise how great was the danger, and how useful medical science might be in ameliorating it. Conservative estimates suggested that around 7% of men in London had syphilis at any one time; the more excitable preferred to suggest that the incidence had reached 'epidemic' proportions.[43] It was not just the health of the English gentleman that was at stake; so too was the health of his family and the Empire. Prostitution, Wardlaw advised, leads inexorably 'to the deterioration of national character'. All 'historically recorded experienced' proves it.[44] The sense of inevitable decline was eagerly embraced by the more pessimistic mid-Victorian of which there were many. In his *History of Prostitution*, published in 1859, WW Sanger hazarded the sober conclusion that the 'malignity' in question had reached such a scale that it now 'almost defies opposition'.[45]

Whilst historians like Sanger and clerics such as Wardlaw shook their heads in weary dismay, others, fired by the march of science and the apparent genius of utility, busied themselves devising strategies and schemes. To fail to address the problem, Greg declared, would be an 'act of culpable moral cowardice'.[46] If prostitution was, at root, a social problem, it could be addressed by more effective social legislation. Greg argued the case for improved housing and education, along with new legislation to suppress brothels and establish public asylums.[47] There was much to be said, he urged, for adopting the strategy of regulatory 'surveillance' favoured by the French authorities.[48] The medical profession also commonly recommended enhanced legal intervention, the Harveian Society publishing a series of reports intended to foster the belief that if Parliament could be persuaded, sexual disease might be eradicated with the sweep of a legislator's pen. A 'new legislative era', to be supplemented by a 'judicious system of emigration', was the

---

[42] Acton, *Prostitution Considered* (above n 24) 38, 49, 59. Judith Walkowitz has recently attested to the credibility of Acton's claim, in her *Prostitution and Victorian Society* (above n 4) 196–97.

[43] Walkowitz, *Prostitution and Victorian Society* (above n 4) 48–50.

[44] Wardlaw, *Lectures on Female Prostitution* (above n 26) 65.

[45] W Sanger, *History of Prostitution* (London, 1859) 18.

[46] Greg, *Prostitution* (above n 3) 449.

[47] Ibid, 468–71, 479–80, 486–88.

[48] Ibid, 482–83.

solution, Acton argued; in passing suggesting that properly written legislation might also reduce apparently soaring rates of 'illegitimacy and infanticide'.[49]

The common law, pretty much everyone agreed, was inadequate. It defined a 'common prostitute' as any woman who solicited men in public streets.[50] Prostitution was not itself illegal, although loitering and importuning for the purposes of prostitution was, and could result in a fine of £2. As Dickens advised Burdett Coutts, enforcement of the law was rare; constables were too easily bribed and too commonly uninterested.[51] Harriet Martineau agreed, opining that the biggest problem in regard to the regulation of prostitution was not the lack of law, but the 'negligence' of the 'police'.[52] Policing strategy, to the extent that such a thing existed, tended to focus on limiting disturbance and using prostitutes as a gateway to uncovering and punishing other forms of criminality. The affinity of prostitution and criminality was commonly assumed. Hemyng made the assertion in his *Prostitution in London*. In like terms, JB Talbot advised that: 'Once a woman has descended from the pedestal of innocence, she is prepared to perpetuate every crime.' For this reason, William Tait confirmed that they should be deemed to have 'abandoned the prerogatives of civil liberties'.[53] Prostitutes, it followed, should be treated as outlaws albeit within the disapproving purview of the law.

The easiest targets were brothels. An 1844 Bill for the Effectual Suppression of Brothels and Trading in Seduction and Prostitution failed, as did Spooner's Bill for the suppression of trade in prostitution introduced three years later; the latter when it was suggested that the names of 'some of the highest and noblest in the land' might be exposed in the press.[54] In 1851, however, Parliament did pass the Common Lodging-house Act which made the registration of brothels compulsory and the arguments for still greater state intervention continued to gather pace, so much so that in 1864 Parliament passed the first of three Contagious Diseases Acts. The Act was intended to reduce the incidence of venereal disease amongst soldiers and sailors by providing for the sanitary inspection of prostitutes in specific military depots in southern England and Ireland. Women identified as 'common prostitutes' by the police could be required to undergo invasive internal examinations every two weeks. Any prostitute found to be suffering from gonorrhoea or syphilis could then be committed to a Lock Hospital for a period not to exceed nine months.[55] The Empire would thus be saved. There was, typically, no statutory

[49] Acton, *Prostitution Considered* (above n 24) ix–x.
[50] This was an 'exceptionally vague legal category' according to Walkowitz in *Prostitution and Victorian Society* (above n 4) at 14.
[51] See Hartley, *House of Fallen Women* (above n 1) 42.
[52] H Martineau, 'The Contagious Diseases Act as Applied to Garrison Towns and Naval Stations' in Jeffreys, *The Sexuality Debates* (above n 29) 85.
[53] See Hemyng's observations in Mayhew, *London Labour* (above n 38) 480–81, 484, 489; J Talbot, *The Miseries of Prostitution* (London, 1844) 43; and W Tait, *Magdalenism: An Enquiry into the Extent, Causes and Consequences of Prostitution* (Edinburgh, 1840) 236.
[54] A Leighton, 'Because men made the laws: The Fallen Woman and the Woman Poet' (1989) 27 *Victorian Poetry* 110.
[55] Lock Hospitals were invariably run on penitential principles, and very commonly sought to exploit their inmates in the same way as the poorhouses, by enforcing cheap labour.

definition of 'common prostitute' or indeed of the extent of police powers. Any woman who resisted the appellation could be prosecuted and would be required to prove that she was not a 'common prostitute'.

Whilst a handful of women such as Martineau and Florence Nightingale, objected to the 1864 Act on the grounds that it legitimated vice, few others made any objection. The public seemed to approve, and revising legislation which extended jurisdictional reach was passed in 1866 and again in 1869. It was at this point that a coherent opposition began to emerge. By 1867, the London Rescue Society had organised a campaign for repeal. Three years later, the Ladies National Association was formed, its membership bringing together evangelicals, radicals and nascent feminists. A broad membership suggested a varied concern though not according to its first chair, the redoubtable Josephine Butler. When asked its purpose Butler replied that it was to 'rouse the country' and to 'Christianise' it again.[56] Butler preferred a 'vital' Christianity. The campaign against the Contagious Diseases Act was, she opined, a 'holy war' against a 'Government established vice'.[57] A Manifesto was produced for precisely this purpose, with agitators despatched to subjected districts to encourage prostitutes to resist compulsory vaginal inspections which the Association recast as a species of 'rape', and to assist the cause by harassing police officers and court officials.[58] The Contagious Diseases Act, it was argued, perpetuated vice and legitimated the systematic 'torture' of women.[59]

The principle of equality was commonly invoked in two different senses: first in regard to the abrogation of supposed common law rights to equal treatment before the law, and second in terms of a 'double standard of morality', the insinuation that as the 'lusts' of men were just as responsible for the 'vice' of prostitution the law should seek to regulate their activity just as much that of the women they bought.[60] So was history, recent and rather less recent. Many campaigners adopted the metaphor of slavery familiar from recent emancipation debates, something which was intended to further align the misfortunes of unhappy marriage and unhappier prostitution. At the same time, Butler reached rather further back in English history, inviting her readers to contemplate the example of Wat Tyler, recently resurrected as a proto-Chartist hero. Legend had it that Tyler was first moved to anger by reports of a girl raped by a government official. The Association

[56] J Butler, *Social Purity: An Address Given at Cambridge in May 1879* (Morgan and Scott, 1879) 173, and Walkowitz, *Prostitution and Victorian Society* (above n 4) 93.

[57] See Butler, *Social Purity* (above n 56) 181. In this she was not alone, as Judith Walkowitz has stressed, noting the same perception of Mary Priestman who attested to the 'influence of religious fellowship' in maintaining the vigour of the campaign. See Walkowitz, *Prostitution and Victorian Society* (above n 4) 122, 134.

[58] Walkowitz provides numerous accounts of such activities in her particular case studies of Plymouth and Southampton. See Walkowitz, *Prostitution and Victorian Society* (above n 4) chapter 9.

[59] See J Butler, *An Appeal to the People of England on the Recognition and Superintendence of Prostitution by Governments* (Banks, 1879), 112–13, 127.

[60] In *Appeal*, Butler further argued that the Acts in effect suspended habeas corpus, and were in sum 'contrary to the entire spirit of English law', ibid, 113–14. The second point was made by Harriet Martineau who wondered why it 'seems never to have occurred to the rulers of the soldier's destiny' that they might more effectively 'apply themselves to preclude temptation'. Letter reprinted in Jeffreys, *The Sexuality Debates* (above n 29) at 81.

published numerous lurid accounts of forced investigations, complete with leering police officers and barely veiled insinuations that the next innocent girl mistakenly forced to undergo such an inspection could easily be the reader's daughter.[61] The Association published, as Butler conceded, in order to create a 'sensation'.[62] The prostitute voice was raised, Butler proudly claimed; and all too carefully edited, her critics responded.

In response, in 1871 the government established a Royal Commission which, while supporting the Acts in principle, conceded that there was a case for ending compulsory inspections. The government, however, declined to act. Repeal bills were introduced into the Commons virtually every year during the 1870s. None was passed but the reform campaign continued. Significantly, *The Lancet* had announced that it was in favour of reform, noting that the Acts had done nothing to affect the incidence of venereal disease in the designated areas. Eventually, the reform campaign secured the support of the Radical MP and Cabinet Minister James Stansfield who assumed control of a Parliamentary Committee of Inquiry. Increased numbers of 'new' Radicals elected to the Commons following the 1880 election gave Stansfield the parliamentary support he needed, and in 1883, the House of Commons passed a motion suspending the compulsory inspections. Repeal of the Acts did not follow until 1886 but, further impelled by Stead's *Maiden Tribute*, it was increasingly obvious that this particular, and unedifying, legislative foray into the murky world of illicit sexuality had reached its end.

The Murder of Nancy Sikes

Prostitutes can be found scattered across the Victorian literary canon, sensational and 'anti-sensational'. In his essay 'Prostitution', Greg cited Gaskell's Esther in *Mary Barton* as an exemplar of the kind of literary representation which might serve to better inform his contemporaries as to the realities of life on the streets, and to urge that, no matter how 'terrible' their fall, any woman who found herself in such an unfortunate condition was still deserving of compassion.[63] A similar argument might have been made for *Lizzie Leigh*, a short story which Gaskell published eight years later in 1856. The tragedy of *Lizzie Leigh* is not simply that the eponymous Lizzie has been spotted working the streets, but that her family cannot ascertain precisely what has happened to her. Lizzie is truly lost; and silenced too. Lizzie never appears in *Lizzie Leigh*. A similar anxiety haunts Thomas de Quincey's *Confessions of an English Opium-Eater*. In a brief interlude, de Quincey records a prostitute named Ann saving his life. They keep each other company for a while, before Ann disappears into the night. De Quincey contemplated trying to save

---

[61] Butler, *Appeal* (above n 59) 144–45.
[62] See Walkowitz, *Prostitution and Victorian Society* (above n 4) 109–10, 138.
[63] Greg, 'Prostitution' (above 3) 502–503.

Ann, but the 'sorrow' had taken hold too 'deeply'.[64] Hers, de Quincey observes, was a 'case of ordinary occurrence' which 'the power of law might oftener be interposed to protect, and avenge' if it could be bothered.[65]

No-one, however, created more literary prostitutes than Charles Dickens. We have already encountered Alice Marwood in *Dombey and Son* and the discomforting insinuation that marriage was a species of prostitution. The same insinuation would be revisited in *Bleak House*, in the unsettling depiction of Esther, Hortense and Lady Dedlock. In *David Copperfield* Dickens would create a more obviously 'common' prostitute in the figure of Martha Endell, alongside the unfortunate, but no less fallen, 'little Em'ly'. Each of these women was cast into the pages of their respective novels while Dickens worked at Urania Cottage.[66] The same cannot, however, be said of his most notorious fallen woman, Nancy Sikes, whose particular fate had been settled a decade earlier. Nancy fell, as we have already noted, just as the Victorian age dawned; an oddly propitious coincidence. Lord Melbourne advised the young Queen Victoria not to read *Oliver Twist* when it first began appearing in serial form in the spring of 1837. It was 'all among Workhouses, and Coffin Makers, and Pickpockets'. But she did read it and apparently found it 'excessively interesting'.[67] So too, did thousands of her countrymen and women; its readership enhanced by the advertisement that it was written by the author of hugely popular *Pickwick Papers*.

The story of *Oliver Twist* is familiar. The eponymous Oliver is an 'orphan of the workhouse', a 'millstone' around 'the parochial throat', his mother having died shortly after his birth (4, 29).[68] He escapes an unwanted apprenticeship to an undertaker and goes to London where he falls in with a gang of young pickpockets and petty thieves who operate under the watchful eye of Fagin, a 'very old shrivelled Jew' and pimp (64).[69] Amongst Fagin's associates Oliver encounters the brutal house-breaker Bill Sikes and his mistress, the prostitute Nancy. Following his reluctant involvement in a failed burglary, Oliver is taken in by the Maylies. It becomes apparent that Oliver is from a respectable and wealthy family; a fact which Fagin gleans when approached by Oliver's half-brother Monks. Monks is concerned that Oliver might make a claim to the family estate and pays Fagin to ensure that Oliver's patrimony is destroyed. For much of the novel Oliver moves between these two worlds: the criminal world of Fagin and the respectable world

---

[64] T de Quincey, *Confessions of an English Opium-Eater* (Oxford University Press, 1996) 20–23, 34.

[65] Ibid, 21.

[66] See Hartley, *House of Fallen Women* (above n 1) 3, and 73–74, suggesting that life in Urania Cottage could be best described as a 'cross between a soap opera and a reality show', and again 134 supposing that his Urania 'Case Book' represented a kind of 'ur-text' of fallen women to which Dickens returned repeatedly during the rest of his professional life.

[67] See Horne, 'Introduction' (above n 17) at xiii. Dickens was granted an audience with Victoria in 1869, at the Queen's instigation. Protocol demanded that both parties stood throughout the full hour and a half, which given Dickens's precarious health was an undoubted strain. Though rather thrilled by the honour, Dickens remained republican in temperament, and later made it plain through private channels that he would prefer not to be offered a baronetcy.

[68] All internal citations are to C Dickens, *Oliver Twist* (Penguin, 2001).

[69] Fagin was named after Bob Fagin, a fellow worker at the blacking-factory where the young Dickens had worked. The character was modelled on that of Ikey Solomons, a notorious London fence.

of the Maylies and another benefactor Mr Brownlow. On hearing that Fagin and Sikes intend to do away with Oliver, Nancy decides to warn Brownlow and the Maylies, and meets them one night on London Bridge. A suspicious Fagin, however, has her followed, and on report of her apparent treachery Sikes flies into a rage and beats her to death. Increasingly paranoid, Sikes returns to London, is chased by a crowd and accidentally hangs himself whilst trying to escape. Fagin, meanwhile, is captured by the police and put on trial as an accessory before the fact of Nancy's murder. He is convicted and executed. Oliver is saved and lives happily ever after.[70]

In truth, as critics have long noted, Oliver is almost incidental to the novel which bears his name. Things happen to Oliver; but Oliver animates nothing. Similar arguments can be made for his various benefactors. Far more significant, in terms of characterisation and plot development, are the criminal characters, Fagin, Sikes and Nancy. Modern criticism has tended to suppose that this concentration on criminality confirms *Oliver Twist* as a late contribution to the Newgate genre of novels, for which reason a case might also be made for it being a very early piece of sensationalist literature.[71] Thackeray set the tone, suggesting that *Oliver Twist* was a novel full of 'startling, pleasing, unnatural caricatures'.[72] Dickens rejected the accusation, as we shall see, whilst other contemporary critics were likewise prepared to excuse *Oliver Twist* from the generally pejorative reputation of the Newgate genre. There was, the *Edinburgh Review* opined, nothing unduly 'romantic' about the criminals who populate *Oliver Twist*.[73] Perhaps not, but Dickens was certainly familiar with both the *Newgate Calendar* and the literature it inspired, and was just as clearly prepared to write to the predilections of the same audience. When Fagin gives Oliver a book of 'great criminals' to peruse, the reader is clearly supposed to infer that this is the *Calendar*. Of course, rather than inspiring Oliver, it merely drives him into a 'paroxysm of fear'; as indeed the same experience did for a young Dickens (164).[74] Only a few years later, moreover, Dickens would be cutting his journalistic teeth chronicling similar cases of spousal violence and indiscretion.[75] The habit stayed with him. For the rest of his life Dickens would scour the morning papers looking for exciting cases which he might recast in his novels and short stories.[76] He may not have liked the appellation of sensationalist,

---

[70] Tantamount, as critics have commonly suggested, to a fairy-tale ending. The salvation theme, which reinforces Oliver's almost angelic nature, has been noted by a number of critics. See, for example, M Tromp, *The Private Rod: Marital Violence, Sensation and the Law in Victorian Britain* (Virginia University Press, 2000) 26–27.

[71] See ibid, 25–26; Collins, *Dickens and Crime* (above n 11) 260–61; and J John, *Dickens's Villains: Melodrama, Character, and Popular Culture* (Oxford University Press, 2001) 129–33.

[72] See John, *Dickens's Villains*, ibid, 124, and Collins, *Dickens and Crime* (above n 11) 257.

[73] J Flanders, *The Invention of Murder* (Harper, 2011) 112.

[74] Dickens later attested that when he read similar works as a youngster they frightened 'my very wits out of my head'. Collins, *Dickens and Crime* (above n 11) 236.

[75] In 1829, at the outset of his journalistic career, Dickens was despatched to Doctors Commons to review salacious separation cases. Within a year he was also reporting from Parliament.

[76] Lisa Surridge suggests that Dickens probably gained his inspiration for Sikes from cases of wife-beating that were prosecuted following the 1828 Offences Against the Person Act. See L Surridge, *Bleak Houses: Marital Violence in Victorian Fiction* (Ohio University Press, 2005) 16–17.

at least not in 1837, but Thackeray was right. At heart, Dickens was a sensational-ist too.

Oliver Twist betrays Dickens's fascination with legal issues, his contempt for its apparent limitations and his anxieties as regards the consequential injustices. The 'law is an ass an idiot' says the Mr Bumble (436). Bumble is ridiculous. Even so we can imagine Dickens smiling, however grimly, as he cast the line.[77] The tone varies, of course; it is sometimes lighter, sometimes darker. Oliver's appearance before the magistrate Mr Fang, following his arrest for pickpocketing, tends to the for-mer. Fang deals in justice 'summarily' and casually, disinclined to worry too much about due process, still less the veracity of evidence brought before his court (84). Later in the novel Fagin tries to pass off the capture of the Artful Dodger in similarly comic terms, wondering how he might 'stand in the Newgate Calendar', and contemplating what it might cost to hire a 'big-wig' with the 'gift of the gab' to defend him; not that he has the slightest intention of spending a single penny (363). Brought before the 'full majesty' of justice, the Dodger blusters his best but is committed for trial all the same (366).[78] The idiocy of the Bow Street Runners who descend on the Maylies looking for Oliver is also written in lighter tones, and the same might be said of Mr Brownlow's companion, Mr Grimwig, who turns out to be a failed lawyer. Rather darker, in contrast, is the depiction of the workhouse into which Oliver is born. Dickens was as staunch a critic of the 1834 Poor Law as Frances Trollope, and the Mudfog 'workhouse' is every bit as grim as that which casts its shadow over Deepbrook.[79]

Darker still is the treatment of Sikes, to whom justice is meted out peremptorily, and of Fagin who is tried as an accessory before the fact of Nancy's murder. In technical terms, Fagin's guilt is uncertain and was indeed questioned by some contemporary reviewers. According to Fitzjames Stephen, Fagin received 'poetical rather than legal justice'.[80] His advice to Sikes not to be 'too violent for safety', to

---

[77] According to Michael Horne, the failure of law is the defining theme in *Oliver Twist*. See Horne, 'Introduction' (above n 17) at xiv–xv. For a recent commentary on Dickens's personal interest in the law, see Tomalin, *Charles Dickens* (above n 5) 34–36.

[78] Dickens would later record a similar incident, when he and a friend Mark Lemon, the editor of *Punch*, chased a pickpocket along Edgware Road. The offender was captured and appeared in the magistrate's court the next day, where he blustered in terms very similar to those of the Dodger, even accusing Dickens of being a renowned 'fence'. For an account, see Hartley, *House of Fallen Women* (above n 1) 56.

[79] An Act which Dickens declared, he would oppose 'to the death'. Nearly 30 years later, Dickens wrote, 'I believe there has been in England, since the days of the Stuarts, no law so often infamously administered, no law so often openly violated, no law habitually so ill-supervised'. The Poor Law was nothing less than a 'disgrace' to the country'. Quoted in J Gold, *Charles Dickens: Radical Moralist*, (Minnesota University Press, 1972) at 25. In *Oliver Twist* Dickens typically assumed a more satirical tone as regards the 'wise and humane regulations' consequent on the 1834 Act, including that which 'instead of compelling man to support his family as they had theretofore done, took his family away from him, and made him a bachelor!' (13). For commentaries on Dickens's treatment of the Mudfog workhouse, and his implicit critique of the Poor Law, see S Zlotnick, 'The Law's a Bachelor: *Oliver Twist*, Bastardy, and the New Poor Law' (2006) 34 *Victorian Literature and Culture* 131–46, and L Berry, *The Child, the State and the Victorian Novel* (Virginia University Press, 1999) 29–62.

[80] In this Stephen likened him to Iago. Quoted in L Rodensky, *The Crime in Mind: Criminal Responsibility and the Victorian Novel* (Oxford University Press, 2003) at 62. The same view was expressed later in the *Saturday Review*. For a rebuttal, see Jonathan Bouchier in 5 ser. *Notes and Queries*

be 'crafty' and 'not too bold' is ambivalent, at best only gesturing towards intent (395). Before 1848, moreover, Fagin could not have been prosecuted as an accessory unless Sikes had already been convicted of murder which was not the case. In literary terms, however, there is no room for doubt. Fagin is guilty; not just of inciting Sikes, but of receiving stolen goods, child assault and, of course, pimping Nancy. There is no possibility of 'sympathy' either in court or, Dickens imputes, amongst his readers (441). Fagin is sentenced to hang. Oliver pays him a last visit, but there will be no confession of the kind which hastened the 'happy' death of Mary Voce. There is no possibility of 'that', as the turnkey confirms (449). The reader leaves Fagin struggling violently and hopelessly, sending up 'shriek upon shriek' (449).[81]

As to the woman for whose murder he is hanged, Nancy too is guilty of myriad offences against both law and propriety. She is most obviously a prostitute; though Dickens failed to actually confirm the imputation in the original edition of *Oliver Twist*. The inference is, however, patent. Nancy is only too familiar with the 'stews' (332).[82] She 'belonged' to a 'particular species of humanity', one that was fully acquainted with casual violence and criminality, driven onto the 'streets' by Fagin 12 years earlier to ply her 'trade' as thief and now whore (131–33). Nancy is very aware that in the common perception there is indeed no trade more 'shameful' (332). Her character owed much to those literary predecessors who walked the streets sketched by Boz. A collected edition of *Sketches by Boz* had been published just a year earlier.[83] The *Sketches* teem with prostitutes, as they do with wife-beaters like Sikes; the two troublingly youthful prostitutes in *The Prisoner's Van*; a 'gaudy' young lady who covered her face in shame and 'burst into an agony of tears' in *The Pawnbroker's Shop*; and perhaps most disturbing of all, the beaten prostitute whose final moments are recorded in *The Hospital Patient*.[84] The *Sketches* were supposed to be read as pieces of journalism, accounts of real people, real sadness and real violence. The death of the beaten prostitute is tragic because it is credible; in her dying breath desperately trying to convince the magistrate that the man accused, her boyfriend and pimp, is innocent. It is, however, 'too late'. She 'cannot save him'.[85] His guilt is established; and in this at least, in the prospect of justice, Dickens permits his readers to be reassured.

The murder of Nancy, this 'foulest and most cruel' crime, occurs in chapter nine of the third volume of *Oliver Twist* (397). Learning of Nancy's treachery, Sikes

---

5 July 1879, 6, conceding only that in reality Fagin would have been more likely to receive a sentence of penal servitude for life.

[81] Dickens was a constant critic of capital punishment, and the passages in which Fagin is driven to the edge of madness as he contemplates his own demise are rightly acclaimed.

[82] Stews was a common nineteenth-century term for brothels.

[83] The *Sketches* had been published in individual form between 1833 and 1836. Aside from portrayals of prostitutes, accounts of spousal violence recur elsewhere in *Sketches*, in conspicuous numbers. See DE Nord, *Walking the Victorian Streets: Women, Representation and the City* (Cornell University Press, 1995) 71–73.

[84] See respectively, C Dickens, *Sketches by Boz* (Penguin, 1995) 314–17, 220–29, and 277–82.

[85] Ibid, 282.

storms into her room 'grasping her by the head and throat' and 'dragged her into the middle of the room'. Nancy begs for her 'life, for the love of Heaven, as I spared yours'. Carelessly she confirms his suspicions by alluding to the possibility that she might, as Rose and Mr Brownlow suggested, go to 'some foreign country' (396). Sikes strikes her with the butt of his pistol:

> She staggered and fell, nearly blinded with the blood that rained down from a deep gash in her forehead, but raising herself with difficulty on her knees, drew from her bosom a white handkerchief – Rose Maylie's own – and holding it up in her folded hands as high towards Heaven as her feeble strength would let her, breathed one prayer for mercy to her Maker. It was a ghastly figure to look upon. The murderer staggering backward to the wall, and shutting out the sight with his hand, seized a heavy club and struck her down. (396–97)

It may not be quite as melodramatic as the stage version Dickens later wrote but there can be no doubting that Dickens wanted to thrill and terrify his readers all the same; as indeed he did his wife. The rhetoric and the imagery of redemption are patent. But so is the intensity of violence, the sheer physicality clearly owing much to the popularity of such scenes in the *Newgate Calendar*.

As we have already noted, it was commonly supposed that prostitution, a necessarily working-class occupation, was inimically related to other species of violent working-class criminality.[86] Nancy was supposed to live a violent life. She is quite prepared to inflict violence if necessary and she is well used to suffering it, and anticipating it, living in evident fear of her next beating. She was supposed to die violently too; most fictive prostitutes did. In his *Confessions* de Quincey agonises over whether the prostitute he has befriended will be lucky enough to die 'before' the 'brutalities of ruffians had completed the ruin they had begun'.[87] Dickens's readers might have hoped for better for Nancy but they would not have been surprised by the realisation of their worst fears. If *Oliver Twist* was indeed supposed to convey a 'true' account of a prostitute's life, they could have expected little other than a violent end for Nancy. Certainly Nancy expected no other, increasingly terrified by 'thoughts of death, and shrouds with blood upon them' (384).[88]

What they may not have expected was the presentation of a flesh and blood prostitute with whose fall and its consequences they were supposed to sympathise. In many ways Nancy bears all the physical hallmarks of her trade, frequently drunk, frequently bruised, more 'pale and reduced' each time she returns to the text (158, 208–209, 318). But appearances can deceive. Nancy has a good heart. It is she who repeatedly saves Oliver from the violence intended by Fagin and Sikes,

---

[86] See Hemyng's observations in Mayhew's *London Labour* (above n 38) at 480–81, 484, 489.

[87] De Quincey, *Confessions of an English Opium-Eater* (above n 64) 34.

[88] She also variously contemplates throwing herself into the Thames, inquiring of Rose 'How many times do you read of such as me who spring into the tide, and leave no living thing to care for and bewail them' (389). As we have already noted, it was a common enough fate for fallen women, and one to which Dickens would later allude in his short story *The Chimes*.

eventually risking everything to warn Rose and Mr Brownlow of the danger which Oliver faces. The fact that she declines to accept money in return for this information is intended to confirm her intrinsic goodness. No fallen woman is beyond redemption; none undeserving of respect and pity. Nancy, in short, is the kind of woman for whom Urania Cottage was established. Mr Brownlow gestures towards the possibility of her finding security in a 'quiet asylum', perhaps in England, perhaps in 'some foreign country' (388). 'It is never too late', Rose urges, 'for penitence and atonement' (336). Nancy is not, however, persuaded: 'I am passed all hope, indeed' (387–88).

Thackeray was not persuaded by Rose's argument. He concluded that in a novel full of 'unnatural caricatures' Nancy was perhaps 'the most unreal fantastical personage possible'.[89] Dickens was particularly troubled by this accusation precisely because Nancy had to be credible if she was to be deserving of the reader's sympathy. There are women such as Nancy, as he confirmed in his 1841 Preface, just as there are 'such men as Sikes':

> It is useless to discuss whether the conduct and character of the girl seems natural or unnatural, probable or improbable, right or wrong. IT IS TRUE. Every man who has watched these melancholy shades of life knows it to be so. Suggested to my mind long ago long before I dealt in fiction by what I often saw and read of, in actual life around me, I have, for years, tracked it through many profligate and noisome ways, and found it still the same. From the first introduction of that poor wretch, to her laying her bloody head upon the robber's breast, there is not one word exaggerated or over-wrought. It is emphatically God's truth, for it is the truth He leaves in such depraved and miserable breasts; the hope yet lingering behind; the last fair drop of water at the bottom of the dried-up weed-choked well. It involves the best and worst shades of our common nature; much of its ugliest hues, and something of its most beautiful; it is a contradiction, an anomaly, an apparent impossibility, but it is a Truth. (460)

Nancy was not just a prostitute. She was a real human being, with the all the contradictions that entails. She is someone's daughter, very probably someone's sister; as might indeed be said of Oliver's fallen mother, Agnes. It was fortune which moved against her, as Nancy is only too aware. 'Thank heaven upon your knees dear lady' she advises Rose, 'that you had friends to keep you in your childhood, and that you were never in the midst of cold and hunger, and riot and drunkenness, and and something worse than all as I have been from the cradle' (334). Nancy, Agnes and indeed Rose, each have a 'stain' upon their name (290)[90] but they also share a common humanity, that 'one feeling' all women have for 'love' (338). Sadly, in Nancy's case it is a love for the man who will kill her.

---

[89] Thackeray's doubts were expressed in his account of the execution of the notorious poisoner Courvoisier. In the crowd watching the execution, Thackeray recorded a girl who might have been 'taken as a study for Nancy', except that the Nancy who appears in the pages of *Twist* was indeed 'fantastical'. Quoted in Horne, Introduction' (above n 17) at xxxii–iii.

[90] There are doubts as to Rose's legitimacy too.

Dickens wanted to do 'great things with Nancy', as he confided to Forster in late 1837;[91] and he did. He made her complex and inconsistent, and thus believable. On the one hand, as Thackeray inferred, there is Nancy the caricature, trapped in an abusive relationship, consorting with criminals, falling ever further.[92] On the other, there is the Nancy preferred by so many later critics including Gissing who suggested that she was made 'credible by force of her surroundings' and who in 'certain scenes' becomes 'life itself'.[93] This is the redeemable Nancy, brave, tragic, deserving of pity, perhaps even respect. There is nothing simple about Nancy Sikes, her life, her fall, or her death.[94] The narratives of fall and redemption were not, as Greg confirmed in his 1850 essay, exclusive; adding that in conveying this ambiguity 'writers of fiction may do much' to aid the cause of saving 'fallen angels'.[95] Similar sentiments could be read in numerous pamphlets emanating from organisations such as the Ladies National Association, as well as the articles and letters published by the likes of Mayhew and Hemyng. If Victorian England was to save its prostitutes, then it would first need to acknowledge their humanity. As Greg concluded, it 'is for the interest of society at large, as well as for that of the guilty individual, that we should never break down the bridge behind any sinner'.[96] It was to this cause that Dickens sacrificed Nancy Sikes.[97]

Contemplating Jenny

As we have already noted, there was nothing particularly unusual in finding a prostitute walking the pages of a Victorian novel, or indeed the pages of a Victorian poem, where the fallen angel as muse emerged as a defining image most notably amongst the so-called 'fleshly' school of pre-Raphaelite poets. It found an original expression in Elizabeth Barrett Browning's influential 'novel-poem' *Aurora Leigh*. Barrett Browning would have been horrified to think that she might be thought a 'fleshly' poet, as indeed would most of the 'fleshly' poets, with the inevitable exception perhaps of Algernon Swinburne. However, Barrett Browning's Marian Erle, the fallen angel who flits in and out of *Aurora Leigh*, set a course for the likes of Christina Rossetti's Laura and Lizzie, as well as Dante Gabriel's Jenny, in much

---

[91] See Rodensky, *The Crime in Mind* (above n 80) 74.

[92] His most recent biographer, Claire Tomalin, suggests that Dickens fell into the trap of writing a 'stereotype' Nancy. See Tomalin, *Charles Dickens* (above n 5) 98.

[93] Quoted in Horne, 'Introduction' (above n 17) xxxvii. Gissing did identify a few weaknesses in the novel, including the 'insufferable' Monks and the 'feeble idyllicism' of the Maylies.

[94] This is one of the reasons why Wilkie Collins would rate Nancy as his favourite Dickensian character; she is seemingly so simple but on closer contemplation so troubling and so complex. On the paradoxes written into Nancy, see Tromp, *The Private Rod* (above n 70) 65.

[95] Greg, *Prostitution* (above n 3) 449, 452, 455 .

[96] Greg, *Prostitution* (above n 3) 494.

[97] For this reason, according to Patricia Ingham, she become 'Dickens's Tess'. See P Ingham, *Dickens, Women and Language* (Toronto University Press, 1992), 59.

the same way as Elizabeth Gaskell's Ruth Hilton did for Hetty Sorrell and Lydia Glasher. When *Aurora Leigh* first appeared in 1856, Swinburne concluded excitedly that there was nothing 'in any way comparable with that unique work of audaciously feminine and ambitiously impulsive genius'.[98]

The 'novel-poem' style, written in deference to Wordsworth's magisterial *Prelude*, was commonly adopted by poets who wanted readers to recognise a testamentary aspiration, as well as a collateral determination to engage broader matters of social justice. The responsibility of the poet, Barrett Browning asserted in *Aurora Leigh*, was not to fashion flights of fancy, but to nurture the 'truth which draws' (761).[99] Marian Erle serves precisely this purpose, contemplation of her real suffering grounding the metaphysical tendencies which periodically capture Aurora's imagination.[100] The reader is introduced to Marian in the second book, in the company of a mother who is regularly and 'badly beat', and who wants to prostitute her daughter to the local squire in the hope that he might 'set' them both 'up' (105).[101] Marian has been 'sold' for the first time, but not the last (109). She runs away. Shortly afterwards, she encounters the young Romney who decides, out of pity but not love, to offer marriage. Recognising that marriage is simply another species of sexual 'contract', Marian runs away again, only to reappear when Aurora, by chance, comes across her in Paris (116). By now she is working in a brothel, 'not dead' but 'damned', and has an illegitimate child (195). At first Marian struggles to tell her story, constrained by poetic propriety, knowing 'that we must scrupulously hint/With half words, delicate reserves, the thing/Which no

[98] McSweeney, 'Introduction' in *Aurora Leigh* (Oxford University Press, 1993) xxi. All internal citations are to this edition.

[99] Barrett Browning conceived *Aurora Leigh* to be 'a sort of novel-poem . . . running into the midst of our conventions'. See M Stone, 'Genre Subversion and Gender Inversion: *The Princess* and *Aurora Leigh*' (1987) 25 *Victorian Poetry* 115, 123–27 commenting on the implications of this peculiar generic hybrid. Further commentaries on the generic implications can be found in A Case, 'Gender and Narration in *Aurora Leigh*' (1991) 29 *Victorian Poetry* 17–32, and J Zonana, 'The Embodied Muse: Elizabeth Barrett Browning's *Aurora Leigh* and Feminist Poetics' (1989) 8 *Tulsa Studies in Women's Literature* 244–45. As we have already noted, Barrett Browning was one of many contemporary female writers of the period who expressed their particular admiration for Gaskell's *Ruth*, in correspondence writing 'I am grateful to you as a woman for having so treated such a subject'. Quoted in Leighton, 'Fallen Woman' (above n 54) 120. For further commentaries on the derivative relation of *Ruth* and *Aurora Leigh*, see M Forster, *Barrett Browning* (Vintage, 2004) 285 and 316–17, and S Gottlieb, 'And God will teach her: Consciousness and Character in *Ruth* and *Aurora Leigh*' (1996) 24 *Victorian Institute Journal* 57–85. The testamentary aspect of *Aurora Leigh* is explored in M Reynolds, '*Aurora Leigh*: Writing her story for the better self' (1987) 17 *Browning Society Notes* 5–11. It is a critical commonplace to identify an obvious parallel with Charlotte Bronte's *Jane Eyre*.

[100] Assuming, according to Leslee Thorne-Murphy, an 'understated yet integral' role in the poem. See L Thorne-Murphy, 'Prostitute Rescue, Rape, and Poetic Inspiration in Elizabeth Barrett Browning's *Aurora Leigh*' (2005) 12 *Women's Writing* 242, 247. Marian's role as muse is extensively considered in Zonana, 'Muse' (above n 99) 243, 250–55. The immediate influence for Marian's character was taken from Eugene Sue's *Mysteries of Paris*.

[101] The negative portrayal of unnatural mothers is common in Barrett Browning's poetry; some unnatural by reason of their unmarried status, others by reason of their 'mother-want'. See B Gelpi, '*Aurora Leigh*: The Vocation of the Woman Poet' (1981) 19 *Victorian Poetry* 39–40, and V Steinmetz, 'Images of Mother-Want in Elizabeth Barrett Browning's *Aurora Leigh*' (1983) 21 *Victorian Poetry* 360–62, 365–66.

one scrupled we should feel in full' (220).[102] Eventually, Aurora gleans that Marian was raped prior to being prostituted for which reason she now has an abiding hatred for the 'common law, by which the poor and weak/Are trodden underfoot by vicious men' (204).[103] Romney pops up to repeat his offer of marriage, but sticking nobly to her principles, Marian again declines preferring to accept Aurora's offer of an altogether sunnier refuge on a Tuscan farm.[104]

Barrett Browning had worried that after all the years of agonising composition *Aurora Leigh* might emerge to barely a critical murmur. There was no need for her to worry. In commercial terms it was a phenomenal success, a first edition selling out in a week, a second by the end of the month.[105] More importantly, the critics were on the whole kind; fellow writers even more so. There were dissonant voices. Emile Montegut in *Revue de Deux Mondes* noted rather too many 'vulgar' passages.[106] Ruskin, however, expressed himself almost as excited as Swinburne. It was, he concluded, the 'perfect poetical expression of the Age'.[107] Female admirers included Frances Power Cobbe, George Eliot, who confessed to the 'profound impression' that the story of Marian Erle had made, and Emily Dickinson, who suggested that *Aurora Leigh* inspired a generation of female, indeed feminist, poets.[108] According to Christina Rossetti, Barrett Browning was quite simply 'the Great Poetess of our own day and Nation'.[109]

[102] On the significance of Marian's fragmentary discourse, and Aurora's role in trying to interpret it, see P Murphy, 'Reconceiving the Mother: Deconstructing the Madonna in *Aurora Leigh*' (1997) 91 *Victorian Newsletter* 25. When Thackeray, as editor of the *Cornhill Magazine*, rejected another of Barrett Browning's poems, *Lord Walter's Wife*, on the grounds that 'there are things my squeamish public will not hear', an incensed author responded that: 'It is exactly because pure and prosperous women choose to ignore vice, that miserable women suffer wrong by it everywhere.' Quoted in D David, 'Art's a Service: Social Wound, Sexual Politics, and *Aurora Leigh*' (1985) 13 *Browning Institute Studies* 120. There is a necessary irony, of course, in the fact that on discovering her personal maid Elizabeth Wilson to be pregnant outside of marriage, Barrett Browning demanded that she either leave her service or leave her baby with relatives. Initially, Wilson took the first option, but as the financial realities became apparent, she reluctantly changed her mind. It is difficult to reconcile the heroic defence of Marian Erle with the stark lack of compassion Barrett Browning evinced in a real case involving a loyal and trusted servant. See Forster, *Barrett Browning* (above n 99) 303, 315–16.

[103] Aurora describes her rape as 'murder'. On the presentation of rape as a species of sexual murder, see L Lewis, 'Rape and Resurrection in *Aurora Leigh*' (1991) 19 *Studies in Browning and his Circle* 56–57, 60–611.

[104] It is evident from correspondence that the disposal of Marian caused Barrett Browning considerable difficulties, primarily because the idea of her disappearing to Italy with Aurora potentially compromised the preferred conclusion which saw the triumph of 'love' in the marriage of the eponymous heroine and the maimed Romney. See Forster, *Barrett Browning* (above n 99) 309.

[105] It went through five editions in the first two years.

[106] See David, 'Sexual Politics' (above n 102) 113, 117–18 and Stone, 'Genre Subversion' (above n 99) 124.

[107] Review of *Aurora Leigh* in E Cook and A Wedderburn (eds) *The Works of John Ruskin* (George Allen, 1903–12), vol 15, 227.

[108] See McSweeney, 'Introduction' (above n 98) at xxi and xxxv. Cobbe's praise can be found in her essay 'What Shall We Do With Our Old Maids?' published in 1862. Virginia Woolf would later admit to being 'enthralled' by *Aurora Leigh*, a poem that 'overwhelms and bewilders; but, nevertheless, it still commands our interest and inspires our respect'. See V Woolf, *The Common Reader: Second Series* (Hogarth Press, 1948) 208. The view that *Aurora Leigh* remains an 'epic of feminist self-affirmation' has been recently pressed by S Gilbert and S Gubar in *The Madwoman in the Attic: the Woman Writer and the Nineteenth-Century Literary Imagination* (Yale University Press, 2000) 575.

[109] J Bristow, *Victorian Women Poets* (Palgrave, 1995) 46.

The fallen angel is a familiar figure in Rossetti's poetry too, recurring in such poems as *Apple-Gathering, Cousin Kate, The Convent Threshold,* and perhaps most famously and enigmatically, *Goblin Market,* a text which might, depending on interpretive preference, be read as a children's fairy tale or a piece of rape-inflected pornography. It opens with two young girls, Laura and Lizzie, peering through the 'brookside rushes' at the goblins as they cry 'Come buy our orchard fruits' (2–3, 33).[110] Laura is the first to succumb:

> She sucked and sucked and sucked some more
> Fruits which that unknown orchard bore;
> She sucked until her lips were sore. (134–36)

She has no money, and so pays with a 'precious golden lock' of hair (126).[111] Stronger willed, Lizzie raises the spectre of 'Jeanie in her grave,/Who should have been a bride' but who, by inference, fell too soon (312).[112]

However, Laura has become addicted to the fruit, neglecting her domestic duties and becoming distracted to such a degree that Lizzie decides to go and buy more fruit from the goblins for her. The goblins are reluctant to accept money and try to force the fruit into Lizzie's mouth. They 'Tore her gown and soiled her stocking' and 'Held her hands and squeezed their fruits/Against her mouth to make her eat' (404, 406–407). But Lizzie 'Would not open lip from lip', and so the fruit dribbled down her face and 'lodged in dimples of her chin' (431, 435). The fact that Lizzie, on her return, then urges Laura to 'Hug me, kiss me, suck my juices' insinuated a further dimension of forbidden sexuality, which was hardly ameliorated by its articulation in the midst of a pervasively Eucharistic imagery (468).[113]

The Godly and the fleshly indeed and none the better, as critics observed, for their imputed affinity.[114] Ruskin was blunt. Christina's poems, like those of her brother Dante Gabriel, were 'full of beauty and power', but also 'quaintnesses and

---

[110] Line references are given from *Goblin Market* in C Rossetti, *Poems and Prose* (Oxford University Press, 2008) at 105–19.

[111] A gesture intended to bring to mind the classical rape of Danae. There are, of course, only two common denominators of commodification and sexuality, prostitution and marriage; insofar as they can be distinguished. See E Helsinger, 'Consumer Power and the Utopia of Desire: Christina Rossetti's *Goblin Market*' (1991) 58 *ELH* 903–904.

[112] The naming of Lizzie imports a further, if again maddeningly elusive, connotation; with Lizzie Siddal, the favourite model of Dante Gabriel Rossetti. Lizzie was seriously ill by 1859, when Christina first conceived *Goblin Market*, and still waiting for Dante Gabriel to make good his promise to marry her. They finally married in 1860, and she died two years later. It is evident that Christina disapproved of Lizzie's relationship with her brother.

[113] See the Prayer of Consecration: 'Take, eat, this is my body which is given for you'.

[114] The extent to which an audience would have registered the various sexual insinuations remains a matter of critical conjecture. See Thomas, *Christina Rossetti* (above n 6) 170–71. On the discomfort which characterises Rossetti's frequently ambiguous association of sexuality and Christology, see S Humphries, 'The Uncertainty of *Goblin Market*' (2007) 45 *Victorian Poetry* 391–413, and Gilbert and Gubar, *The Madwoman in the Attic* (above n 108) 566–69. The sexual insinuations are strongly pressed in D Mermin, 'Heroic Sisterhood in *Goblin Market*' (1983) 21 *Victorian Poetry*, observing at 113, that Christina 'knew what she was doing' when she wrote such passages. For more cautious discussion of the imagery written into these passages, see Bristow, *Women Poets* (above n 109) 50–51, and L Kooistra, 'Modern Markets for *Goblin Market*' (1994) 32 *Victorian Poetry* 263–65.

offences'. They should not be placed before the 'public'.[115] But they were, and Ruskin was right; the 'public' was not ready for *Goblin Market*. Christina had feared as much; but as ever deferred to her brother's apparently superior sense of audience propriety. By 1861 Christina had anyway suffered another nervous breakdown, for which reason, as part of her projected recovery, she had begun visiting St Mary Magdalene Penitentiary in Highgate. In truth, she never fully recovered, remaining troubled by related disorders until her death in 1894. She certainly never wrote another poem like *Goblin Market*. But while Christina spent more and more time with real prostitutes, Dante Gabriel focused increasingly intently upon imaginary ones,[116] so much so that in 1870 Jeanie would be spectacularly resurrected in the shape of 'Poor shameful Jenny' in a collection of poems the tenor of which was to ignite a furious debate amongst critics as to the responsibility of authorship (18).[117]

Not that Jenny has anything to say on the subject. The reader first encounters 'Lazy, laughing, languid Jenny,/Fond of a kiss and fond of a guinea' as she is about to nod off in the lap of the young gentleman who narrates his thoughts over the ensuing 391 scandalous lines (1–2). It is again the disarticulation of Jenny which is so significant. The reader is invited to contemplate a 'thoughtful man of the world' as he in turn contemplates the woman whose body he has just bought.[118] Though it silences her, sleep also keeps Jenny safe; not only precluding sexual intercourse, but preserving an ultimate anonymity, leaving the narrator to speculate on her life and feelings, and then his own. 'Poor shameful' Jenny draws in the narrator and the reader (18). She frustrates them too, as the narrator confirms when he likens her to a 'rose' trapped between the pages of a closed book, the real story of her fall left to conjecture. Jenny is a 'riddle that one shrinks/To challenge' (280–81). Jenny might be regularly bought, but she is a 'volume seldom read', and seldom understood; something which gestured towards a supremely discomforting affinity between the poet and the prostitute. As Dante Gabriel observed in correspondence with Ford Maddox Brown: 'I have often said that to be an artist is just the same thing as to be a whore, as far as dependence on the whims and fancies of individuals is concerned.'[119]

[115] Thomas, *Christina Rossetti* (above n 1) 200–201.

[116] Though not, as has become apparent, to the exclusion of visiting real ones. See N Shrimpton, 'Rossetti's Pornography' (1979) 29 *Essays in Criticism* 325.

[117] In fact, Dante Gabriel had begun sketching *Jenny* before his sister began *Goblin Market*. Thereafter it went through numerous revisions prior to publication in 1870. A provisional draft also spent eight years interred in the grave of Elizabeth Siddall before being exhumed, Dante Gabriel coming to the eventual conclusion that he was not quite as grief-stricken as he had originally thought; a realisation that accompanied a new affair with William Morris's sister, Jane. The writing of *Jenny*, as modern critics have noted, was clearly a tortuous experience, evolving over 20 years. On the composition of *Jenny* and its inter-textual relation with *Goblin Market*, see A Chapman, *The Afterlife of Christina Rossetti* (Palgrave, 2000), 148–50, Helsinger, 'Consumer Power' (above n 111) 919; R Sheets, 'Pornography and Art' (1988) 14 *Critical Inquiry* 332–23; and J Bristow, 'What if to her all this was said? Dante Gabriel Rossetti and the silencing of Jenny' (1993) 46 *Essays and Studies* 96–99.

[118] Rossetti raised his 'thoughtful young man' in his 'The Stealthy School of Criticism' in D Rossetti, *Collected Poetry and Prose* (Yale University Press, 2003) 338.

[119] Quoted in Bristow, 'Jenny' (above n 117) 106.

Eventually, the narrator begins to contemplate the extent of his own responsibility, and also his shame. Lounging about in Jenny's meagre apartment, he is not merely a client but also a *flaneur*, stimulating his sexual faculties by gazing at a prostitute's body. As he leaves, he tosses a few 'gold' coins into Jenny's hair.[120] Their relationship is concluded:

> I think I see you when you wake,
> And rub your eyes for me, and shake
> My gold, in rising, from your hair,
> A Danae for a moment there. (376–9)

And gesturing towards the possibility of redemption also, his as well as hers:

> And must I mock you to the last,
> Ashamed of my own shame, aghast
> Because some thoughts not born amiss
> Rose at a poor fair face like this?
> Well, of such thoughts so much I know:
> In my life, as in hers, they show,
> By a far gleam which I may near,
> A dark path I can strive to clear. (383–89)

It is this sense that the narrator, and thus the poet and the reader, share the responsibility for Jenny's fall which was so challenging. Dickens also challenged readers insofar as he invited sympathetic consideration of Nancy's plight, but the reader was never deemed to be responsible for her murder. Attribution of guilt is not so simple in *Jenny*. The idea that men, in their inability to control their sexual urges, were responsible for prostitution could be found, repeatedly, in the writings of Josephine Butler, as well as those of Greg and Acton. The sexual urge was alien to women. It certainly is to Jenny. Men, conversely, are constantly 'excited'; their lust the 'toad within a stone', as Dante Gabriel's 'young gentleman' muses, before gently placing Jenny's head on the pillow and masturbating over it (282).[121] The question as to what the young 'gentleman' has really learned, still less the extent to which he might be thought redeemed, hangs in the air.

Importantly, Jenny is not the only woman contemplated in *Jenny*. There is also Nell, the cousin who is yet to fall, and to whom the young 'gentleman' is intended. In an 1858 editorial on the subject of prostitution, *The Lancet* reminded its readers 'after all the prostitute is sister to those by our firesides'.[122] Besant cast the same allusion: 'If a man realised that in buying a prostitute he was buying the womanhood of those he loved at home, he would shrink back from such sacrilege as from

---

[120] On the alternative interpretations of the tossed coins, see L Starzyk, 'Rossetti's *Jenny*: Aestheticizing the Whore' (2000) 36 *Papers on Language and Literature*, 239–40, and D Bentley, 'Dante Gabriel Rossetti's Inner-Standing Point and Jenny Reconstrued' (2011) 80 *University of Toronto Quarterly* 710–11. Masturbation was a subject of peculiar interest, and the cause of considerable consternation, in Victorian England. See E Rosenman, *Unauthorized Pleasures* (Cornell University Press, 2003) 19–27.

[121] Greg, *Prostitution* (above n 3) 456–57.

[122] 'Prostitution: its Medical Aspects' (1858) 2 *The Lancet* 198.

the touch of a leper.'[123] The same insinuation could, of course, be read into the alignment of Nancy and Rose Maylie in *Oliver Twist*. If Rose and Nell might be the reader's sister or cousin, or indeed prospective wife, so just as easily might Nancy or Jenny.[124] The introduction of the pure woman, yet to be corrupted, engages once again the issue of readership. In her *Girl of the Period*, Elizabeth Lynn Linton worried that young women were trying to emulate literary fallen women in order to appear sexier.[125] WT Stead had warned that such behaviour might easily lead to prostitution. It is Jenny's craving too, her 'magic purse', which the narrator surmises has precipitated her fall (345–46).[126] Nell meanwhile is worryingly 'fond of fun/And fond of dress, and change, and praise', the kind of woman who troubled Linton, who might read a 'book/In which pure women may not look' (185–86, 253–54). It might have been thought that poetic prostitutes were, for reason of audience, less threatening than those found in novels. Alexander Macmillan's letter to Dante Gabriel confirming his willingness to publish *Goblin Market* gave the lie to this supposition:

> I took the liberty of reading the *Goblin Market* aloud to a number of people belonging to a small working-man's society here. They seemed at first to wonder whether I was making fun of them; by degrees they got as still as death, and when I finished there was a tremendous burst of applause.[127]

The audience may not have been on the same scale as that which attended Dickens's readings, but the response was clearly as remarkable. Moreover, if the working-men of England were entranced by the story of Laura and Lizzie, and Jenny and Marian Erle, it might be reasonably supposed that this could just as easily be true of their wives and daughters.

Such a thought underlay Robert Buchanan's notorious attack on the 'fleshly school' of poets which appeared in the *Contemporary Review* a few months after the publication of Dante Gabriel's collected *Poems*. Buchanan made two accusations. The first suggested that 'the fleshly gentlemen have bound themselves by solemn league and covenant to extol fleshliness as the distinct and supreme end of poetic and pictorial art'. Such poetry was 'emasculated', Buchanan added, citing *Jenny* as being especially culpable; 'fleshly all over'.[128] The second, just as damaging, was to suggest that the 'Mutual Admiration Society', as he termed it, had pursued a critical strategy 'mutually to praise, extol, and imitate each other'. It was a view that might have resonated with readers of the *Fortnightly Review*, in the

---

[123] Besant, *The Legalization of Female Slavery* (above n 30) 99.

[124] According to Daniel Harris, stripped to its bones, *Jenny* boils down to one question 'is a whore a person?' See his 'DG Rossetti's Jenny: Sex, Money, and the Interior Monologue' (1984) 22 *Victorian Poetry* 197.

[125] EL Linton, *The Girl of the Period*, (Bentley, 1883).

[126] The association of purse and vagina was familiar in Victorian culture. If Jenny unlocks her purse, she might access untold wealth; except that in the end, as the narrator, confirms, her dreams are dashed, her purse 'clogged with shrivelled flies'.

[127] Thomas, *Rossetti* (above n 6) 207.

[128] R Buchanan, 'The Fleshly School of Poetry: Mr DG Rossetti' *Contemporary Review*, August 1871, 335, 343–45. The article was published anonymously.

pages of which Swinburne was busy asserting that *Jenny* alone was 'worthy to fill its place for ever as one of the most perfect and memorable poems of an age or generation'.[129] In short, Dante Gabriel and his acolytes had wilfully crossed the line between art and pornography, and they knew it; for which reason they were now engaged in a desperate strategy designed to add some measure of critical lustre to their pornographic musings.[130]

Whilst he had anticipated 'impending charges of recklessness and aggressiveness', Dante Gabriel was horrified by the sheer ferocity of Buchanan's attack, by the insinuation that he had tried to load critical responses, that he had further emasculated the poetic form, above all by the assertion that he was little more than a grubby pornographer masking his trade with classical allusions and the clever deployment of fancy verse-forms.[131] For a while he was catatonic, falling into deep depression.[132] When he did respond, in an essay entitled 'The Stealthy School of Criticism', he did so in much the same terms as those articulated by Dickens, Eliot and Gaskell when they were similarly berated. Jenny was real and, poetic though its form might be, the purpose of *Jenny* was political to its core.[133] In correspondence with Ruskin in 1860, Dante Gabriel had confirmed that *Jenny* was 'the most serious thing I have written', the poem he later confirmed that he 'most wanted' to write.[134] Emphasising the importance of approaching familiar problems of social injustice by means of an 'inner-standing point', a contemplative as opposed to utilitarian faculty, he thus urged not just the humanity and the reality of Jenny, but the ensuing responsibility of all those who, in their different ways, continue to pay for her services. Some were persuaded, Joyce, Yeats and Pound amongst them;

[129] A Swinburne, 'The Poems of Dante Gabriel Rossetti' *Fortnightly Review*, 1 May 1870, 572. Buchanan unsurprisingly alighted on the particular example of Swinburne. See 'The Fleshly School of Poetry' (above n 128) 344. Swinburne's devotion to Rossetti has been likened to Coleridge's devotion to Wordsworth. The affection was not entirely mutual. As he sank into depression, Rossetti was increasingly given to blaming Swinburne for the ferocity of Buchanan's attack. See C Murray, 'DG Rossetti, AC Swinburne and RW Buchanan: The Fleshly School Revisited I' (1982/83) 65 *Bulletin of the John Rylands University Library* 209–10, 216–19.

[130] Although Buchanan identified Dante Gabriel as the ringleader, in the opinion of many, the most culpable of the 'fleshly' poets was Swinburne. When Swinburne's *Poems and Ballads* was published in 1866, John Morley was moved to incandescence in the *Saturday Review*. Swinburne, he famously concluded, was an 'unclean fiery imp from the pit', the 'libidinous laureate of a pack of satyrs', his mind 'aflame with feverish carnality of a schoolboy over the dirtiest pages of Lempriere'. See 22 *Saturday Review*, 4 August 1866, 145–47.

[131] Rossetti, *The Stealthy School of Criticism* (above n 118) at 337.

[132] Troubled by chronic insomnia, for which he regularly overdosed on chloral, Rossetti even contemplated suicide, or alternatively challenging Buchanan to a duel which might well have had the same result. It has been suggested that Buchanan's attack 'certainly hastened' his death; which if true implies that Jenny had as lethal effect on Rossetti as Nancy did on Dickens. See Murray, 'The Fleshly School Revisited I' (above n 129) 206, and C Marshik, 'The Case of *Jenny*: Dante Gabriel Rossetti and the Censorship Dialectic' (2005) 33 *Victorian Literature and Culture* 577.

[133] Rossetti, *The Stealthy School of Criticism* (above n 118) 337. For the extent to which the commitment to reality or 'truth' defined the pre-Raphaelite movement as a whole, not just the poetry, but the painting and iconography too, see J Rees, *The Poetry of Dante Gabriel Rossetti: Modes of Self-Expression* (Cambridge University Press, 1981) 7–9.

[134] See Sheets, 'Pornography and Art' (above n 117) 334, and Bentley, 'Reconstrued' (above n 120) 695. See also Jerome McCann's observation that *Jenny* was intended to present an 'all-too-present nightmare', in his 'Introduction' to *Poetry and Prose* (above n 118) xxv–vi.

others less so. The *North British Review* accused Rossetti of 'debauching the minds of a certain number of' his readers.[135] In the *Pall Mall Gazette*, Sidney Colvin concluded that whilst its artistic merit was undoubted, *Jenny* was 'unfit for the drawing-room table' before concluding rather mournfully that it appeared that 'the day of drawing-room decencies in literature is nearly done'.[136] Two decades later, Evelyn Waugh still felt moved to advise that no matter how beautiful his poems, Dante Gabriel Rossetti lacked an 'essential rectitude'.[137]

Because Men Made the Laws

Reflecting on his own prosecution for offending morals which occurred just a few months after Flaubert's, Baudelaire concluded that: 'A true work of art has no need for a prosecution speech. The logic of the work suffices for all postulations of morality, and it is left up to the reader to draw conclusions from the conclusion.'[138] Rossetti might have agreed, but an increasingly vociferous number of his country-men and women, their anxieties exercised by the Society for the Suppression of Vice and aligned organisations, did not. At precisely the same moment that Baudelaire found himself arraigned before the Parisian *Tribunal Correctional*, Lord Chief Justice Campbell was busy piloting through Parliament an Obscene Publications Act, which 'authorized the seizure and destruction of all copies of an obscene publication'. It was not a coincidence.[139] Whilst Fitzjames Stephen sought to reassure his readers that there was little 'fear' that English writers would 'out-rage public decency' in the way that Flaubert and Baudelaire evidently had, others thought it better not to take any chances.[140] There was, Campbell advised, a 'tide of poison' rushing through the streets of the capital, 'more deadly than prussic acid, strychnine or arsenic'.[141]

The Act was widely welcomed, not least as a prospective antidote to the possible consequences of the Matrimonial Causes Act which had staggered through Parliament at the same time. *The Times* was 'confidant' that the Act would 'power-fully tend to the purification of public morals'.[142] In rather more sober terms

[135] Quoted in Marshik, 'The Case of *Jenny*' (above n 132) 572.
[136] Ibid, 571.
[137] Ibid, 560.
[138] E Langdon, *Dirt for Art's Sake: Books on Trial from Madame Bovary to Lolita* (Cornell University Press, 2007) 35.
[139] Two prosecutions for obscene libel under the common law in spring 1857 had further sharpened Lord Campbell's attention. See C Manchester, 'Lord Campbell's Act: England's First Obscenity Statute' (1988) 9 *Journal of Legal History* 226–27.
[140] Stephen's comments were made in the context of his review of *Madame Bovary* which was, he warned, 'one of the most revolting productions ever issued from a novelist's brain'. See B Leckie, *Culture and Adultery: The Novel, the Newspaper and the Law 1857–1914* (Pennsylvania University Press, 1999) 20, 30.
[141] Ibid, 36.
[142] Manchester, 'Lord Campbell's Act' (above n 139) 231.

Campbell had repeatedly assured fellow Members that his Act was essentially prosaic and precautionary. Lord Brougham, concerned as to whether the poetry of
Ovid might be proscribed, wanted to know how the term 'obscene' was to be
defined. Lord Roebuck wondered if there was a 'line' to be drawn; perhaps. But it
was not going to be drawn in the Act. There was no intention to prosecute serious
literature, Campbell inferred, just the kind of things that might be found in 'railway stations' and other 'low thoroughfares'; for which reason there was no need
to venture a definition of obscenity either. A gentleman would surely be able to
recognise a 'bad book'.[143] Campbell's immediate target was indeed prosaic: a select
group of London publishers who, rather too obviously, were not fulfilling their
responsibilities as 'sentinels' of public decency. On these terms, Hemyng welcomed a 'salutary reform' which he hoped would visit a 'blow' upon a 'disgraceful
trade' from which it 'will never again rally'.[144] Because publishers were concerned
about the Act, so necessarily were authors. Blackwood was certainly troubled when
he urged George Eliot to revisit any parts of *Adam Bede* which might be thought
'highly objectionable'.[145]

In reality, there was little immediate need for concern. Following a series of
initial prosecutions of targeted booksellers, the authorities seemed disinclined to
prosecute the Act too rigorously.[146] The publishing landscape assumed a rather
more threatening aspect, however, a decade later, when Campbell's successor,
Lord Chief Justice Cockburn, handed down his judgement in *R v Hicklin*. If the Act
was to be properly prosecuted, Cockburn observed, the 'test of obscenity' must be
defined, and it 'is this, whether the tendency of the matter charged . . . is to deprave
and corrupt those whose minds are open to such immoral influences, and into
whose hands a publication of this sort might fall'.[147] It was accordingly no longer
a question of whether a text might be considered artistic or not, but whether it
might 'deprave and corrupt' an impressionable reader; something which rather
obviously made the identification of an obscene text irreducibly subjective and
impressionistic. The intention of the author, moreover, was rendered necessarily
irrelevant in considering the question of guilt. Rossetti published his *Poems* in the
shadow of *Hicklin*, and successive drafts of *Jenny* suggest that he was acutely aware
of its implications. The Jenny of 1870 is notably less sensual than her various predecessors. Gone are the breasts, thighs and other 'beautiful secrets' described in
the 1860 draft.[148] However, if she is less sensual, it might be argued that the Jenny
of 1870 was no less provocative. Indeed, it could be argued that she was more so.

---

[143] For accounts of the passage of the Act through Parliament, see Manchester, 'Lord Campbell's Act'
(above n 139) 223–41, Leckie, *Culture and Adultery* (above n 140), 35–48; L Sigel, *Governing Pleasures:
Pornography and Social Change in England 1815–1914* (Rutgers University Press, 2002) 21–22, 26–27;
and G Robertson, *Obscenity* (Weidenfeld and Nicolson, 1979) 28–29.

[144] Mayhew, *London Labour* (above n 38) 437.

[145] Quoted in Bristow, 'Jenny' (above n 117) 102.

[146] Within a couple of months the police had raided a number of notorious booksellers in the
Holywell and Wych Street areas of London. See Manchester, 'Lord Campbell's Act' (above n 139) 228–
29, 233.

[147] *R v Hicklin* LR 3 QBD 371 (1868).

[148] See Marshik, 'The Case of *Jenny*' (above n 132) 562–68.

Either way, as an approving William Morris observed of Dante Gabriel's poem, whilst the 'subject' of prostitution is undoubtedly 'difficult for a modern poet to deal with', it was just as surely 'necessary for a man to think of'[149] and woman too, it might be added. Elizabeth Barrett Browning and Christina Rossetti clearly thought about it, as did Elizabeth Gaskell, Angela Burdett Coutts, Frances Trollope and George Eliot, and the tens of thousands of women who rolled up, with or without their husbands or fathers, to watch Dickens ham his way through 'Sikes and Nancy' in theatres up and down the country. There was much that was obviously different about the cases of Nancy and Jenny, and Marian Erle and Lizzie Leigh and de Quincey's Ann. But each account had at least two things in common. First, they brought to the fore a socially instantiated, and jurisprudentially embedded, injustice. Second, and perhaps most importantly, in narrating their respective falls and their consequences, the prostitutes were humanised. Nancy was written, as Dickens urged, to be 'real'. Jenny, according to Dante Gabriel, was his most important poetic muse, for which reason she also had to be his most credible. The prostitute, moreover, no longer lurked in the shadows of English literature. She took centre stage; in Nancy's case quite literally.

The Obscene Publications Act was perhaps inevitable; a testament both to the rise of the literary text and its presumed danger as well as to residual Victorian concerns regarding the depiction of sexuality. The very fact that it was thought to be necessary is significant, regardless of its rather obvious legislative inefficacy. It was not, of course, the only ineffective piece of legislation of the period. The Contagious Diseases Act was just as ineffective in its attempt to regulate prostitution. It was also dramatically more distasteful. It comes as no surprise to find Victorian legislation inscribing gender prejudice. Indeed it would have been odd if it had not. The Victorian age, like any other, cherished its prejudices. The 'double-standard' written into the 1857 Matrimonial Causes Act therefore comes as no surprise, and neither do the provisions of the 1803 Infanticide Act or the 1834 Poor Law. Writing at little later in 1881, Elizabeth Blackwell referred to a broader 'despair of legislation':

> Always remember that the laws of a country possess a really terrible responsibility through the way in which they influence the rising generation. Inequality between the sexes in the law of divorce, tolerance of seduction of minors, the attempt to check sexual disease by the inspection of vicious women, whilst equally vicious men are untouched, all these striking examples of the unjust and immoral attitude of the legislator, will serve to show how law may become a powerful agent in producing prostitution, through its direct attitude towards licentiousness.[150]

Of course, the case for reforming certain common law principles, most notably those of coverture and criminal conversation, remained as the likes of Caroline

[149] He went on to conclude that *Jenny* did so 'with the utmost depths of feeling, pity, and insight, with no mawkishness on the one hand, no coarseness on the other'. Review published in *The Academy* and quoted in ibid, 571.
[150] Blackwell, 'Prostitution' (above n 29) 103, 109.

Norton vigorously attested. But the greater problem, it seemed, lay with the belief cherished in successive Parliaments that the 'question' of England and its women might be resolved by legislation. Quite the contrary, as Elizabeth Barrett Browning famously exclaimed in her *Casa Guidi Windows*:

> Christ, no cure!
> No help for women sobbing out of sight
> Because men made the laws.[151]

Resolution did not lie in Parliament. Parliament was the problem.

Even those such as WR Greg, who continued to argue the case for greater statutory intervention, particularly in the matter of prostitution, recognised that the 'force' of law in such matters is 'often very weak'.[152] Elizabeth Lynn Linton, as we have already noted, said precisely the same in regard to the utility of the 1857 Matrimonial Causes Act. The legislators did not give up, of course. As the century progressed there would be more Matrimonial Causes and Matrimonial Property Acts, more Infant Custody Acts, further attempts to regulate brothels, most notably within the provisions of the 1880 Infant Schools Amendment Act of 1880, which empowered the police to remove children from brothels and place them in Industrial Schools, and the 1885 Criminal Law Amendment Act, which made it easier to bring summary proceedings against brothel keepers. However, it was becoming ever more crisply apparent that the law, as Greg and Linton conceded, could no more eradicate sexually transmitted disease than it could ensure connubial bliss.

In this context the literary text assumed a still greater significance as what Lisa Surridge has termed a site of 'active resistance'.[153] Here, it can be argued that the Victorian novelist, poet, and indeed critic, presumed to able to do at least three things which the lawyer could not, or more commonly did not seem particularly interested in doing. First, the writer could bring to the court of public opinion incidences of injustice. As Blackwell suggested, no amount of new statutes would be of use without the 'enlightenment of public opinion'.[154] Butler was of the same opinion: 'It is public opinion which gives sense to the letter and life to the law.'[155] At the same time, they could also humanise the consequences of this injustice. According to George Eliot 'our moral progress may be measured by the degree in which we sympathise with individual suffering and individual joy'.[156] The cause of female emancipation, Butler advised, depended not upon law, which as often as not simply criminalised them, but upon an ability to nurture 'human

---

[151] H Scudder (ed), *The Complete Poetical Works of Elizabeth Barrett Browning* (Bucaneer, 1993) lines 637–39, at 251.
[152] Greg, *Prostitution* (above n 3) 489.
[153] Surridge, *Bleak Houses* (above n 76) 9–10
[154] Blackwell, 'Prostitution' (above n 29) 106.
[155] Butler, *Purity* (above n 56) 174.
[156] Quoted in 'Introduction' to G Eliot *Adam Bede* (Penguin, 1980) at xix.

tenderness'.[157] Third, and finally, the same writer could raise voices. 'Is it not time that the woman's voice should be heard?' Butler inquired.[158]

Oliver Twist was written to raise such a voice, as were *Aurora Leigh* and *Jenny*, and whilst there were other voices raised in the literature of the period, of frustrated adulteresses, abused wives and abandoned mothers, the issue of prostitution undoubtedly served to concentrate the emergent feminist mind. As one harassed MP opined, the campaign for the repeal of the Contagious Diseases Act seemed to have brought to the surface an incipient 'revolt of the women'.[159] Of course, few of these revolutionaries were prostitutes. But many of them were married, and many might have registered the particular insinuation written into novels such as *Dombey and Son* and *The Newcomes*, that their respective marriages were a species of legalised prostitution. A few might have known what it was like to live in fear of the next beating, or might have known somebody else who did. A fair number, we can reasonably suppose, liked to read a good novel, maybe even a 'fleshly' poem. Not everyone who read them necessarily sympathised with the adulterous wives and languid prostitutes whose stories could be found lying around thousands of Victorian drawing rooms but many, it was feared, did, which is why, in part, Parliament was persuaded that England might benefit from an Obscene Publications Act.

By the middle of the century the women of Middle England, or at least enough of them, were increasingly literate and increasingly animated; for which reason, as Frances Power Cobbe confirmed, there was 'morally' no more 'serious thing' than writing a book, or indeed reading one.[160] Again, this did not mean that every book was written to incite resistance. Even the most sensational of tales was as likely to recommend conformity. *East Lynne* did so, as did *Aurora Floyd*. Braddon identified herself as an 'old Tory' by 'birth and instinct', and much the same might also be said of Wood, Eliot and Gaskell.[161] Even if Dickens and Thackeray betrayed more reformist tendencies, it did not mean that they were radical in political temperament. In an intriguing memoir written in 1912, towards the end of her life, Braddon looked back half a century to 1859 recalling a 'very shy' girl, a 'vigorous chicken in a shell of thick glass', one who could see 'a wonderful world outside and [was] hopeless of getting to it', who 'could go nowhere, see no one, spend nothing, read nothing, think nothing'. That Mary Elizabeth Braddon, she concluded, was 'hemmed round with conventionalities, stifled with respectability'. Half a century

---

[157] Butler, *Appeal* (above n 59) 129, and also *A Letter to the Members of the Ladies National Association* (Brakell, 1875) 151, reaffirming that her purpose in writing essays on the subject of prostitution was to generate 'pity' amongst her readers.

[158] Butler, *Purity* (above n 56) 177.

[159] Before adding, in presumably despairing tones, 'what are we to do with such an opposition as this?' Walkowitz, *Prostitution and Victorian Society* (above n 4) 1.

[160] F Cobbe, 'Celibacy v Marriage' in S Hamilton (ed), *Criminals, Idiots, Women and Minors: Victorian Writing by Women on Women* (Broadview, 1995) 105.

[161] Braddon was a regular church-goer and loyal member of the Church of England, what Wolff terms a 'sensible, no-fuss-about-it, Church of England Christian'. 'I love', she once observed, 'old things, old habits, old houses, old customs, old trees, old halls, old costumes'. See R Wolff, *Sensational Victorian: The Life and Fiction of Mary Elizabeth Braddon* (Garland, 1979) 266 and 323–24.

on, women 'have everything now'. 'The world', she concluded, 'is theirs in a century that ought to be called the Golden Age of Womanhood'.[162] The insinuation was clear; the 'golden age' to come was founded on the 'age of the lady novelist' which had gone before.

There is an evident sense of the fabulous as well as the nostalgic in Braddon's remembrance. The 'age of the lady novelist', though narrowly conceived in the pejorative by Dallas, could be broadened into a wider celebration of a distinctive genre of women's literature. No text did more to establish the myth, not just of its particular subject but also the broader genre, than Elizabeth Gaskell's *Life of Charlotte Bronte*. Gaskell's *Life* was written in order to bring Charlotte out of the shadows whilst also restoring the reputation of the Bronte family. Charlotte, of course, preferred the shadows, as did most of her fellow female writers of the period. The true authorship of *Adam Bede*, Eliot advised, should remain hidden precisely became readers might be scandalised if it was discovered that the creator of Hetty Sorrel was a woman.[163] Even Braddon had her secrets. The thought that the female writer might be somehow prostituting herself was commonly insinuated and just as commonly felt. In her poem *A Castaway*, published in 1870, Augustus Webster went a step further aligning writer, prostitute and lawyer, all engaged in the same business of deception and dissimulation: 'Our traffic's one; I own it. And what then?'[164] She might just as easily have added the critic to the list. GH Lewes liked to envisage himself as assuming the kind of responsibility defined by Senard. Writing in 1856, he advised that the 'vast increase of novels, mostly worthless, is a serious danger to public culture' which 'can only be arrested by an energetic resolution on the part of critics to do their duty with conscientious rigour'.[165] Certainly many authors lived in fear of the critics, not least Lewes's later wife, George Eliot. Small wonder perhaps that Dante Gabriel was tempted to skew the critical market.

The critic, Victorian or modern, is always troublesome, their employment necessarily inserting still further layers of prejudice and uncertainty between author, reader and text. As the nineteenth century wore on, the matter of who wrote what and who read what caused increasing concern. The Obscene Publications Act, though never intended to regulate the kind of literature we have encountered in this book, can again be interpreted as being symptomatic of this concern. At an immediate level, the fact that Isabel Gilbert contemplated adultery was concerning. The fact that she was addicted to reading the wrong kind of novels, the kind that encouraged her ultimately harmless contemplation, was the greater worry. Looking back a century and a half, it is easy to dismiss such anxieties. There is

---

[162] See ibid, 379–80.

[163] When *Scenes of Clerical Life* was first published, the *Saturday Review* pictured its author as a bearded clergyman with a large brood of children running around his rectory. See N Thompson, *Reviewing Sex: Gender and the Reception of Victorian Novels* (Macmillan, 1996) 1, and D Kreisel, 'Incognito, Intervention, and Dismemberment in *Adam Bede* (2003) 70 *ELH* particularly 542–45.

[164] A Webster, *Portraits* (London, 1893) 38–39. Webster is largely forgotten today. Christina Rossetti was, however, a huge admirer.

[165] Thompson, *Reviewing Sex* (above n 163) 4.

nothing in a Braddon novel that troubles us today. Dickens, Eliot, Gaskell, Barrett Browning, even the Rossettis, are firmly ensconced within the canon. They are respectable. Literature students read them all the time. Law students could if they were so moved. They would, it is suggested, learn much not just about the state of English matrimonial and criminal law in mid-nineteenth-century England, but about its condition today. The nature of the debate, and the anxieties which shape it, has changed. It is no longer about the broader propriety of reading such novels as *Dombey and Son* or *Aurora Floyd* or *East Lynne,* or poems such as *Goblin Market* or *Jenny.* It is about the narrower disciplinary propriety of reading them in a law school classroom. It should not be controversial. Whether or not we can learn much about Victorian jurisprudence by reading Austin or Stephen, it is surely unarguable that we can learn so much more by reading Dickens or Eliot or Barrett Browning. Their contemporaries did.

INDEX

Index